CW01506718

YEAR OF THE RAT

Year of the Rat

Undercover in the British Far Right

HARRY SHUKMAN

Chatto & Windus

LONDON

1 3 5 7 9 10 8 6 4 2

Chatto & Windus, an imprint of Vintage, is part of the
Penguin Random House group of companies

Vintage, Penguin Random House UK, One Embassy Gardens,
8 Viaduct Gardens, London SW11 7BW

penguin.co.uk/vintage
global.penguinrandomhouse.com

First published by Chatto & Windus in 2025

Typeset in 11.6/15.8 Calluna by Jouve (UK), Milton Keynes
Printed and bound in Great Britain by Clays Ltd, Elcograf S.p.A.

The authorised representative in the EEA is Penguin Random House Ireland,
Morrison Chambers, 32 Nassau Street, Dublin D02 YH68

A CIP catalogue record for this book is available from the British Library

HB ISBN 9781784746049
TPB ISBN 9781784746056

Penguin Random House is committed to a sustainable future
for our business, our readers and our planet. This book is made
from Forest Stewardship Council® certified paper.

For Hattie

Introduction

The smell of the crowd hits us before the sound does, a chemical tang from the hand-held flares sparking up in central Warsaw. It tickles our throats and itches our eyes. As we get closer to Solidarności Avenue, the capital's main street, the yells of 100,000 Polish demonstrators charge around the corner to meet us: *Bóg! Honor! I Ojczyzna!* God! Honour! And Fatherland!

Six of us are here from the UK. This rally is nominally meant to celebrate Polish independence on 11 November, but has become an annual meet-up for the European far right. Groups from across the Continent come to forge connections, sell copies of *Mein Kampf*, stamp on LGBT rainbow flags, and get drunk. Clad in skull balaclavas, they march through the city waving banners emblazoned with neo-Nazi symbols and slogans like 'DEFEND WHITE EUROPA'. Hosted for the last decade by a fascist party called the National Radical Camp, it has become a significant date in the extremist calendar. It is controversial even within Poland – the mayor of Warsaw has tried in previous years to ban it. Journalists reporting on the event have been attacked with mace by participants.

We are delegates from Britain First, an extreme political party run by Paul Golding. At the march, he points his camcorder at passing anti-abortion banners that depict bloody foetuses. 'This is how Britain should be,' Paul shouts over the noise. 'This is what a country without a left-wing ideology looks like – united and patriotic.'

The crowd moves east through the city, dodging fire-crackers and plumes of red and white flare smoke. Ashlea and Alex, two other Britain First members, look around in wonder. The biggest rallies they have attended back home had a fraction of this turnout. They marvel at the discipline of the crowd – their own events in the UK are beset by drunkards carrying beer cans and urinating in public.

Nick, a senior figure in the party, puts an excited arm around my shoulders and pats my chest. I tense up, feeling like I have been plugged into a socket. Nick's hand – not that he knows it – is touching the hidden camera underneath my shirt. Will he ask why a weird plastic box is taped to my chest? Will he expose my hidden wire in the middle of a mob of neo-Nazis? But he doesn't seem to notice, and we march on through Warsaw, my heart racing. Later, over dinner in a five-star hotel with a Polish MEP, I am convinced my camera is visible and keep dashing to the toilet to check. But I'm safe – for now.

We go out to a bar adorned with white pride stickers to down shots of frozen vodka. I listen to them talk about how the Holocaust was 'the big lie', and Auschwitz – a four-hour drive away – didn't have gas chambers, but swimming pools and cinemas for Jews to enjoy. When two of the guys suggest a strip club, I head back to my hotel, up the road from the Jewish cemetery of Warsaw which is filled with the mass graves of ghetto victims. I lie on my bed with my hands on my face, smelling the booze and fag ash on my fingers, thinking about how much longer I'll be able do this.

I was undercover in the British far right for more than a year, pretending to be a racist named Chris while feeding information back to my colleagues at HOPE not hate, an anti-fascist organisation. I put my normal life as a journalist on hold to spend time among racists. Britain First, who I was with in Poland, is one of the extreme groups I infiltrated. There was also a far-right community network, a white nationalist campaign, a neo-Nazi conference, a circle of Holocaust deniers, and a movement of race scientists, including one well-funded organisation financially backed by Silicon Valley.

Each of the groups had their own beliefs and attracted members for different reasons. Not one of them knew my real identity, although I repeatedly came close to being found out.

For a year, I was constantly frightened. It felt like there was an exclamation mark stamped onto my brain. Exposure was my biggest worry, and I imagined it happening in two ways. Either I would make a small but irreparable slip-up, like introducing myself as Harry instead of my fake name, Chris. Or I would be in a pub, wedged into a corner, when a friend from my normal life would approach shouting my real name and I would be unable to explain myself.

Before a meet-up, I thought about all the ways it could go wrong, obsessing over possible conversations and how to escape if the worst happened. An hour undercover required three or four to prepare. As a naturally nervous person, I found that my habit of mentally rehashing past conversations and planning future ones was helpful in preparing for undercover meetings. I would rehearse dialogue and try to anticipate potentially difficult questions about who I was, or why I wanted to know something. Afterwards, I would be unable to sit still, my fingers palpitating with a five-espresso jitter. Having kept myself steady for so long, I would have a lot of nervous energy to release. Every night after a meet-up, I had nightmares about being exposed.

I put myself through this because I wanted to get close to the British far right, find out what kind of people join, and, if possible, do what I could to disrupt their operations. The far right now makes up around a third of terrorism convictions and a majority of referrals to the government's Prevent counter-radicalisation scheme. The threat of terrorist activity was frequently in the headlines during this time. A man firebombed an immigration centre in Dover. A white supremacist from the Midlands made firearms and explosives to kill ethnic minorities and was convicted on terrorism charges. Another man was charged with the attempted murder of an asylum seeker in Worcester. Understanding where these people come from, what they believe and how they organise has never been more important.

As I was writing this book in the summer of 2024, the biggest wave of far-right violence in the post-war period swept England. After a teenager born to Rwandan parents stabbed three young girls in an attack on a Taylor Swift-themed dance class in Southport, race riots exploded across twenty-seven English towns and cities. Far-right agitators, wrongly believing the perpetrator was Muslim, targeted mosques and Muslim neighbourhoods in the violence that followed, while arsonists set fire to hotels housing asylum seekers and rioters set up whites-only roadblocks. Around eight hundred people have been charged in relation to the disorder.

A moment that sticks in my head from the riots was a mob in Hull ambushing a BMW. They jumped onto the car, yanked the door open and dragged out the driver and his two passengers. None of them were Muslim – the three men were Christians from Romania, who thought they were about to die as one rioter attacked them with a metal bar. They survived by escaping to a nearby hotel housing refugees.

Far-right activism takes many forms. There are sophisticated, educated and resourceful campaigners working towards ridding this country of anyone not considered white and British. I became close to well-connected, well-funded extremists who sought to widen the Overton Window – the range of ideas acceptable to the mainstream – to include race science and eugenics. Some of them enjoy the support of American tech tycoons and Conservative policymakers, work in the right-wing think-tank scene and, in one case, write policy papers for Downing Street.

All this matters. We cannot allow our democracy to become undermined by those who want to implement eugenicist policies or abuse and forcibly deport British citizens because they have a different religion or skin colour. Extreme organisations in the UK are looking to capitalise on the election of five MPs from the far-right Reform Party. They have furthermore been energised by the re-election in the US of Donald Trump. Italy now has a far-right prime minister, the first since the Second World War. In Holland the anti-Islam Freedom Party of Geert

Wilders won the most seats at the last election. At the time of writing the AfD is polling nationally at 23 per cent in Germany, a record high, and leading polls in three states. Britain First, a party I spent time with, is developing connections with Continental partners to learn electioneering and seek funding.

Getting close enough to the far right to understand it is difficult. Extremists on the fringes of society are rarely open to approaches from reporters, who are typically believed to be controlled by dark establishment forces. Just as Oswald Mosley, the most famous icon of the British far right, denied the extent of his extreme activity (notably his relationship to Nazi Germany), today's organisations also believe the path to success depends on hoodwinking the public with lies of their moderation. Far-right activists will try to deceive the media to seek a favourable write-up on the occasions where they do speak to them. Undercover, however, they will tell you things they never otherwise would. They reveal their true views and intentions, and not the ones they think you want to hear.

I had found this out while experimenting with undercover reporting for my blog, Scout. Inventing a false name, I got in touch with conspiracy theorists and far-right activists, asking to join. I spent Sunday Mass at a renegade church of antisemitic Catholics in Southport, an afternoon in Birmingham at the house of an anti-satanic activist, and a day among the sleepy members attending UKIP's annual conference in Skegness. I became fascinated by the idea that in every town there is a community of conspiracy theorists whose beliefs are completely unrecognisable to the mainstream.

These reporting trips usually had a narrow journalistic objective: hear the racist comments and get out safely. I never stayed long enough to find out what the people in these movements are really like. Why do they join? What do they want? Do they get along with each other? Do they find it fulfilling? What do they tell their partners, parents and kids about their activities? What do they talk about when they're not being racist? Why do they give up Saturday after Saturday to hand out scaremongering leaflets or picket refugee accommodation and get insulted by passers-by? Why do they listen to the leaders in these movements, who to outsiders seem pretty obviously to be money-hungry grifters or aggressive cranks? How does a leader maintain power and momentum?

A long-term infiltration project in which I tried to get close to the most extreme, sinister groups in the British far right would, I thought, be the best way to answer these questions. It would also be a useful way to learn about their capacity to organise events, draw funding and forge international connections. The thrill of working undercover was a draw, but I also had a personal stake in this. I am not spiritually or culturally Jewish, but I come from a Jewish family – one side fled the Nazi invasion of France; the other emigrated from the Russian Pale of Settlement that restricted how Jews could live and work. I am fascinated and maddened by the persistence of antisemitic prejudice, and the adaptation of old tropes that targeted them also being used against Muslims.

While researching stories for my website, I would consult with HOPE not hate, which in addition to monitoring the far right runs infiltrators into extremist groups to disrupt their operations. In 2017, their mole inside a far-right terror group foiled a plot to murder a Labour MP. Another helped to identify the 1999 nail bomber who detonated explosives in areas of the capital known for their Bangladeshi, black and gay populations.

HOPE not hate's reports on the far right always displayed an encyclopedic knowledge of extremist campaigners and their activities. I contacted their research team in late 2022 to discuss working together. We couldn't meet at their office because, as the targets of death threats and harassment campaigns, their location is kept secret. Instead, they invited me to a gloomy central London pub, where I met David Lawrence, Patrik Hermansson and Joe Mulhall.

Over a pint of Guinness, Joe, the head of the research team and a veteran anti-fascist, asked what I was hoping to hear. Would I like to team up for a long-term infiltration project? It would be more intense, but with any luck much more revealing than the day trips I had so far been doing. An undercover project in which I joined and became close to the leaders of a far-right group could, Joe explained, meaningfully disrupt their operation. He told me to think carefully if this was what I really wanted, given the dangers involved. I didn't have to think long. I was already spending time undercover in extremist circles. This was a chance to do it more safely, with more guidance. Far better, I thought, to work with the professionals than risk bumbling about on my own. I told Joe I'd let him know, but as I left the pub, I had already made up my mind.

Patrik Hermansson became my handler. He was a perfect choice. In 2016, he had pretended to be a master's student on exchange from Sweden in order to infiltrate extremist think tanks. He was appointed to help with vetting for a far-right group. Over a year, Patrik befriended the Holocaust denier David Irving and captured on film for the first time the identity of the secretive white nationalist Greg Johnson. His last meeting was at the Charlottesville rally in 2017, where American neo-Nazis lit torches and chanted antisemitic slogans; one of them murdered the anti-fascist activist Heather Heyer by running her over in his car. Patrik saw it happen.

During our project, Patrik was patient, attentive and calm. He understood the difficulty of undercover work, having done it himself for so long. I quickly grew to like him and trust his advice. We brainstormed how to respond to messages and phone calls from my new far-right friends, and how to go safely in and out of meetings.

My first assignment was to infiltrate a far-right group he had identified. It was a community network set up by a disgraced academic booted out of the University of Surrey for peddling race hate. On his website, he advertised a cryptic link to meet-ups, and so Patrik and I began looking for a way in. The British far-right scene, he explained, is a giant Venn diagram, with a small number of activists belonging to more than one organisation. He suspected that we might encounter people in one group who could refer me to a more extreme one. We would take a year to see what we could find, and then stop. Any longer might risk my safety and sanity.

Together, we built my new identity, planning my debut in far-right society. First, we created Chris. Fake identities are easier to remember if they are anchored to the truth, so I inverted my biography to create an altered version of myself. My parents and siblings now went by their middle names, for instance.

We wanted Chris to avoid too much attention, so we gave him a job that sounded so tedious people would be unlikely to ask a second or third question about it. Chris was a strategy consultant working in support function optimisation. Clearly we'd chosen well because the eyes of everyone I met glazed over at the mention of my job title and people rarely wanted to know anything more about it. To look the part, I chose the most boring clothes in my wardrobe, selecting a white shirt, a zip-up fleece, a pair of navy trousers, and a practical yet sad anorak, complemented with a fake lanyard around my neck.

In each of the groups I joined, being undercover tended to mean the same thing. I had to show up and fit in. That could mean participating in a conversation about the Jews controlling global politics, canvassing for votes with an extremist party, or doing the washing-up at a house full of Holocaust deniers. Patrik and I thought that Chris should be dependable, affable and, above all, normal.

Right-wing extremists tend to think that infiltrators will be easy to spot: slippery and sneaky, asking cackhandedly obvious questions like 'What does everyone think about the Jews?' or 'Committed any good hate crimes recently?' Among the far right, this is known as fed-posting, which is when heavy-handed police investigators appear in online groups and say especially racist things in order to prompt admissions of illegal activity. I wanted to avoid fed-posting, not just to keep my cover, but for ethical reasons – I didn't want to entrap anyone into saying something they wouldn't ordinarily discuss.

As Chris, I would sit there politely, buy rounds of drinks if it was my turn, and contribute to conversations. I couldn't pretend to be an Aryan *Übermensch*, coming, as I do, from a long line of short-sighted, short-statured dyspeptics. Patrik and I thought Chris should be an interested layman concerned about demographic replacement – the fear that white people will one day become a minority due to high immigration and low birth rates. When asked, I would mention growing up in an ethnically homogeneous village and feeling alienated upon moving to diverse London; how I enjoyed the videos of far-right content creators; how I was lonely and bored and didn't have anyone to talk to about my politics.

Patrik advised me not to speak too much. A lie becomes weaker the more details you try to pack in, he explained. Another piece of advice was often in my mind. A former colleague at *The Times* once told me that in undercover work, you can avoid suspicion by convincing people that you are a bit dim, a bit dopey. Fortunately, this has never been a problem for me.

Next to sort was the camera. This is much less cool than its Hollywood equivalent. In spy movies, there are glasses, lapel pins and even contact lenses that send a clear live feed back to an operations room. The real thing is clunky and frustrating. It's a plastic cube an inch in size, and can be screwed onto a shirt button, placed under your clothes where it rests on the sternum. This box has a cable that dangles down your chest and feeds into your trouser pocket through a hole made with scissors. The wire connects into a heavy battery the size of a cigarette packet, and there it rests, about as comfortably as a hernia.

I never got used to the camera. Its low position meant that footage was recorded at gremlin height, and I would try, when conversing with tall people, to lean backwards so I could capture their faces. The whole thing felt as conspicuous as a 'kick me' sign.

It was some consolation to know that in the past these devices were even more obvious. Undercover journalists used to rely on cameras that recorded footage onto cassette tapes which would emit a loud click at the end of the reel. Paul McMullen, a former *News of the World* reporter, once described hanging out in the back of a van with violent cocaine smugglers, unable to remember if he had put a 45-minute or a 90-minute tape in his device, panicking that it was about to make a strange noise. The equipment may have improved, but the fear remains that it will somehow malfunction and expose its user.

I learned the hard way to keep checking if a tape was working. On a day out with Britain First, I listened, with horror, to senior members telling me Auschwitz was 'made up'. Gas chambers weren't used except for delousing, they said. Here was proof that Britain First is a nasty party whose activists traffic in some of the vilest conspiracy theories – and I was capturing it on camera! At the first opportunity, I slipped into a pub toilet to check the recording equipment. I pulled it out of my pocket, pushed a button, and saw with soul-mangling despair that the camera had been off the whole time. Next time, I taped bits of plastic over the off button to make sure it couldn't be touched while in use. The snapped-off covers of dental floss boxes, I learned, fit perfectly.

My biggest worry at the beginning was maintaining

my cover. As Chris, I had to repeat the name in my mind whenever I was walking into a meeting in order to remind myself who I was pretending to be. It would be so easy, I knew, to slip up, so I made sure to pause whenever anyone held out their hand to shake, to think *Chris* before introducing myself. I was pleased that, before long, I would turn my head if I heard a shout of 'Chris!' although I was never able to stop myself from reacting if someone called out 'Harry!' On one occasion, when another Harry was part of the group I was with, I found myself automatically – helplessly – answering questions not meant for me. Thankfully, nobody noticed.

There were many near misses. Once at a Wetherspoons with a white nationalist influencer, I offered to buy a round on the pub's app. I pulled out my phone and in full view of the table, started typing in my real email address, getting halfway through before noticing. I quickly deleted the name, muttering that I sometimes borrowed my girlfriend's account, and got away with it.

The heartstopper came when I logged onto a video call with an American eugenicist on my personal email account. Five minutes in, I saw my real name on the screen. I hung up and waited until I could breathe normally again. I rejoined using my Chris account, my face burning, ready with a lie about how I had been using a borrowed work laptop. Luckily, my contact didn't remark on it, and she continued speaking.

Apparently when bigamists cross the threshold of their secret family's front door they forget about their other partner and children. Something similar happened to me. I noticed that after arriving for a meeting, once I had greeted everyone and no longer had to mentally repeat my pseudonym, I was in Chris mode. Thoughts from real life intruded sometimes – *cancel Amazon Prime, get flea medicine for dog, what am I doing here?* – but so much of my focus went on pretending to be Chris that I could bat these away.

Chris mode was like a flow of concentration. It could last for hours but break unexpectedly. If someone looked at my chest, I became convinced they had spotted my hidden camera and I began catastrophising. Once, a far-right campaigner directed his gaze at my shirt. Straight into the camera lens. I was sitting in his house, with a dozen other activists, far from the door, with his eyes drilled at exactly where the device was. Had he seen it? I counted all the steps I would have to take, all the people I would need to pass – *his eyes were still on me!* – before I'd have to unhook the tricky latch on the back door and escape. Then he yawned and looked elsewhere. He had just been zoning out.

Going undercover is an extreme strategy, and readers may ask if it is justified. Activists and politicians on the far right are intensely distrustful of the media, and many of them believe it is controlled by malfeasant Jews. Had I walked into a meeting of a far-right group and openly presented myself as a journalist, there is no chance that I could have spent time with them and learned their inner workings. In the rare event that I would be allowed to interview them at all, I would have been presented with a more moderate front. The groups I infiltrated had vetting procedures and were obsessed with 'opsec' – operational security – like redirection points, secret handshakes and phone checks designed to keep reporters out.

Even those few on the far right who do interact with

journalists have devised tactics to mislead them. I met an American couple with connections to the far right who gleefully described their successful manipulation of the British press. To secure more favourable coverage, they downplayed objectionable beliefs in interviews and dropped progressive soundbites to protect themselves from accusations of bigotry. By mentioning their support for LGBT rights, or their disavowal for white nationalism, this American couple sought to garner positive write-ups and avoid accusations of belonging to the far right.

Far-right organisations seek to expand using disingenuous methods. Take Britain First. Its leader, Paul Golding, would have you think it has a patriotic manifesto, somewhere to the right of the Conservatives, honouring broken Tory promises to curb illegal immigration. What you don't see in the pamphlets and the social media posts is the reality of the organisation, which is vicious and racist. The party's head of security, when I became a member, had been convicted of slashing the throat of a policeman; their national organiser told me about how he thought the gas chambers at Auschwitz were hoaxes; their candidate for London mayor revealed his 'hatred for coons'.

Leaders in the far right conceal their true nature to present a more acceptable version to potential voters, donors and sometimes their own members. One prominent eugenicist who works in Westminster admitted this tactic after I'd befriended him. 'Everyone puts on the mask,' he said. Only by spending prolonged periods of time with them, winning their trust and being deemed safe is it possible to see those moments when that mask slips, and the truth peeks out from underneath. If the far right are using subterfuge to gain ground in politics, then it makes sense to turn their tactics back on them. It takes a thief to catch a thief.

What follows is an account of the year in which I wore my own mask in the British far right. It is not a complete picture of radicalism in this country. I did not spend time with any Islamist groups, for example, or extremists of other stripes. Nor is it a complete picture of the far right. Safe infiltrations are done slowly, and I could only join so many groups in the time I had. Each upcoming chapter deals with a different group I joined, but the account is not chronological as my time with each organisation overlapped.

Far-right activity in the UK takes a number of forms. There are political parties contesting elections, hoping to build a supporter base that will take them to power. These range from large parties, like Reform UK, which has MPs in Parliament and millions of voters, to much smaller operations such as Britain First, which has no elected officials and an inner circle of just forty activists.

Some groups are dedicated to campaigning, on the street or online. A handful plan or in rare instances commit terrorist acts. Sometimes groups or the people within them will be involved in multiple forms of activism. Although I met people who had been convicted of crimes in the past and in some cases broken terrorism laws, I did not encounter anybody who was at the time planning a terror attack.

Of course, not all far-right campaigning in this country is coordinated by an organisation. In the days of the British Union of Fascists, members belonged to a regional branch, their subscriptions noted in a ledger. Today, a great deal of far-right activity is called 'post-organisational'. This means that extremist influencers like Tommy Robinson – real name Stephen Yaxley-Lennon – can use their enormous audiences on social media to mobilise followers for anti-immigrant demonstrations or financially support them without the need for a traditional organisation. This limited what I could infiltrate.

There were also some groups too risky for me to join. There are a number of activists who hound asylum seekers landing in small boats at Dover. One of them is called Steve Laws, and I had written about him when he contested an election for UKIP. In response, he shared my name and photograph to his many thousands of online followers, warning them to watch out for me. I was always worried that I would bump into someone who had seen this alert. As Chris, I disguised myself as best I could by cutting my hair short and growing a moustache. It did very little to change my appearance.

This book is also incomplete in the sense that I didn't learn everything I would have liked to. I couldn't call up my new friends with the questions I really wanted to ask about their childhoods and family lives and hobbies. Sometimes I would detect a sensitivity threshold that I might have been able to cross as a nosy journalist, but not as a stranger among clandestine racists. There are only so many times you can ask 'Sorry, what was that you said about the Jews?' before it sounds odd.

While it might be ironic that I lied and cheated for a year, what follows is all true. The conversations described below are based on video recordings, audio tapes and notes I took. Halfway through the year undercover, the film director Havana Marking began making a documentary about HOPE not hate, and recorded some of the briefing and debriefing sessions I had with Patrik. *Undercover: Exposing the Far Right* was broadcast on Channel 4 in October 2024. At the same time, the *Guardian* and HOPE not hate published reports about some of the material that we uncovered in the shady world of race science.

So what did we find? Contrary to the perception that the British far right is only composed of the kind of lagered-up, English Defence League skinheads you see on TV, I met people from all walks of life. In the first group I infiltrated, a far-right community called the Basketweavers, I saw that they came from all classes and educational backgrounds – I met aristocrats and the unemployed; people with PhDs and school dropouts (see Chapter 1). Some were happy just meeting up once or twice a week, while others wanted to travel overseas to far-right conferences and develop connections with foreign activists. This is how I ended up in Tallinn, Estonia (see Chapter 2). Curiously among groups dedicated to white nationalism, not all of them were white. I could only speculate about what made a half-Japanese man or an Indian Muslim, for instance, join a racist community devoted to ending race-mixing. I felt the same confusion when women arrived at these events. For every nine men, there was one woman – who inevitably had to listen to a discussion on the higher IQ of men and the unsuitability of women to intellectual life.

Not all of the groups I joined were that proficient at activism, and were just as interested in getting drunk as talking about demographics (see Chapter 3). In one case, I saw how a leader obsessed with power manipulated his activists into volunteering their time, energy and, above all, money, in his service (see Chapter 4). Some activists have come down on the wrong side of the law, and after prison sentences, question their future in the movement (see Chapter 5).

I learned, as the year went on, that a great deal of what my new associates were discussing was not confined to fringe groups. Some leading activists were reaching the ears of powerful people (see Chapter 6). Ideas about falling birth rates, for instance, have become one way to slip extreme views about race science and demography into the mainstream. This is known as pronatalism (see Chapter 7). There are concerning links that this particular movement has with genetic testing companies that offer screening of embryos produced during IVF to see which will have the highest IQ (see Chapter 8).

One advocate of race science told me about policy papers he was writing for the prime minister at the time (see Chapter 9). 'Most elites actually know the score,' he said. 'You're talking about race and IQ?' I asked. 'Yeah,' my contact replied. 'People know that. It's not some huge secret.'

Among the rank and file members of far-right organisations, however, I was struck by their loneliness. In discussion groups, in city pubs, at secret meetings in the countryside, many of them spoke about feeling like outcasts, alienated and bored. They described their days of working in tedious, unfulfilling jobs, and evenings spent listening to hours-long fascist livestreams online. When they attended conferences, many of them tuned out of the talks (I used to count the nodding heads of sleeping audience members, frequently reaching double figures) and looked forward most to the coffee breaks and post-event pints. Wanting connection is a common reason people give for arriving at these groups, and also what makes it hard for them to leave, even if they're not enjoying themselves.

A lot of the people I met were conspiracy theorists. Many claimed to have discovered the far right during the Covid pandemic, when lockdowns and masks and vaccines prompted baroque fantasies about the government trying to launch a genocide on its own people. Conspiracy theories can appeal to people who feel isolated, ignored and insignificant. Believing that a small elite controls the outcome of major world events could explain why one's own life might not be unfolding as planned. Rarely would adopting a conspiratorial outlook improve one's overall happiness and satisfaction, though.

What surprised me most was that despite my revulsion for what my new associates said and did, I often felt myself becoming friendly with them. It was hard not to. To fit in, I had to endear myself to new groups by being friendly and smiley. Naively, I hadn't reckoned on them being friendly and smiley back. They thought I was one of them. On long bus journeys with Britain First, they would shout at South Asian drivers, jeer at black people, and tell jokes about the Holocaust. Then they told me about their weight-loss goals and divorce proceedings, their grandchildren's birthday parties and their garden renovations, their girlfriend troubles and their summer holidays.

As they greeted me with cheers and handshakes, I told myself that what I was feeling was merely relief at their acceptance of me. But was there also warmth? I felt a confusing mix of disgust at what they said and did, fear about my own exposure, and guilt. Guilt at befriending dozens of people with the intention of betraying them. As abhorrent as their views are, and as nasty as some of their actions may have been, these people invited me into their homes and shared intimate details with me about their lives and hopes and dreams. One day, I knew, I would have to sell them out.

I told myself that my new extremist friends, who frequently asserted the conspiracy theory that Jews control global affairs, would not have been so welcoming were I not white and male or had they known I came from a Jewish family. That it was only by making friends with neo-Nazis and Islamophobes that I could gain their trust and earn access to yet more extreme groups. That journalists covering the far right are lied to, and that only by spending time with these people undercover would it be possible to see what they're really like. This was all true. But the people I met are still human beings, and I felt like I was judasing them. It was grubby: that's why this book is called *Year of the Rat*.

Sometimes I was worried about the efficacy of undercover reporting. A hardcore conspiracy theorist is unlikely to ever change their mind. When my new friends eventually found out I had hoaxed them, might they feel more ostracised? Would they feel justified in their paranoia that mainstream society is out to get them, and double down in their beliefs?

There is dirt on my hands. I never wanted to entrap someone by prompting a hateful conversation, but I did join in. On the Britain First battle bus, members shared antisemitic jokes and looked to me for one. I had to spend weekends canvassing votes for extremist candidates, holding my breath on election night in case they actually won (thankfully they didn't). For a white nationalist activist group, I put up offensive stickers at London universities. To get close to a race-science website, I had to give them editorial advice to make their operations run more smoothly. I could tell myself this was justified, but I was nonetheless complicit.

Much of the activism I participated in, particularly the anti-immigrant protests, can be traced back almost a century. In 1932, Oswald Mosley founded the British Union of Fascists, known for their blackshirt uniform inspired by the Nazi SS. During his years as a far-right campaigner, Mosley created a template that groups still follow. The techniques and talking points that he developed as an agitator first against Jews and then non-white immigrants seem indistinguishable from the extremist activism of today, with Mosleyite propaganda from the 1930s echoing in the groups I infiltrated.

Take, for instance, this article in *Action*, the official newspaper of Mosley's British Union of Fascists, dated 24 June 1939. I dug it out of the HOPE not hate archives. Headlined 'Behaviour of Jewish Exiles Disgusts Sandwich People', the report was about the arrival of Jewish men who had fled Nazi Germany and were now housed in a refugee camp in Sandwich on the south coast. The anonymous reporter complained of 'alien invaders' wrecking a 'picturesque Kent village'. The Jews, we learn, were enjoying a 'life of leisure' in fancy new clothes provided by the British taxpayer; they were also riding bicycles and going to the cinema. Local parents were apparently forming a vigilante group to prevent these Jews from 'forcing attentions on English girls'. The reporter concluded: 'If anyone wishes to discover the real cause of anti-Semitism, I advise them to take a trip down to Sandwich.'

This article could have been written by Britain First, were it focused on Muslims instead of Jews. While protesting at a camp for Afghan refugees – in Folkestone, just half an hour's drive from Sandwich – I repeatedly heard that native communities are being wrecked by the arrival of violently lascivious foreigners who enjoy luxury perks that white Britons go without. Paul Golding is forever posting on social media about 'native girls' and 'foreign sexual predators'. To him, refugee facilities are an insult to all patriots. While a cost of living crisis bites white citizens, sponging foreigners are enjoying the high life. 'Working-age chancers,' Paul calls them.

It is not just Britain First using the same language as Oswald Mosley. Government ministers spoke in his hateful vernacular while this project was going on. In spring 2023, Robert Jenrick, immigration minister at the time, delivered a speech about refugees that was remarkably similar to what was being said in the groups I infiltrated. 'Those crossing tend to have completely different lifestyles and values to those in the UK,' he said. Suella Braverman, then the home secretary, talked about refugees as an 'invasion' and a 'swarm', adding: 'Let's stop pretending they are all refugees in distress, the whole country knows that is not true.' The former prime minister Liz Truss said Enoch Powell, who made the incendiary 1968 'Rivers of Blood' speech, 'had a point' on immigration.†

Powell, at the time a Conservative shadow minister, was sacked. Now I worry that views like his, once considered incompatible with public life, are becoming mainstream. Reform UK, whose leader Nigel Farage is an admirer of Powell's, was elected to Parliament in the 2024 election, along with four of his colleagues. His party has opened a front against multiculturalism, scapegoating it for Britain's underfunded public services. 'The unprecedented population explosion has pushed Britain to breaking point,' he writes in Reform's manifesto. It is alarming to think that four million people voted for his party, giving him the power now to influence the Conservative Party in opposition, and drive them further to the right.

This book draws on a definition of the far right as outlined by Cas Mudde, a political scientist at the University of Georgia. He describes it as an 'anti-system' ideology, hostile to liberal democracy. Far-right beliefs tend to encompass a mix of authoritarianism, sexism, xenophobia, racism and populism. 'Extreme right ideologies believe that inequalities are natural and outside of the purview of the state,' Mudde writes. 'They celebrate difference and hierarchy, and their core feature is elitism, which holds that some groups and individuals are superior to others and should therefore have more power.'

---

† In the speech, Powell quoted a man, purportedly a constituent, who told him: 'In this country in 15 or 20 years' time the black man will have the whip hand over the white man.'

The far-right belief I most commonly encountered was the view that shadowy forces are coordinating the mass migration of Asians and Africans into Europe in order to weaken and ultimately extinguish the white population. Known as the Great Replacement, it was perhaps first articulated by Adolf Hitler in *Mein Kampf*, who claimed that Jews were responsible for bringing colonial troops into occupied Rhineland after World War I so they could breed with Germans. Their children, insulted as *Rheinlandbastarden*, were among the first victims of Nazi sterilisations – eight hundred mixed-race children were forcibly castrated.

Academic researchers often draw a distinction between the extreme right and the radical right. Where these two tend to differ is in their views on democracy and violence. A radical right political party broadly believes in the democratic process, even if it opposes the rule of law or full rights for religious minorities or certain sexual orientations. An extreme right organisation, on the other hand, rejects democracy and is more likely to believe in violent action to achieve its goals.

While undercover, I noticed that this boundary between radical and extreme right could be messy. I saw radical-right politicians speaking at extreme-right conferences, cheered on by neo-Nazis as they described their growing poll numbers. Similarly, I met extreme-right members of radical-right parties who expressed a fondness for violence and a disdain for democracy, even as they handed out election leaflets. This book, which is a work of journalism and not academia, uses the more general term of 'far right'. More specific definitions are helpful when considering the differences of opinion across the political spectrum, but as

I was not always able to ask those I met for their beliefs on the function of democracy and the rule of law, I hope readers will forgive this more simplistic definition.

Some names in the following chapters have been changed for legal reasons. These are represented by an asterisk.

1

It's November 2022. Patrik invites me to the cafe in the Wellcome Collection, a museum in central London, for a test. He shakes my hand and the smile leaves his face. In a voice too quiet for the tourists around us to hear, he asks my name. 'Chris,' I reply, and the interrogation begins.

Where do I work? Where did I grow up? What A levels did I do? What did I study at university? What modules? Where was my student accommodation? What are the names of my parents? What does my brother do for a living? My sister? What films do I like? Music? TV? Where do I live now?

I hesitate on this last question, and Patrik pauses the interview. 'You can tell them you don't want to get doxxed,' he says. Doxxing means the identification of an anonymous activist. I write down his answer in a notepad, hoping I can remember it when the time comes. The questions resume.

What are my political views? What do I think about immigration? What is going on with British culture? Which internet streamers do I watch? Was there a moment when I started to realise the truth?

He's building to a big one.

What do I think about the JQ?

The JQ is the Jewish Question. Where do I stand on the Jews?

I think for a moment. You can't just ask me on the first date, I reply, making a joke about it. At least buy me a few more drinks.

Patrik's smile returns. He's satisfied with my answer, and offers me a tip. For the biographical questions, I must have a quick response. When it comes to politics, it is OK not to have a perfectly constructed answer. Lies follow a script, but the truth can sometimes be messy. An alternative response to the Jews question, he says, could have been a shrug, a grin, and a 'you tell me'. I scribble this in my notepad.

For a month, I have been developing my alter ego. I write out my biography, and practise answering personal questions in the shower, pacing the flat, walking the dog. My wife shouts out 'Chris!' so I can turn my head to look. I've been reading racist books and watching online chat shows to immerse myself in the language and talking points of the British far right.

At the same time, I've deleted my social media profiles, removing traces of my old life from the internet. The first lies I have to tell are to my friends and colleagues, asking if they can delete their photos of me and remove my byline from articles I've written. I pretend that I've been getting some internet abuse and want to lie low for a while. It feels like I'm preparing to abandon my old life.

With the drill complete, Patrik says I'm ready, and briefs me on the beginning of the year I'm about to spend as Chris. He has identified an organisation called the Basketweavers. They have a sparse presence on the internet and that appears to be the point. On an obscure website, they advertise themselves as a kind of clandestine discussion group:

> In a time when most communication is performed online – hiding behind avatars and screen names – we have forgotten the importance of meeting face to face. In the parts of the world where many of us have to hold our tongues and never reveal our beliefs to anyone, finding a place where you don't need to hold that pretence is enormously valuable.

It doesn't add much more, except that applicants are made to go through a vetting process, to be sure that everyone has 'just as much passion for the craft as you do'. But what is that craft? It certainly isn't weaving baskets. Whatever it is, it seems to be popular. The Basketweavers' website features a map with pins in every major UK city – London, Manchester, Liverpool, Sheffield, Bristol, Birmingham – with additional locations in the US, Ireland, Germany, Poland, Switzerland, Belgium and the Netherlands. What are all those Basketweavers doing?

Patrik has good reason to believe that this is no ordinary community. In addition to their secrecy, there is another fact about the Basketweavers that is especially worrying, and it has to do with their supporters.

The Basketweavers are advertised on the home page of a disgraced academic called Neema Parvini. A former literature lecturer at the University of Surrey, Parvini once wrote books about Shakespeare and the occasional comment article. But he led a double life, producing a far-right internet show under his pseudonym, Academic Agent.

In 2020, a clip of his programme was uncovered by students at his university. Discussing the murder of George Floyd, Parvini explained he didn't want to live in the same country as black people. 'They don't deserve to survive,' he said. The university fired him.

Why Parvini detonated his promising career is a mystery, but he relishes his new life as an overtly racist influencer. He has become a fixture of the British far right, swapping academic conferences for secret extremist gatherings. Parvini has 100,000 followers on YouTube, 37,000 on X/Twitter, and a further 3,000 on Telegram. On these social media channels, he says black people are a 'different species', 'closer to homo erectus', 'impulsive' and with a 'low IQ'. He also fantasises about the need to 'recreate rightwing victories in mid-century Europe with street-level supremacy', calling for 'an underground army' in the mould of the Nazi Brownshirts.

Parvini is inspired by the twentieth-century philosopher Julius Evola, a self-described 'super-fascist' who collaborated with Mussolini's Italy and Hitler's Germany. In his essay 'Negrified America', Evola wrote: 'We are witnessing a negrification, a mongrelization, and a decline of the white race in the face of faster-breeding inferior races.' Curiously, Parvini, who is part-Iranian, says this essay was 'obviously correct'.

Although his career as an academic is over, he continues to style himself as an educator and mentor of young people. On his website is a recommended reading list for his fans. It features two books by Francis Parker Yockey, an American Nazi, and five titles by Kerry Bolton, a Holocaust denier.

Parvini also recommends *The Jews* by Hilaire Belloc, who wrote that they should be segregated from Gentile society.

It looks like Parvini did not found the Basketweavers, but was rather an early supporter. Only months later do Patrik and I find out who created the group.

The Basketweavers have also been promoted by some vicious far-right influencers. Patrik shows me a video by Keith Woods, an Irish white nationalist. In the clip, Woods holds up a small wooden basket. 'Alone these pieces of tree bark are weak, but when brought together, they make a mighty basket,' he says cryptically. A new group has formed that is 'totally apolitical, for people to come together and discuss basket-weaving'. Deadpan, he explains: 'There will be no discussion of economics, politics, philosophy, religion, or any of the kind of controversial topics that might be discussed on somewhere like this YouTube channel.' Woods once described himself as a 'raging anti-semite', so what does he see in the Basketweavers that is so promising? And what to make of his assertion that it would not discuss controversial topics?

Patrik and I agree that the Basketweavers are an intriguing target. Given their commitment to secrecy, there is no way to understand what goes on inside the organisation – what they do that so impresses Neema Parvini and Keith Woods – without joining.

The Basketweavers had been on Patrik's radar before I started speaking to HOPE not hate. Several months earlier, he created an account on Discord, a social media messaging app, and joined the Basketweaving server. The access link is publicly available – he found it underneath Keith Woods's promotional video. Once there, Patrik had to undergo a vetting process. It was surprisingly quick. An administrator asked him by text to describe his political views and what he hoped to gain by joining.

'I'm on some sort of journey regarding my politics,' Patrik answered. 'I'm a nationalist and a traditionalist.' He said he hoped to make friends and learn from them.

'Good answers,' replied the admin. It worked. Patrik was now, under an alias, a member of the Basketweavers.

The name he chose for this Discord account was Chris.

Patrik had discovered an enormous organisation. In the Discord server today, there are more than 2,000 members worldwide, with hundreds of them in the UK. At its peak, Patriotic Alternative, the white nationalist organisation that was perhaps Britain's biggest far-right group, had a membership of a few hundred. Aware that the Basketweavers would attract the attention of journalists, anti-fascist researchers and perhaps even the police, they ban online discussions. Members are told to delete messages that stray off the only acceptable topic of organising in-person events. So what are they trying to hide?

Patrik and I set out our goals. We want to find out what the Basketweavers are up to, determine the role of Neema Parvini, and if possible identify the group's creator. Infiltrating a group that seems to be less focused on street activism and thus less risky will help to establish my far-right credentials without putting me into too much danger early on. A bonus ambition is to chart any links that members have to other far-right groups and see if we can use the character of Chris to infiltrate them.

I say goodbye to Patrik and start preparing for my first

undercover assignment in a week's time. The Basketweavers release a calendar of events every month, and December begins with a Friday-evening meet-up in a central London pub called the Crosse Keys, near Bank. I spend the next days excitedly getting ready, buying a cheap Android phone and memorising the number. This will be Chris's new device.

On the day of my first meet-up, I don't want to take any chances. Although it is certainly overkill, I head to the site of my fictional company offices in west London before taking the Underground to the Crosse Keys. This adds half an hour to my journey, but just in case I later meet a Basketweaver who saw me on the same carriage, I will be able to pretend I was leaving work. I reach Bank at 6 p.m., repeating the name Chris in my head, and arrive at the pub, not quite believing what I'm about to do.

Patrik has a safety protocol: I am to text him on entry, again after twenty minutes to say I'm safe, then an update every hour. I don't have the hidden camera, as I am unsure what security checks the Basketweavers might enforce. Instead, I have my Chris phone and some cash. I take a deep breath and send my 'going in' message to Patrik.

The sound of a hundred drunken Londoners explodes through the door. The Crosse Keys is a sprawling, raucous pub packed with City boys conducting competitive experiments on the male stomach's volumetric capacity for alcohol. What are the Basketweavers doing in a place like this? They text me that they're in a quieter room at the back on the first floor. I squeeze through the crowd to find them occupying a sticky table near the revellers of an office Christmas party.

Are you the Basketweavers? I ask. They nod and I shake

hands with four unsmiling young men who watch me as I pull up a chair.

A member introduces himself as Mitchell,* and I notice the other three listening to him.

'How did you come to find the Basketweavers?' he asks.

This is the interrogation that Patrik and I had practised for. It's finally happening. I try to keep cool. Mitchell has a stern, unblinking expression on his face.

I reply that I found the group through Neema Parvini's website. I'm a fan of his, I add.

'How did you become interested in him?' Mitchell asks.

I remember Patrik's advice about verisimilitude and vagueness – it goes against my nervous inclination to blurt out a word-perfect answer.

I don't really know, I respond. I watch a lot of YouTube and listen to a lot of podcasts, and can't recall exactly how I found Parvini. I list the other streamers I like: Paul Joseph Watson, Colin Robertson aka Millennial Woes, and Carl Benjamin, who blogs under the name Sargon of Akkad.

Will they buy it? Patrik had warned me that exposure is always a danger but the more likely risk during the first meet-up is that I will simply not fit in. He had told me about wannabe activists during his time undercover who failed an indefinable sniff test. They might have been too loud, too quiet, too keen, or too bored – in any case, they just didn't look right and were banned from returning. It could happen to me, Patrik said. The four Basketweavers process my answer silently, eyes on me. Have I passed?

'Sargon is a good way in for a lot of people,' says Mitchell, finally softening up. The test is over, quicker than I expected. It helped, I think, that Patrik had completed the application several months ago, and lurked in the Discord server without interacting, giving me the appearance of a shy member, rather than a rat desperate to sneak in.

Other Basketweavers arrive, providing a welcome distraction. Soon there are a dozen of them, all men in their twenties and thirties. After a drink or two, they become friendlier, and chat about their work weeks and the weather and Christmas plans. I learn that they come from a variety of backgrounds – there are delivery drivers and university graduates, factory workers and investment bankers. I shake hands with all of them, including Robert.* He is more easygoing than Mitchell. We strike up a rapport, and he invites me to work out in his local gym. I am beginning to wonder whether the Basketweavers might be what Keith Woods said it was – no discussion of controversial topics – when Robert talks about his plans to attend an upcoming far-right demonstration.

Perhaps it was Robert's mention of the protest, but Basketweavers around us change gear from small talk to politics. Edward,* a fellow member, joins our conversation and he and Robert discuss their admiration of Julius Evola. 'A nation is only strong when it has a pure stock,' says Robert, citing the super-fascist philosopher. Others discuss their fears about Muslim immigration and falling birth rates among white people. I hear members talk about videos they have watched on the JQ and others describe their admiration of Patriotic Alternative and its leader, Mark Collett.

I had expected the Basketweavers to be extreme, but this is a dizzying experience. Here, in a Wetherspoons pub, a group of out-and-out racists are meeting for their fortnightly drinking session. I'm sitting among them, feeling weird and jittery, my mind lurching every so often when I hear something unexpected. 'I'm surprised that HOPE not hate hasn't tried to send in an infiltrator to do an exposé on the Basketweavers,' Robert says, looking at me. Does he suspect me? I laugh it off, trying to stay calm.

The Basketweavers discuss the Covid pandemic being fake, calling it the 'holo-cough'. I head downstairs to the bar to get another drink and check in with Patrik. Searching for my phone, I happen to touch the back of my trousers, and notice, with an adrenalising jolt, that an old face mask is poking out of my pocket. I can't believe they haven't seen it.

Patrik advised me to leave early, a precaution against getting drunk and forgetting my backstory. There's no danger of that – I've been ordering non-alcoholic beers out of sight and pouring them into a pint glass. It's 11 p.m. and plenty of Basketweavers are still here, even if they have slumped a little in their chairs. The priority tonight is to fit in. All the questions I have about who created Basketweaving and what they hope to achieve are secondary to securing an invitation to the next meeting. Tonight, it is enough of an achievement to leave with enthusiastic hugs and a few see-you-next-times. I walk away from the pub, looking over my shoulder.

Every fortnight that follows, I go to the Crosse Keys. The Basketweavers also arrange weekend trips to art galleries and cinemas, but I avoid these as they offer less chance for conversation and a greater risk of bumping into someone I might know. There is a regular midweek trip to a pub in Croydon, but as the Basketweavers think I live on the other side of London, they look surprised when I show up

36

one night. I lie about finishing work early and having a free evening. A very drunk man pukes on the carpet, filling the pub with the stench of vomit. I decide against returning.

As Chris, my life as a corporate consultant is dull enough not to merit much attention. I present myself as an interested layman new to far-right politics, which explains why I stay quiet during Basketweaver events. I buy drinks when it is my round and do my best to get along with them. It works with everyone but Mitchell, who always seems to look at me askance. He has an annoying habit of correcting me. Every conversation we have, he loudly tells me I am wrong. I find myself bringing up increasingly odd topics to see if he will offer his opinion. He lectures me on the merits of medieval siege engines (trebuchets have greater range, catapults are easier to set up) and traditional French methods of preserving meats in aspic.

Only once am I able to correct him, on something very niche: the pronunciation of the word Circassian. Mitchell says 'Circ-asian' and I say that it's pronounced 'Cir-cassian'. He glares at me.

In January, several weeks into the infiltration, the Basketweavers feel comfortable enough in my presence to talk about frighteningly extreme things. At the Crosse Keys again, members fantasise about gunning down migrants in the English Channel and murdering civil servants believed to be enacting progressive policies. 'Shoot them dead, so the streets run red with their blood,' spits Edward.

He says he's keen to visit the countryside in the spring.

Oh yeah? I reply, not paying much attention.

'Yeah!' he shouts, surprising me. ''Cause there's no blacks!'

The Basketweavers talk about which European cities have been 'ruined by Arabs', and delight in using racial slurs. Robert, like Neema Parvini, brings up the Julius Evola essay, 'Negrified America'. 'It was remarkably prescient about the problems in America in culture and crime caused by ni . . . ni . . .' he stutters, unsure whether to cross the line. Two other members encourage him. 'Say it! Say nigger! Nigger!' Robert, having been egged on, says the slur with glee.

Despite the occasional outburst, the Basketweavers tend to use coded language to mask their racism. I learn that 'elves' means Jews ('funny little people wearing funny little hats'), and 'TND' means 'total nigger death', a policy objective. The codes are not always subtle: they talk about 'the Austrian painter' and 'the Bavarian corporal' to refer to Hitler. If the number six comes up in conversation, someone will joke that it is fake – the six million dead Jews of the Holocaust being, to them, a fiction.

While black people and Muslims are frequently the targets of the Basketweavers' ire, Jews are the ultimate enemy. According to the Great Replacement conspiracy theory that animates the group, Jews are responsible for importing Asians and Africans into Europe in order to subvert white society.

Replacement theory is articulated by the books on Neema Parvini's recommended reading list. In *Babel Inc: Multiculturalism, Globalisation, and the New World Order*, Kerry Bolton, a far-right author from New Zealand, accuses Jews of plotting 'the destruction of national and cultural cohesion through "cultural pluralism" or multiculturalism'. By promoting Muslim immigration and women's rights,

Bolton says, Jews are creating a 'dumbed-down global slave race' that one day they will control.

The Basketweavers have absorbed this message and talk about 'the Ashk' or 'the tribe' with contempt. Edward, one night, talks about Jews being responsible for the death of Jesus Christ, and accuses them of unfair moneylending practices. 'Is it any wonder they're persecuted?' he says. Others believe Jews have taken over the food industry to sell products filled with inflammation-causing seed oils to weaken and control Western men.

I never get used to hearing these conversations. In the mind of the Basketweavers, there is no limit to Jewish villainy. There are always new atrocities that Jews are plotting. Jews, I am told, exploit their control of the media to encourage race-mixing through TV adverts depicting multiracial families.

'It's always a black man and a white woman,' says Robert. 'They're trying to lay the groundwork for white women to give birth to mixed-race babies.'

Ricky* nods. 'It's in the interest of Talmudic forces,' he says. 'Jews want us weaker so we are easier to rule.'

If Jews are so powerful, I think, how come after all the centuries they have been accused of scheming to take over the world, it still hasn't happened? They must be the most powerful yet ineffective cabal in existence.

After several weeks, I feel like I'm getting more used to undercover work. After every meeting, I note down every lie I told about myself, so I don't trip myself up later with a contradictory statement. But the threat of exposure means I am never comfortable.

In January, I head towards a pub meet-up, texting Patrik

when I go in. I hit send, then feel a hand grip my shoulder. My body freezes with alarm. It's Edward. Was my phone in view? Did he see the messages on it? We walk to the bar together, thoughts zipping around my head about what might happen next. How could I have been so stupid? Edward looks angry and doesn't say much. I offer to buy him a pint, and we head into the back room where the other Basketweavers are waiting. Is he angry because he knows, and he's going to tell them what he saw? I picture all these weeks of preparation going down the toilet because of one brainless error. Why didn't I check that nobody was nearby? Edward instead rants about his difficult work week and the train delays that made him late to the meeting. He can't have seen.

Chris mode becomes increasingly easy to slip into, but some mistakes are unavoidable. No matter how many times I practise saying my new name, I come close to saying my real one. After one long evening, again in the Crosse Keys, a member I don't know approaches and offers his hand. He introduces himself and for a horrible split second, I make an aspirated 'H' sound for the beginning of 'Harry' before catching myself and saying 'Chris'. Luckily, it goes unremarked. On the train home, I knead my palms into my head thinking about how close I came to being found out.

After six weeks with the Basketweavers, I make a breakthrough, when I overhear another new member down the table complain that he wasn't invited to the Basketweavers' Christmas dinner.

'That's because there's a secret, invite-only group,' replies Luke,* a senior member, offering to let him in.

It sounds like another online messaging group for especially trusted members. I think about a way to ask for permission to join. Later on, Luke shows me a meme about an Israeli hiker who died after falling off a cliff at the Eagle's Nest – Hitler's retreat in southern Germany. '6,000,001' says the caption. Spotting an opportunity, I tell Luke this is hilarious.

If I find a picture like that, is the main Basketweaving Discord the right place to share it?

'No,' he replies. 'There's a secret group, I'll invite you in.'

It feels like a small victory. After most meet-ups, I worry unnecessarily that Basketweavers are on to me, that I'm going to be found out next time. Here is a sign that the infiltration is working. I click on the join link, and look through the secret group of the inner circle of London members. There are forty people here, a fraction of the full membership, those who have come to multiple events and been deemed safe.

Unlike the main channel, where Basketweavers are banned from making conversation, in this one they are unleashed. There are video clips of far-right influencers calling Jews 'filth', complaining that they rule the world. There are comments and photos that advocate against race-mixing and deny the number of Holocaust dead. Members post photos of their shelves stacked with Julius Evola books. They rail against 'joggers', a code for black people, and joke about a fictional police officer called 'DCI Nate Higgers'. Although these are things that the Basketweavers have said in person, it feels important to see proof, laid down on my laptop screen, that the group is masking just how extreme it is. The Basketweavers are totally apolitical, Keith Woods claimed. The photos in the secret chat glorifying the Nazi SS speak for themselves.

The male composition of our nights in the pub is a constant topic of discussion. 'No women ever set foot in here,' grumbles one member. It is indeed so rare for women to come to events that in my first six months of attending Basketweaver events, I never encounter any.

Were women to join the group in greater numbers, they might not feel very welcome. I hear members talk about how women are dressed 'too provocatively' these days.

'Misogyny is the natural position,' I overhear a Basketweaver say one night in the Crosse Keys.

Another member turns round. 'I heard misogyny!' he says, joining their conversation.

Most of the members are single, and some try to meet women using pickup-artist techniques. Robert tells me that he has been practising methods of approaching strangers in the street to ask them on dates. It has, on occasion, worked. Given that I am pretending to be Christian, I take a chance and ask Robert if he would agree that some pickup artists have a pretty bleak view of women. Daryush Valizadeh, a famous pickup artist, once wrote about legalising rape in private settings (a blog he later defended as a 'satirical thought experiment'). Aren't they a bit creepy? 'Yeah,' says Robert, 'but you've got to meet the world as it is, not as what you want it to be.' I'd like to push him, but I also worry about breaking my cover.

Robert later sends me a video by Chris Dangerfield, a far-right influencer. He tells me which part to skip forward to. I click on the link, and see Dangerfield, his shirt off, a vape in his hand, telling his male listeners to choke their girlfriends: 'Hold her ponytails and fuck her. I'm fucking getting in there, forearm on the neck. "You having trouble breathing, you bitch?" They love it.' Robert says he found it funny. I close the lid of my laptop.

In public, the Basketweavers maintain the fiction that theirs is merely a discussion group. In private, however, they describe themselves as 'dissident right'. Basketweavers like the label of dissident for its renegade allure. The majority of members are Millennial or Generation Z, and as far as I can tell, many of them appear to have come to the far right influenced by two key events that made them feel like dissidents rebelling against an authoritarian regime.

The first was the 2016 US election, when being racist on the internet looked like fun. As the young men who joined the Basketweavers saw it, elites wanted Hillary Clinton to win but the grassroots digital activism for Donald Trump's campaign put him in the White House. It was now acceptable to joke online about Jews being evil and talk openly about creating a white ethnostate in America. The older Basketweavers still talk fondly about 2016 as a formative moment, watching from across the Atlantic as the social barrier to being in the far right began to drop.

The second event was the Covid pandemic. It profoundly affected the future Basketweavers, convincing them that the authorities were lying to them about everything: politics, education and, above all, health care. They were angry, and wanted to do something about it – and not just on the internet.

I meet Basketweavers whose first foray into real-world activism was at the anti-vaccine demonstrations that were so popular during the pandemic. Over pints of Doom Bar ale in Croydon, one young man – smartly dressed in a suit and tie, his hair gelled into an elegant quiff – explains that he was so galled by coronavirus restrictions that he co-founded an anti-lockdown group. It was hard to find a place to meet – he lived with his parents, and they weren't going to open up their home. He instead joined the Heritage Party, a conspiratorial offshoot of UKIP, whose manifesto claims 5G phone signals and water-based fluoride are poisoning the country. He has unsuccessfully contested council elections for them.

Many of the Basketweavers – indeed many British people – were angered and confused by the government's response to Covid. There was lots to be angry about: the Conservative Party cronies who got rich by selling unusable protective equipment, the restriction of movement in garbled 'tiers', the failure of leaders to follow their own rules. Amid the uncertainty, conspiracy theories about sinister elites flourished: they had engineered the pandemic! They exaggerated a disease no more dangerous than the flu! They wanted to take control of people's lives! Lurking behind the Covid measures was an ulterior agenda to keep people inside and pump them with toxic chemicals.

Feelings of anxiety, powerlessness and uncertainty are all associated with belief in conspiracy theories. These appeal because they simplify our confusing, messy reality into a much more digestible message: the bad guys are in charge. Ironically, because conspiracy theories remove one's agency, they are likely to exacerbate anxiety and powerlessness and uncertainty.

Out of the pandemic came a conspiracy theory about

the World Economic Forum, the annual conference of business leaders and politicians. I meet many Basketweavers who believe that by the year 2030, the World Economic Forum will attempt a coup to impose a one-world government (although this conspiracy theory is by no means exclusive to the far right). The takeover is already under way, according to some Basketweavers, in the form of net zero climate policy.

'They're coming for our petrol,' says one member. Some have begun to prepare for this by stockpiling fuel. One Basketweaver keeps fifty jerry cans of petrol in his garage to which he adds a stabilising liquid every two years to keep it fresh.

The Basketweavers have been so affected by the pandemic that they now seem to have a complete distrust of conventional medicine. At the pub one night, I meet a member named Russell.* Everything about him, apart from his membership of the Basketweavers, suggests he is an ordinary guy, and we make small talk about keeping fit. Russell reveals that weightlifting has given him a hernia, which he refuses to get treated.

Aren't they easy to get fixed? I ask.

'No,' he replies. 'I'm just going to see if I can heal it naturally. I've been reading a lot about how modern medicine has got it wrong on hernias.'

This sounds like nonsense, and later I google 'can hernias heal naturally?', and the answer, resoundingly, is no.

I've been with the Basketweavers for about two months now. A member posts a list on our private group chat of Christian-themed nicknames, and includes me on it. My name is 'EuChaRISt'. As spring approaches, the Basket-weavers plan new events like trips to other national chapters. They particularly like walking in the countryside, joking that a 'magic force field' protects the outdoors from black people. A member interested in martial arts holds an unarmed combat class in Hyde Park. Although I'm not in the city when it takes place, he says it will be about 'self-defence in the kali yuga', using Evola's term for the dark age.

Curious of any discontent within the group, I discreetly ask what members think about Neema Parvini. They buy his books and donate 'superchats' to his internet show, paying £5 or £10 to pose a question to him mid-broadcast. What interests me most about his fan base is their reaction to his online courses on entrepreneurship (£99) and economics (£350). I wonder what a former lecturer on Shakespeare would know about either of these topics. I take a risk and ask, as politely as possible, what the Basketweavers think of them. Unsurprisingly, they are fans. One of the members explains he has purchased the entrepreneur pack and plans a session for us all to go through the coursework.

Despite his wish to be recognised as a public intellec-tual, Parvini runs a social media tournament called WWYD, or 'Who Would You Do'. On X/Twitter, he posts photo-graphs of famous women like Cindy Crawford and Eliza-beth Hurley and asks his followers to rank them based on who they would rather have sex with. He then posts longer descriptions of each woman on an internet forum dedi-cated entirely to WWYD. At the time of writing, Parvini has made 1,641 edits to the website.

What do the Basketweavers make of this? On this, they concede, Parvini is mistaken. 'It's unbecoming and undignifying,' grumbles one Basketweaver. 'He's meant to be an influential academic, a thought leader. He's undermining his credibility.'

Around this time, a message drops into the Basketweaver Discord from an administrator I've not met in person. He identifies our organisation as part of a bigger group called the Beowulf Foundation. I had the sense that there was an operation somehow in charge of the Basketweavers. Senior members had alluded to a founder, but seemed coy whenever I asked them who they were. Nobody else is as curious as I am, so I don't want to ask too much.

Inspired by the Old English poem, the Beowulf Foundation has a website with a rousing call to arms:

> Let us pledge ourselves to this noble cause, and let our deeds shine forth like the gleaming armour of the hero Beowulf, for we are the champions of the weak and the defenders of the downtrodden.

The Beowulf Foundation has all kinds of plans for the future. Suddenly, the Basketweaving network appears even larger. They launch another social media forum dedicated to off-grid living, where more than a hundred members share tips on building houses in the countryside and how to home-school children. There is a group of artists who hire an art gallery in west London and host 'The Exhibition' to display sculptures of muscular men looking strong and nude women posing suggestively over sofas. A team of developers works on a payments app to provide users with financial services if they get barred from their own banks.

The most enterprising team in the Beowulf Foundation

is called Scyldings, an events organisation named after Beowulf's family. In August, they book the conference centre at a swish country hotel in rural Oxfordshire. One hundred people pay £400 each to listen to speeches by Neema Parvini and Carl Benjamin, a far-right content creator and failed UKIP candidate. Benjamin once told the Labour MP Jess Phillips: 'I wouldn't even rape you,' and later added: 'With enough pressure, I might cave.' He is notorious for using racial and homophobic slurs in his videos, calling people 'faggots' and 'a bunch of niggers'.

The level of organisation that has gone into this conference is remarkable. There are three days of events, and guests from across Europe come to the grand Milton Hill Hotel, an old manor house near Abingdon. I arrive for the final day only, hoping to catch, at last, the creator of the Basketweavers himself. I have heard that he might be attending this conference. I ask around, and a fellow Basketweaver points him out in the crowd: a suited man with black hair and a beard. As he leaves the lecture hall, I jog over to meet him in the corridors. I introduce myself as a Basketweaver, and ask why he set up the group.

He says his name is Mark Houghton, and it turns out that he has an obscure YouTube channel under the name NotSoObvious. He says he wanted to create a group with low social and political risk, which perhaps explains why so many people have joined. Mark says he has a thirty-year plan culminating in 'the self-actualisation of young men in our circles'. He elaborates: 'We want them to all have a place. My dream is you can go to any town in the UK, or globally, and have somewhere you can be safe and have resources, like embassies.'

Mark tells me that Basketweaving was his idea, although the name was Neema Parvini's – chosen for its innocuousness. I look up his YouTube channel and there, in a 2021 video, he elaborates on the concept of Basketweaving. In the clip, he claims that young men need a community where they can forge connections. He identifies poor mental health, social media addiction and a lack of in-person friendships as aggravating factors. While it's hard to disagree, Mark also includes 'the crimes of Islam' in his assessment, plus 'hypergamous dating'. This is the belief that women can be ranked according to looks, and thanks to dating apps like Tinder, they ignore men of equal rank in pursuit of more attractive matches.

Islam and hypergamy aside, Mark sees loneliness as a key problem in modern society, and he wants his new organisation to help. In the video, he says:

> Basketweaving and the idea it upholds is a commitment to meaningful local connections, promoting healthy and positive values. It has the scope to heal the longing that we have for real human connections and takes away the fear of reprisal for expressing ourselves.

Watching this video, I think about all the Basketweavers I meet. Many of them are indeed lonely, and share their disappointment that the friendships and relationships they expected from life have yet to materialise. Loneliness, in fact, seems to be a major reason why they sought out the Basketweavers to begin with.

At the Crosse Keys one night, I talk to Jimmy.* When his children came back from school talking about their history lessons on Nelson Mandela or LGBT rights, Jimmy would argue with them. He calls it 'counter-subversion', and his wife hated it. 'It's why we broke up,' he says quietly. Everywhere he goes, he says he is surrounded by wokeness. The museum where he took his kids had a 'multi culti' exhibit. The office where he works apparently held a lecture on how hard it is for disabled gay men to go clubbing. 'They had balloons the colour of the trans flag, and I just thought, "Oh my God."' After six pints, he sounds glum. 'I can't talk to anyone about this stuff,' he says. 'I feel like I'm really on my own. I've had two intellectual conversations in the last year and both of them were in this room.'

There are other members who talk about spending long nights alone listening to marathon far-right livestreams, three or four hours of racist philosophy. They describe complicated family situations: one Basketweaver says he still lives at home but isn't on speaking terms with his parents. Another tells me he enjoys arguing with his mother at the dinner table over her liberal views on abortion, considering it a victory when he berates her into silence. Another believes his romantic prospects are slim. 'I consider myself pretty low down on the totem pole of society,' he says, tragically. 'I spent most of my formative years being rejected by people.'

Listening to the social difficulties of Basketweavers makes me feel not just sympathy but an enormous sense of guilt. I hadn't expected this. For so many weeks, I have seen the Basketweavers as targets and not as the people they are. When I learn about their social isolation, I am crushed.

What makes me saddest is that unhappy young men are turning to the Basketweavers in search of friendship and not finding it. In creating the organisation, Mark Houghton hoped that it would provide people with meaningful communities, although I'm not sure his dream has been realised. Basketweavers maintain a nasty hierarchy. They mock members who are sexually inexperienced, informing each other which ones are still virgins. Rich Basketweavers insult poor ones who can't afford to attend more expensive events. I hear mutters of 'for fuck's sake' when members arrive who are disliked.

Before one meet-up in the summer, I listen as a veteran Basketweaver named William* talks about who he hates the most. Ian, another member, is 'a twat, a fucking liability', he says. 'I find him insufferable. I saw him around the street last weekend and I blanked him. I pretended I didn't know him.' I never learn why Ian is so disliked, he seems no different to the other members – if anything, a little nicer.

William hears that another member named Gary* may be on his way, and the group jokes about attacking him. 'I'll hang Gary off the ceiling and use him as a punching bag,' says William. At an event a few weeks later, the Basketweavers learn that Gary has moved overseas. They cheer. 'That man is a dredge upon society,' someone says. 'He is first into the gas chamber . . . I hope his plane crashes, and a fucking mutt dies.'

The viciousness with which Basketweavers sometimes treat each other is shocking, particularly the way they target the most maladjusted people. Senior members berate more junior ones over their beliefs, which also seems to push the latter in a more extreme direction. In the Crosse Keys, a Basketweaver named Freddie* says he caught Covid at the height of the pandemic, and it 'floored' him. 'It's real,' he says. 'It's no joke, it's not just a flu.' Freddie seems distressed at remembering the time he lost to being sick. He describes a painful recovery process in which he experimented with different diets to get back on his feet, even going vegan at one point. Mitchell interrupts. 'Why the fuck did you do that? Was it just "following the science"? Did you also start believing in trans bullshit?' Freddie looks shaken. He mutters that he didn't stay vegan, and Mitchell turns away, affronted.

I see this happen again and again. A Basketweaver will be humiliated for bringing up their belief in climate change, for instance, and someone more extreme like Mitchell will loudly admonish them. 'I've not got the intellect to debate him,' moans one member to me privately. He gets hounded by Mitchell for trying to argue Russia should not have invaded Ukraine. 'It's mental! But you can't talk about it.' By doing this, the Basketweavers force members either to accept more radical opinions or to shut up. Ironically for a group that claims progressive culture silences critics and bans dissent, it too has orthodoxies that cannot be questioned.

Mark Houghton certainly wanted his organisation to radicalise new members. In his 2021 video, he describes bringing 'a brother or a cousin or simply a friend from work' to events. In person, potential recruits will be 'much more amenable to listening to what you have to say', he explains. 'It will humanise you to them.'

The Basketweavers have taken this on board. Together, they discuss tactics on convincing friends and colleagues that Jews are the cause of the world's problems. 'I have tried to bring up how much they control certain industries,' says one member.

On one occasion, I see how the Basketweavers try to radicalise potential members. In March, we are invited – through a slightly unclear connection – to a meet-up at a pub in Battersea. There, a member of the New Culture Forum, a right-wing pressure group based at 55 Tufton Street (a London town house home to other right-wing think tanks), has organised a get-together. Among the thirty-odd crowd, I see Andy Ngo, an American commentator, and Amy Gallagher, a nurse suing the NHS for anti-white discrimination.

After several drinks, I overhear Mitchell recommending the books of Neema Parvini to people he meets. He tells one man to research the Kalergi Plan, a conspiracy theory about an Austrian-Japanese politician named Richard von Coudenhove-Kalergi who, extremists claim, devised a scheme in the early twentieth century to allow mass immigration into Europe, weaken the white race, and make it easier for Jews to rule.

'Look it up, see what you think, and next time we can talk about it,' Mitchell says, smiling.

'I heard it might be some racist thing,' replies the man, a little uncertain.

'Just check it out and read into it before you make any judgements,' says Mitchell, with much more patience than he has for the vegans in our group.

It is remarkable that the Basketweavers have been in operation for more than two years, grown to the size of at least 2,000 members, and have so far escaped media attention. Their secrecy and vetting procedure has, until now, been effective, allowing them to maintain a high level of activity.

The harm they cause is hard to quantify, although the existence of an underground community that is ferociously antisemitic and harbours fantasies about shooting migrants is obviously concerning. The group continues to organise, radicalise new members with angry conspiracy theories, and network across the country and overseas.

Mark Houghton says modern life keeps us 'in a constant stress state', and that Basketweaving provides young men with a refuge. It seems like his organisation will only help members suffer more stress. The Basketweavers believe they are under threat. On the website that Patrik found before we started the infiltration, they describe how too many of them are 'hiding behind avatars' in cyberspace or else holding their tongues in the real world. In person, they worry about attention from the press, the police, and anti-fascist researchers, calling them 'the eye of Sauron', watching their every move.

The explosion of extremist online activity following the 2016 election and then the Covid pandemic has perhaps given the misleading impression that far-right campaigning mostly takes place on the internet. The Basketweavers represent the next generation of far-right activism: eager to put their ideas into practice by meeting up in person and yet attuned to the risks of doing so. Their offline-focused organisation speaks to a growing sophistication among extremists wary of outsiders. Over the months I spend with them, the more I hear them talk about progressing their activism and taking more tangible action. That's when I hear about a trip to Estonia.

2

In early spring, I hear the Basketweavers excitedly discuss an upcoming conference. Organised by a Faroese white nationalist called Fróði Midjord, the Scandza Forum is one of the biggest intellectual far-right gatherings in Europe. After a hiatus during the pandemic it is being relaunched, this time in Estonia's capital, Tallinn, and promises three days of speeches and socialising. In previous years, the conference has attracted guests from across the Western far right.

This year, Fróði has invited a grim roster of lecturers. Best of all for the guests, he has booked Jared Taylor, a famous advocate of segregation who has written: 'Blacks and whites are different. When blacks are left entirely to their own devices, western civilization – any kind of civilization – disappears.' The Basketweavers are all fans of Taylor, and enjoy imitating his blue-blooded American accent.

Conferences are an ideal target for infiltration. For a brief period, it becomes normal to meet and talk to strangers. Paranoia and secrecy surrounds the organisation of such an event, but once inside, attendees feel safe to speak more freely. Having spent around four months in the Basketweavers, I know a few of the conference guests, and will be able to fit in. The overseas location, however, adds an alarming edge of unpredictability to the trip. Patrik's advice, if I ever become exposed, is to quickly leave the meeting and, if possible, jump into a taxi. It becomes harder in a foreign country that neither of us is familiar with.

I try not to think about this when I fly to Estonia in May. The strangeness of it all hits me when Tallinn's grid of Soviet-era tower blocks comes into view. Meeting the Basketweavers in a pub is one thing. But an international conference of neo-Nazis in a country I don't know? It seems reckless.

I walk uneasily through the warren of cobbled streets that make up the old city centre, and find my hotel, which is between a loud sports bar and an even louder nightclub. In my room, I carefully screw together the pieces of my hidden camera. It's my first time using it. Until now, I've been taping events on an audio recording app on my phone, but as there will be so many new faces in Tallinn, I need an upgrade.

At Patrik's hotel, a ten-minute walk away, we plan the evening over a takeaway bowl of ramen. The first conference event is a dinner for VIPs who can buy their way in for €200. We debate the ethics of paying this – it's going into the pocket of a neo-Nazi, after all – but decide that only by getting as much access as possible to the senior figures of this conference can we have any hope of understanding and sabotaging it. Plus, it might help my cover if I had the chance to befriend other guests before the main event begins.

Patrik hands me a pack of Marlboro Lights, advising me that a cigarette is a helpful way to exit boring conversations and enter better ones. I test the shirt camera again, and see the picture quality looks clean and sharp, and nervously head out.

Tonight's dinner is held in the upstairs room of a medieval-themed restaurant in the city centre. Outside, the late-spring air is full of blossom and hope. The only light inside the Olde Hansa, true to its dingy historical decor, comes from flickering candles. Robe-clad musicians play a dirge on lutes, bagpipes and kettledrums, and I wish I had the powers of a feudal lord to banish them to a dank and soundproof crypt.

There are two long tables, and I'm unsure where to sit, not recognising any of the other VIPs. I take a spot and turn to my left, introducing myself to a man in charge of filming the conference speeches. After exchanging preliminaries and a handshake, he promptly turns to talk to the person on his left, where he remains for the rest of the dinner. On my right is Ruuben Kaalep, a former Estonian MP, the first speaker tomorrow. 'Muslim demographics are a "time bomb" for Europe,' he writes in his book, predicting sectarian conflict. Tonight, he seems glum. He slowly tells me about his pagan beliefs and how he shunned a political career for a life in the countryside.

I wonder if I should change seats, but it's too late. A waiter claps his hands and announces that as part of Estonian tradition, a feast master must be appointed: the wisest and strongest man at the table. Fróði, the conference organiser, gestures at a Danish race scientist named Helmuth Nyborg, in his late eighties. After protesting, Nyborg stands up to applause. He gamely goes through the rituals, tearing a loaf of bread in two, sprinkling a chunk with salt, and eating it. The VIPs cheer.

The food arrives, and soon there are so many species of animal on the table that it looks like a barbecue on Noah's Ark. There are sausages of bear, boar and elk, veal cheeks, pig's lard, grilled salmon and duck legs stewed in goose grease. Waiters offer two types of medieval beer: honey or herbal. I ask for a pint of the honey beer. It tastes like fizzy Calpol.

Oil splatters onto the table as the dishes are passed around. I start talking to Emily* across from me. She is one of the first women I have met in this project, and easily the most fascinating person at the table. Emily describes a plan to found a new community in the US. She wants to buy five hundred acres somewhere in the Appalachians, the mountain range that stretches from Pennsylvania down to Alabama, to 'escape the coming collapse'.

Who will be invited to live on the commune? I ask. Can anyone show up?

'Oh no, it's whites only,' she says.

Later, Emily says twenty-three people have already expressed an interest in her community. 'Some of them are pregnant, so the real number will soon be higher.' She runs through the list of skills that her followers have: farming, gardening, medicine, hand-to-hand combat and proficiency with small arms. 'There will be an inner circle where the buildings are,' she explains, 'then a protective layer of forest, and then maybe a wall. Walls are expensive but when the collapse happens, we will become a target for everyone in the area.' One possible site she looked at was just an hour away from the nearest town: not isolated enough.

Her vision for this community is ambitious. 'What I really want to do is build a nuclear reactor on the site,' she tells me. 'It would actually be really easy.'

How come it took the Iranians almost fifty years to make one, I think, but I keep this to myself. Instead I ask how she would get hold of all the necessary materials.

'The only difficult thing is sourcing the uranium, but with money I'm sure you could go to Russia and find some on the black market,' she replies matter-of-factly. 'You really don't need that much of it.' I imagine a compromised reactor blasting radiation into a blood-red sky over Pennsylvania, fallout cascading down like carcinogenic snow.

Emily is integral to this conference. She confides that she contributed $5,000 for the flights and accommodation of the American speakers, plus two of her friends. Later, I hear a rumour that she is worth $60 million. She invites me to join her community. I reply that I don't have many skills to contribute but will think about it.

She is obsessed with the idea of a giant solar flare destroying life on Earth. This, she tells me, is a Carrington event and it happens every 12,000 years. 'We are overdue for the next one,' Emily says, her eyes wide. 'The only way to survive will be a hundred feet below ground.'

I say it sounds like a different commune to the one she is planning. She concedes that it's not possible to build both, and an above-ground community is her priority.

The unctuous dishes have thankfully been cleared away, and with dinner over, it seems like the real business can begin: getting wasted. I try to leave my half-finished pint of honey beer in different spots around the restaurant, but other diners keep reuniting me with it. We spill out of the restaurant to the smoking area. Here I run into Derrick,* a fellow British Basketweaver. He praises Estonia for its 'lack of diversity', but then pauses to glare at a South Asian man who walks past the restaurant. 'There's one now,' he says, puffing on a roll-up cigarette.

At an outdoor bar called Mad Murphy's, I listen to the conference guests mingle. A bearded Italian man enthuses over how many European nationalities fought in the Waffen-SS ('the Swiss defended the Führerbunker against the Russian invaders!'). I sit next to Edward Dutton, a former academic from England, now a race scientist. He lives in Finland and runs a YouTube channel where he talks about racial differences in IQ. I don't know it yet, but Ed is going to return later in the undercover project.

He is the only one of the conference speakers who has joined the night out. Although Ed is in his early forties, making him a millennial, he inhabits a different era, talking about British TV shows from the fifties and sixties. Ed is the author of a book called *Why Islam Makes You Stupid*, and another called *Breeding the Human Herd*, in which he writes about falling IQ levels. 'A lot of people would have to be prevented from breeding simply to halt the decline,' he writes. Tonight he seems particularly animated, and obscenely refers to the female fans who watch his speeches as 'the wet chair contingent'.

Alcohol has loosened the tongues of the conference guests, who are now braying and chanting and delightedly shouting racial slurs. It's around midnight, and I slip away to Patrik's hotel, looking over my shoulder. I take off the hidden camera, handing him the memory card. He plugs it in, and we are both dismayed to see that the footage has no sound accompanying it. Some unknown technical glitch means that we have video but no audio. With only a few notes on my phone for some of the conversations I heard, it is devastating. Patrik tries to console me, saying this is a common occurrence with shirt cameras.

Fortunately, he has a spare device – the one he used for his infiltration six years ago – and he hands it to me to screw into my shirt tomorrow morning. I dejectedly return to my hotel, listening to the bass of the next-door nightclub rattle my bedroom windows.

For the conference itself, Fróði has booked the Von Stackelberg hotel, a nineteenth-century mansion in central Tallinn. To prevent leaks, he keeps the exact location a secret until the day before it begins, and puts up signs referring obliquely to the 'Spring Seminar'. Fróði has chosen well. The venue is a converted carriage house in a courtyard out of sight from the street, making it harder for Patrik to snap guests with a long-lens camera. So he rents a room from a neighbouring hotel, and is able to photograph conference attendees as they go in and out, feeding back information to the London office about who has come.

Although approximately a hundred people have signed up for Fróði's conference, this morning's turnout is much lower. Everyone seems to be struggling with a hangover. This may be a scholarly gathering, but the attendees are so far treating it like a stag do. Derrick the Basketweaver doesn't arrive until the late afternoon because he was being held in a police cell. He apparently caused such a ruckus in his Airbnb last night, partying and smoking weed with random Estonians that his neighbours called the cops, who hauled him off to the drunk tank. He looks sheepish and sweaty when he returns, and is only able to communicate properly several hours later, having resumed drinking. 'I felt like I was on the moon earlier,' he moans.

The conference theme is 'The Year 2050' and Fróði introduces it with bad news. Jared Taylor, the American segregationist, will not be speaking this weekend. He was banned from entering the Schengen zone in 2018, and had not checked that the interdiction was still in place. When he landed in Poland for a connecting flight, he was stopped and turned back. 'Rest assured this has nothing to do with our event,' Fróði tells the guests, aware that the loss of his top speaker is an inauspicious start.

I listen to Francis Roger Devlin, a heavyset man in a tweed jacket, lecture about 'the capture of America by non-whites'. Francis began his career in mainstream conservative commentary, having completed a doctorate in political philosophy at a university in Louisiana. Now he is much more extreme. Taking the stand, he laments that white people are 'destined for minority status' in the US. Francis hopes one day that the 'humane repatriation of African and Asian immigrants' will take place. 'It would be easily feasible to return the immigrants if the will to accomplish this was sufficiently widespread, although it will undoubtedly take some time,' he explains. The audience nods appreciatively.

Fróði has arranged for the speeches to be taped and posted online, so I feel able to sit at the back and slip out when I think nobody's looking. I'm determined to make up for yesterday's ruined footage. I walk out of the hotel, and once I'm outside, run to a cafe round the corner where Patrik is waiting. We perform a nerve-tightening pit stop where he checks the camera to confirm it is working while

I keep an eye out for other conference guests. Patrik downloads the footage and hands me back a fresh memory card. He also passes me a takeaway cup of coffee that I can use as a prop to explain my absence. I dash back to the venue, panting. A conference organiser by the door shoots a quizzical look at me. I hold up my coffee cup, and she smiles. Phew.

Next up is Mark Weber, a Holocaust denier, who takes the stage in a baggy grey suit. Although he's in his seventies, he energetically gesticulates and paces around. Like Francis, he wants to talk about removing racial minorities from the US. 'The question that every American should ask himself is: can whites and blacks live in the same society on the basis of equality and mutual respect?' he asks. 'No. The answer is no. It's not going to happen. The only answer is to remove blacks from North America.' Mark does not specify how this should happen, only that great historical changes are 'difficult'. His speech finishes to applause.

Repatriation is a key goal of the far right. In reality, it would be impossible. In May 2023, Britain is ruled by Rishi Sunak, a prime minister of South Asian descent. Would he be repatriated? What would happen to the then home secretary, James Cleverly, born to a Sierra Leonean mother and a white British father? Repatriation is always presented as an eminently achievable task – merely a question of logistics – and in my time undercover, I never hear anyone address the fact that somehow the British establishment is expected to deport itself.

There's a break for lunch, and I set out to meet as many people as I can. Fróði is out of reach, rushing around to organise the next speaker. The speakers themselves, I notice, are hard to engage with – Francis and Mark just want to repeat the talking points of their lectures. I walk around the courtyard and I hear an English accent. It's coming from a tall moustachioed man in a Barbour jacket and polo neck. I shake hands with Ryan Williams, who tells me he is dressed like his idol, Oswald Mosley. Did Mosley have a Barbour? 'He was a gentleman, so I'm sure he owned a hunting jacket,' Ryan replies. Together we eat from the buffet laid on by the conference venue: sweaty croque-monsieurs and quiches made with tarmac pastry.

Ryan tells me about the podcast he used to host, *The Absolute State of Britain*, or *TASOB*. It was a popular audio show among the far right. The hosts called it 'Britain's most racist podcast'. On the programme, Ryan would describe Muslims as 'parasites', speak about how the Jews are 'very good at manipulating people', and praise the terrorist who rammed his car into Finsbury Park mosque in 2019, killing one person and injuring eleven, as a 'saint'. He also shared his belief that women shouldn't be allowed to have their own bank accounts.

The *TASOB* podcast aired until 2021, when Ryan claims he ran out of things to talk about. Plus, there was a personnel crisis. His team had made a sacred pagan oath pledging to defend the white race, but it emerged a week later that a co-host was dating a woman of Indian heritage. The other *TASOB* hosts sacked him. Ryan is still aghast. 'It's like, mate: you're on a white nationalist podcast every week, ranting about the Jews, and you've got a half-Indian girlfriend!'

He says the police had started arresting far-right podcasters, and decided that the time was right to end *TASOB*.

What he doesn't say is that two of his co-hosts on the show had drawn the attention of the police and will this year be convicted of terror offences.

One of them, Kristofer Kearney, a former soldier in the British Army's parachute regiment, pleads guilty in June 2023 and is sent down for four years and eight months. He shared dozens of documents that encourage far-right violence. In addition to the terrorist manifestos of the 2019 Christchurch mosque shooter and the 2011 Norway attacker, which together killed more than a hundred people, Kearney posted a letter entitled 'Punish a Muslim Day', which awarded points for assaulting, stabbing and throwing acid in the face of Muslims.

In August, the other co-host, Ashley Podsiad-Sharp, a prison guard, receives an eight-year sentence for possessing a far-right 'murder manual'. He ran a group called the White Stag Athletics Club, which trained far-right activists, including Ryan, in unarmed combat. Unrepentant, he arrived at court wearing a T-shirt emblazoned with the slogan of Benito Mussolini's blackshirts: 'Me ne frego', Italian for 'I don't care.'

Kearney and Podsiad-Sharp are both seen as martyrs to the far-right cause, silenced for speaking the truth. Extremist social media channels raise money for their families and send letters of encouragement to them in prison.

Their friend Ryan is a minor celebrity at the conference. He attracts a small crowd of Brits who seem to hang on his every word. I find myself among them, and over coffee and cigarettes in the sunny conference courtyard, listen to him discuss his plans for the future. He's finding it hard to meet women in Britain – hardly a surprise when he believes they shouldn't control their own finances – and is instead looking in Eastern Europe. It's whiter, cheaper and, apparently, more racist. 'You can meet someone in the gym, and within five minutes you can be talking with them about how Hitler was right,' he explains. I daren't compare his own plans to the immigration he so despises. Estonia and Romania are now top of his list. Croatia was almost an option, but he ruled it out because he found it 'rather difficult to get a local girl'.

This is his real priority: finding a wife. It has proved hard. Ryan is so obsessed by racial purity that he has broken up with women because they weren't white enough, even though he felt a connection to them. 'I almost fell for a Lebanese girl but I decided against it because she's not racially white,' he says. 'Her parents looked really European. She was a Catholic virgin, one of the best girls I've ever met. But the race thing was a big one, and she was older than me.' This is his other concern. He wants his wife to be much younger than him so he can have as many children as possible. 'She was thirty-three when I met her, and I was twenty-eight,' he laments. 'So the maximum I could have had with her was two kids.'

Another love interest turned out to be '12 per cent negroid', so Ryan broke up with her too. 'Lovely girl, but I'm a bit of a purist,' he says, ruefully shaking his head.

Ryan tells me about the problem with women, or 'the battle', as he puts it: they talk to their friends and family. 'I had that with an ex,' he recounts. 'She started saying stuff to her friends, mum, and even priest: "Oh, he's a tyrant, he's a fascist, blah blah blah."' He laughs that he is 'a fascist in politics and a fascist in the bedroom, in the household'.

Ryan thinks sexual equality is a 'lie' and says women are influenced on how to vote based on 'evolutionary biology'. He gives a glimpse of what his relationships are like. 'Any future wife I have, they will never have another man in the house, on pain of redacted.' He actually says that last word – redacted – and leaves it hanging in the air, letting me imagine what he means.

Over another meat-heavy dinner, this time in the hotel's basement restaurant, Ryan reveals he may have finally found someone willing to be his girlfriend. He met her on a dating app in Tallinn a couple of days ago, and is especially excited about her IQ (135) and her age (twenty-two). He is currently thirty-three. 'We can get a good six children,' he says proudly. Where does she stand on politics? I ask. What does she think about the Jews? With a dismissive wave of his hand, he replies: 'She knows all that stuff, she's very logical about everything.'

Ryan likes to give off the impression that he has cracked the code to life. He claims to be wealthy, well connected and adept at seducing women, and frequently crafts messages on dating apps for his tongue-tied friends. 'I just gave him every single response for, like, three days and now she's saying she's dreaming of him,' he says about one friend. He's turned this into a business, offering real-time chat-up lines to single men, like a digital Cyrano de Bergerac. 'We mostly got wealthy Pajeets,' says Ryan, using a derogatory term for South Asian men. 'And we outsourced the messaging to poor Pajeets online.'

I wonder how he found his way into the far right, and he explains that his conversion came in 2017. He was active on Twitter the year before as an 'anti-sharia kinda guy', and followed an account called Andrew Joyce. 'I got red-pilled on white nationalism in about three weeks,' he says, using a term to describe acceptance of far-right views. 'I couldn't sleep. I was like, Hitler was right.' He became obsessed with Andrew Joyce's Twitter feed, where he spoke about Jews apparently masterminding the demise of the white race.

Andrew Joyce is the pseudonym of an unknown man with a Northern Irish accent. Today he is less active but in the late 2010s, his essays and podcasts were popular among the online far right. Joyce claimed to have a PhD (sometimes he said it was in Jewish studies, other times it was in history and literature), and used a dispassionate veneer to mask a ruthless antisemitism. In measured tones, he talked about Jews being an 'incredibly parasitic minority' subverting Europe by controlling its political and financial systems. 'I look at Jewish history and I see the history of a people which has exploited the population among whom it has settled,' he told listeners in one podcast. 'This is not controversial what I'm saying here.'

Ryan spoke with Joyce back in 2017, who encouraged him to be even more extreme. 'He was fully racist against Indians,' says Ryan. 'I was like, "Don't you think Indians are OK?" I interacted with him a bit, and then accepted everything he was saying not long after.'

Now that Ryan mentions being inspired by Andrew Joyce, I can see the link. Like his mentor, Ryan presents himself as a rational intellectual whose studies have led him to the conclusion that the Jews are evil and must be expunged from white society. Both men are fond of macho posturing – Joyce by going on about his skills as a mixed martial artist, Ryan with his weightlifting strength. They both talk about a glamorous international life of travelling to far-right events, their connections to important thinkers, and their influential position within the movement. Ryan plays a similar mentoring role to the next generation of extremists, who look to him the way he once did to Andrew Joyce.

I overhear him share dating advice with his fans. He has studied pickup-artist techniques to approach strangers in the street. 'Sometimes I'll go out for a deliberate session, at a busy time of day when the girls are coming home from work,' he says. 'Get in front of them – big smile – and say "Hey, sorry, we caught eyes back there, I know I'd regret it if I didn't speak to you."' He brags that for every ten girls he approaches, he gets one phone number. 'You have to be the prize,' he adds. 'You can't beg, that's a low-value approach.' With this advice in mind, I ask for Ryan's phone number, and we agree to meet up back in London. I wonder what he sees in me. Braggarts need an audience, and I laugh at his jokes and coo at his boasts. I get the impression he likes to collect fans.

The shadows in the courtyard grow longer and the grip of this morning's hangover finally softens. The audience becomes livelier, anticipating another night swept along by a tide of cheap Estonian lager. We head out to a brewery in town, where I meet Veiko Hessler.

In his early thirties, he is a cynical veteran of the British intellectual far right, and has been attending extremist conferences for over a decade. A former civil servant now applying for history PhDs, he is a writer for Counter Currents (a white nationalist website that Patrik infiltrated in 2016). I find myself drawn to him because of his laid-back demeanour and his willingness to admit that many of the speeches we watched today were arse-numbingly dull.

Veiko, despite (or because of) the time he has spent in the far right, has little patience for its leaders. It is a pleasure to hear. Finally, I have someone to talk to about the inarticulate, meandering dryness of these events. Even when guests fall asleep during lectures or tune out to watch football on their phones, they will, puzzlingly, not admit to boredom. He complains that many of the talks have been indistinguishable from the livestreams he has heard for free online.

Together, we joke about white nationalists we find lame. He mocks Nick Griffin, the former BNP leader, for dressing up in the flowing white robes of a Templar Knight. He laughs at the cringeworthy social media habits of Colin Robertson, aka Millennial Woes. 'Since Woes got unbanned from Twitter, he's gone full Facebook mum, posting stuff like "I've got Mini Cheddars!" Really advancing the white race.'

He particularly dislikes Neema Parvini – whose books and livestreams I have long found to be dull – and recounts going to a particularly dreary event in London. 'He didn't practise his speech, and it was massively running over time. He kept saying, "I've got to skip this bit." He had, like, four hundred slides. He was the last speaker of a long day. "This fat man is bamboozling me and I wish him to stop" – that was my review of his talk. It was a really convoluted model explaining how elites work. It was incredibly long-winded. And, like: it's Jews, bro.'

Veiko's cynicism about the intellectual far right makes me wonder: why is he here? If the speakers at these conferences are so bad, why spend money coming here at all? Perhaps, like the other guests, he's lonely. He seems to recognise a lot of people in Tallinn – as he does when I see him at a London conference in October. His mention of a 'normie' girlfriend who doesn't engage in politics, or fully know about his views, makes me hope that he might one day drift away from the far right through sheer tedium.

The conference has attracted people from all over the Western world. The refrain I hear from everyone – isn't it great to have someone to talk to? – fills me with sadness. If anything, the individuals in this crowd are lonelier than the Basketweavers, who at least have each other. Many of the Tallinn attendees don't know anyone in their communities they can hang out with. Some of them flew several thousand miles, spending several thousands of pounds, to get here.

I meet Sam,* who comes from the US and works in finance. Before discovering far-right politics, he used to date Asian and Jewish women. Now he won't. Sam describes a girlfriend who dumped him because he spoke in favour of *The Bell Curve*, a book that claims black people are less intelligent than white people. It didn't go well. 'I have never seen someone –' he pauses, searching for the right word – '*break* like that in real time. She ranted at me for, like, ninety minutes, and wouldn't back off. Not that I kept my cool. I was like, are we really going to break it off over this? It doesn't mean I hate them' – them being black people – 'but, like, they're not as smart as us.' Sam is still looking for a partner.

The brewery closes for the night. A crowd of around thirty head over to a bar on the main square. One of the

British conference guests crashes to the ground, his body making a loud report against the plastic furniture. 'I just fell!' he laughs inanely, before shouting at a waiter for another beer. The words 'strip club' ripple through the group. 'Yeah!' shouts an American man. 'Strip club it is! Come on, let's go!' He walks off unsteadily, hoping the crowd follows. It does not. Though Ed Dutton asks with unrestrained delight, 'Are we going to a strip bar?' There is a drunken horniness in the air. Ryan says he knows of a place filled with 'Russian hotties'. They troop off together in search of them. A clip posted on Ryan's Telegram channel shortly after shows Ed in a bar puffing uncertainly on a shisha pipe, only blokes around the table.

The sexual desires of most conference attendees – except Nathan,* a fellow Brit I see cosying up to a blonde woman – remain thwarted. I meet one man in a double-breasted jacket, who says he's from Helsinki. His name escapes me and sounds garbled on my audio recorder, which nonetheless captures his bizarre description of the previous night.

'I got conned yesterday in the strip club,' he says. 'They charged my card €500. They kept getting me drinks and said that stuff was going to happen. But it didn't happen.'

What stuff? I ask. Did you think you were going to get laid?

'I thought I was going to, but it never happened. It was just a massage.'

Did you take your clothes off?

'Yeah.'

And they gave you a massage?

'Yeah. Three women.'

But nothing else?

'I think there was a bit of touching, but nothing else.'

And it cost you €500?

'Yeah, they kept charging my card all the time. I think they must have put something in my drink, because I can't remember anything after that. I sort of blacked out.'

Are you feeling all right today?

'Surprisingly, yeah.'

The Helsinkian doesn't look too embarrassed. I ask if he's been to brothels before, and he says he has, in Vietnam and Thailand. This rings a warning bell, and I ask if the sex he purchased in South East Asia was from adults. 'Yeah, of course,' he replies. I don't know what else to say. It's time for me to go.

On the last morning of the conference, the audience is even thinner. There are lots of grey-faced people in the room. Even the immaculately coiffed cameraman filming the talks looks tired and glassy-eyed. He yawns frequently. An Italian political scientist takes the stage in a tiny suit that makes him look like an overgrown child. His name is Guido Taietti, and he is introduced as an activist in Casa-Pound, an organisation inspired by Italian fascism. Taietti's accent is thick and chewy. Every point he makes has sub-sections, addenda and definitions he wants to clarify. The title of his speech is 'A Snake of Planetary Dimensions', but I miss what the snake represents and how it came to be so big.

Taietti holds a stack of A4 pages in both hands and reads them at the speed of treacle. He's talking about In-stagram, I think. 'It's an agent of socialisation stronger than the school for young people, and I will speak of absolute socialisation as a theoretical category when 100 per cent of the sources of socialisation will be mediated by the same few actors.' What? His voice is unbearably soporific. I wiggle my toes, gnaw my fingers, move my head, but after three sleepless nights, I feel myself slipping into unconsciousness. As I try to stay awake, my vision distorts. Taietti seems to undergo mitosis, and for a confusing moment, I see two of him. I bite down hard on my hand. Finally, mercifully, he finishes.

The conference also begins to wrap up. Fróði's closing speech echoes the common refrain that the Great Replacement was never put to countries in a democratic vote. 'I don't think it's a coincidence that they haven't had a referendum on mass immigration in any country. They know the outcome, and they don't want to have that referendum. Should we have mass immigration, or not? It will never happen. You get a trivial option. You can choose the tax rate of 32 per cent or 33 per cent. But: "Hey, we're going to make the biggest change in the history of civilisation, we're going to replace the population!" You don't get a say in that.'

There are nods and murmurs of approval.

Another Italian, neatly dressed in a suit and tie, is given the floor to ask a question. He was the man who, two nights ago, praised the European nationalities who joined the SS. Now, he is asking a question that is a little obtuse, but, listening between the lines, can only be about one thing.

'This might be a bit controversial,' he begins. 'You mentioned Nuremberg, and that's a good starting point for this. We talk about a negative founding myth in modern European cultures that is based on this "good guys and bad guys" story. It seems like Generation Z having less direct interaction with people who were actually alive at the time will make them less susceptible to the myths of World War II. Maybe I'm exaggerating a bit here, but do you think if you can destroy that specific myth, some big cultural and political changes can come out of that?'

I recognise what he's asking, but Fróði hasn't. 'I don't understand,' he says, asking the Italian man to rephrase his question.

He tries again: 'Do you think desensitising people to the propaganda that is founded on what happened in World War II could have big ramifications in destroying much of the premises of the story of fake liberalism, and all that?'

Fróði finally twigs. It's surprising that it took him this long, given he runs a podcast with a Holocaust denier. 'Yeah, I think when history moves on, people see historical events more clearly, and less cartoonishly,' he says. 'World War II will just be a historical event because the problems we have here and now are much more important.'

We applaud. The conference is over. A very hungover-looking Nathan shows up in search of coffee. He missed the closing remarks, still drunk from last night. He sways unexpectedly, like he's trying to stay balanced during an earthquake. Nathan says he spent the night with a woman and manages a smirk. He invites me to a post-conference drinking session but I have to catch my plane home.

I return from Tallinn with some useful contacts. Ryan Williams is top of the list. He belongs to perhaps the biggest and best-known far-right organisation in Britain, Patriotic Alternative (PA). Founded in 2019 by a neo-Nazi named Mark Collett, PA has hundreds of members campaigning for a whites-only society. It is vehemently antisemitic.

Collett describes himself as a 'Nazi sympathiser' and recommends *Mein Kampf* to his followers.

In 2023, five activists from PA are handed prison sentences for hate crimes. One of them is James Allchurch, a Welshman in his fifties, who distributes songs about hanging Jews and black people, and is convicted in May of stirring up racial hatred. Another is James Costello, who I met while reporting on an anti-vaccine rally in Liverpool, back in 2021. I watched him shout 'Resist! Defy! Do not comply!' while two older people, likely his parents, filmed him for social media. He declined my interview request. Costello gets sent down for five years.

Patriotic Alternative is a priority for anti-fascist researchers. However, because of that encounter I had with Costello, plus the fact that some of my articles about PA have been read and commented on by its leaders, it is too risky for me to join. When Ryan Williams arrives in London, asking to hang out, it seems the closest I will be able to get to the group.

Ryan is an influencer with a following of 5,000 fans on Telegram. He is unique in that he has been able to make activism a full-time job. Ryan seeks to radicalise young extremists and feed them into PA, travelling across Europe, developing connections with Continental far-right groups.

He funds this by gambling on sports, mostly cricket. In Tallinn, he pulls out his phone and opens a betting app, pointing to a part of the screen that shows a balance of £30,000. Or at least, that's what it appears to show. During our time together, I often wonder how much Ryan is bullshitting me, and to what end. He later says that he shows women his betting app balance to seduce them. Why did he show it to me? Do the same tactics work on recruiting new far-right activists?

Ryan has gathered around him a circle of associates, hardcore campaigners within the far right, but also novices like myself. In the summer of 2023, he brings me in. He loves an audience, and as Chris I am willing to listen. Ryan sees himself as the alpha of the group:

- 'Normally I'm one of the strongest guys in the gym.'
- 'I went to one of the best schools in the country.'
- 'Every girl that's been into me just loves my smell.'
- 'When I think about all the girls who've liked me, they've all put out on the first date.'

His chest is always puffed out, his brow is twisted into a scowl. He likes to steer his followers in a more extreme direction. In Tallinn, Ryan spots two young men from the suburbs of London, Liam* and Henry,* who question his admiration of Hitler. 'Look how well that turned out,' Liam scoffs over dinner. Ryan doesn't respond, but later tells me he thinks they could be 'red-pilled further'. It sounds like a subtler approach than the hectoring I saw in the Basketweavers.

In July, Ryan puts his plan into action by inviting the three of us to gamble on the horse races at Ascot. The trip nearly ends in my exposure and hospitalisation for heart attack.

We meet at Waterloo to take the train south, in our suits. Ryan spends the journey boasting about how much money he has available to spend today (£3,500) and talking not-so-subtly about 'the Js' and 'Uncle A'. The carriage fills up with women in dresses and fascinators. Two men in tails and top hats sit down next to us and pause their conversation while Ryan complains about 'J families' controlling global politics. I'm stunned that he is willing to talk so openly inside a packed train, but maybe a confrontation is what he wants. He doesn't get one.

Ryan says he belongs to a circle of extremist gamblers, and I ask if he thinks there is a connection. Are far-right people attracted to betting? He ponders the question. Both gambling and politics are like a 'puzzle that you can solve', he replies. Far-right gamblers capitalise on their racial prejudice to make money, he improbably claims. 'There are all these great angles that apply to race. Caribbeans play cricket with a certain attitude, Anglos play cricket with a certain attitude.' The two men next to us look at their feet.

The train reaches Ascot and disgorges hundreds of suited and bejewelled passengers onto the platform, who head towards the racecourse. Before going, I tried to find out what security measures there are at the main gate, but couldn't confirm if there were metal detectors. There are only so many ways to ask Ascot's customer services 'how strict is your door security' without sounding like a terrorist. What I want to know is whether a hidden camera could be sneaked past the guards. Would they ask me to empty my pockets in front of Ryan? Patrik and I decide to take the risk, and the device is now strapped self-consciously to my chest.

As the grandstand comes into view, the movement of the crowd slows down, thickening into a queue several people wide. We climb a pedestrian bridge, and from up here I can see the security barricade. To my horror, the guards have portable metal detectors in their hands. I try to stay calm. Step by step, I am pushed forward by the impatient line of racegoers behind me. I can hear the beeps of the metal detectors getting louder and louder. It looks like the guards are making people unpack their bags and show the insides of their pockets. They're going to find me out, I think. I'm going to be exposed, right here, in front of a Hitler fanatic and his acolytes.

I wait behind Ryan and the others, feigning a phone call to my wife, hoping to stall so we don't all pass through the gates at the same time. It is a stupid miscalculation. Ryan, Liam and Henry get scanned and searched long before me. They stand on the other side of the security barrier and turn to watch my progress.

There are just a few people between me and the guard, whose scanner emits a frightening robotic screech when it registers metal. I shuffle forward, feeling panicky. There's one man in front of me now. The guard asks him to turn out his pockets. My camera's battery pack is in my right-hand trouser pocket, connected via a wire to the recording unit on my chest. Both contain metal, both are going to be discovered. There's no time to disconnect it, and nowhere to hide it even if I could. I'm stuck now, too close to back out.

Moments before the man in front of me moves, I slip my phone into my trousers next to the battery and a cigarette lighter into my shirt pocket. The guard waves me forward, his metal detector raised like a cosh. He sweeps it over my arms and then my chest, where it shrieks. I take the cigarette lighter out of my top pocket and show it to him. The guard disinterestedly points me to go to the ticket turnstiles where Ryan is waiting. He didn't even check my trousers.

The relief, the elation, is overwhelming. Giddily I walk through the gates. While Ryan orients himself inside the grounds, I walk away, pretending to admire the stand while my breathing slows down. I can't believe my luck.

Ryan leads us through the concourse. We walk through the bars where the air is filled with the sickly burps of gamblers drunk on Moët & Chandon. Out on the turf, next to the fence that separates the horses from the crowd, we watch King Charles, red-faced and grinning, and Queen Camilla riding past in an open carriage. Ryan takes a photograph of them on his phone.

In the stands, with a view of the course, he begins his lecture. First, he talks us into placing an accumulator bet that I lose on the very first race. Then, in between researching horses, he offers Liam and Henry tips on how to chat up girls. Both single, they accept his advice like fire from Olympus. Nodding at a woman in a peach-coloured frock, he tells them how he would approach her. He beams, raises his eyebrows and mimes sauntering over to her. 'I'd say, "You're looking *peachy* today!"' He finishes his demonstration and the smile vanishes from his face. The scowl returns. The effect is disquieting.

Getting ripped off isn't my idea of a good time – one pint of beer costs £7.50 – so perhaps Ascot isn't meant for me. Ryan doesn't seem to be enjoying himself either. He loses money in the first four races of the afternoon, and is thousands of pounds in the hole. Fidgety and silent, he anxiously texts his friends for a hint that might end his unlucky streak. I head over to a blackboard listing the favourites selected by the newspaper pundits. There is no consensus for the fifth race, and none of the runners look like obvious winners. 'That's what you want,' says Ryan, worse odds meaning a greater potential payout. He thinks about putting down £1,000 for a runner called 'Ahorsewithnoname'. That's peanuts for you, I tell him. 'It's all I've got,' he responds nervously, face in his phone.

Having held off from gambling in the previous three races, I jog over to a bookie and put £20 on Ahorsewithnoname. 'Come on,' Ryan mutters as the race begins. A note of optimism appears in his voice as our horse accelerates and gallops to the front of the pack. 'Come on!' Approaching the finish, he gets louder. 'Yeaaaaaah!'

Ahorsewithnoname wins by almost two lengths. I'm delighted with my own win – £130! – but the joy gives way to guilt. The cash I pick up from the bookie feels tainted. Ryan made £5,500 from that one bet, turning a profit for today. Liam and Henry look at him in wonder.

Buoyed by his winnings, Ryan buys us a round of Guinness and cadges one of my cigarettes. He animatedly tells us more about his girlfriend, the 22-year-old he met in Tallinn, and the children he plans to have with her. If she has six, he will buy her a *Mutterkreuz* medal, which Nazi Germany used to give to mothers. In the Third Reich, four children merited a bronze medal, six a silver and eight a gold.

'You can get one for about 150 quid,' he says. 'The real thing.'

That cheap? I ask. Although now I'm unsure how much Nazi antiques should cost.

'No one wants one apart from us: weird Anglos with a breeding fetish,' Ryan replies. 'My one's super-fertile. She's got, like, a crazy amount of eggs.'

Ryan says the cigarette has gone to his head. He points out a woman in the crowd who has apparently been checking him out. 'The best opener for a bird is, "Does that count as a hat?" With your cock out. She'll fucking love that.' I don't quite understand the logistics of this, but laugh for his benefit.

Compared to the far-right influencers I saw in Tallinn, Ryan has a more appealing message when it comes to finding romantic partners (cock-out chat-up lines aside). Francis Roger Devlin, for instance, writes in his book that the push for sexual equality has 'made it impossible for many decent men to find wives'. His solution? 'Restoring shotgun marriage – but with the shotgun at the woman's back.' What Ryan says, on the other hand, resonates more with the young men in his orbit: get strong in the gym, study his pickup-artist techniques, and women will throw themselves at you.

Liam and Henry seem amazed by him. Their conversation is not on equal terms: Ryan speaks to them like a teacher imparting wisdom. They listen to his stories about shrugging off the loss of £12,000 on a single bet and laugh at his interpretation of Greek philosophy ('As Thucydides said, he who is only a scholar is a pussy, basically'). In between conversations on how to talk to women, Ryan encourages both of them to commit themselves to far-right activism. They have already been to the Tallinn conference, so they're ideologically aligned, but now they are ready to get involved in campaigning.

'I want to do something constructive, I don't want to just sit there talking about it,' says Liam.

'That's what you've gotta do, boys,' Ryan tells them, recommending Patriotic Alternative. He explains there has never been a better time to be involved in the far right. In a way, he's correct. Ryan doesn't have to worry about what his employer might think about his political views, he can make a living online. As long as he stays on the right side of hate-crime laws, he won't suffer any social cost to openly admiring Hitler. When he mentions two school friends who learned about his activism and stopped returning his texts, he laughs. He says he's got lots of other mates.

'People are living the life, properly networking. It's what I've been calling for. It took me ages to get eight lads together to do some boxing in the park.' Ryan is now a walking advertisement for the far right, promoting his politics the way some social media influencers recommend gym shorts or stainless-steel water bottles. Branding is clearly important to him, as he hints that the far right has historically suffered from a problem of coolness. 'If you're not offering money or women, it's an uphill struggle,' he says.

And this is where he comes in. Ryan presents himself as a woman-scoring moneymaker who wears his extremism on the sleeve of his expensive grey suit. He wants to be known as the guy with the secrets to getting rich, getting laid and saving the white race. He is trying to zhuzh up far-right activism, and judging by the way Liam and Henry stare at him, he is successful. In Tallinn, they laughed at his support of Hitler. They're not laughing at him now.

'London-based nationalists enjoyed a day at Royal Ascot

getting in touch with our Indo-European heritage, he later writes on Telegram, alongside a photo of King Charles in a top hat. 'In true Anglo tradition, we hailed the King and speculated on the market, securing a profit.' Around 1,500 people see the post.

Ryan is a valuable influencer for the likes of Patriotic Alternative and the wider far right. The person he claims to be – a wealthy jet-setter, a weightlifting intellectual – is miles away from the archetypical far-right activist. Not that long ago, they were either perceived to be stuttering fanatics in dandruffy suits or skinheads fired up on vandal-strength lager. Someone like Ryan, who boasts of a costly wardrobe and extensive reading list, is much more influential. His appeal is perhaps an intellectual version of Andrew Tate, the former kickboxer turned men's rights activist (the two even bear a slight physical resemblance, although Ryan mocks him for being mixed race). Both present themselves as sophisticated alpha males enjoying a high-octane life outside the confines of the mainstream.

It's working for Ryan. He has built a network of extremists that serve his ego and ideological ambitions. In July, Ryan invites me to St James's Park to hang out with some of his friends. Nathan, who I met in Tallinn, is here. There's also Harry, a far-right podcaster and his friend Jasper.* Leo,* a Basketweaver, is due to show up later. I find them sitting on the grass, in between an office party playing giant Jenga and two Australian tourists throwing a Frisbee back and forth.

Ryan is texting on his phone. Nathan has just returned from Germany, where he saw his girlfriend, the one he met in Tallinn. 'We spent the whole time in bed,' he grins wickedly. Nathan says he now needs to 'recharge', which is a little bit more information than I needed. 'There's probably some element of truth,' he adds, 'to semen retention.'

I first heard about the practice of semen retention as a youth-news journalist in America writing about oddball health trends like urine consumption or weight-loss pills that claim to magically negate the calorific value of food. Advocates of semen retention say abstaining from masturbation gives men special powers of strength and concentration.

Harry and Jasper are nodding. I ask if they retain their semen.

'Yeah, absolutely,' says Harry. 'Probably now, like, 160, 180 days. The longest I've gone is nine months.'

Ryan looks up from his phone to say his record is twenty-three days.

'I'm only on, like, forty,' says Jasper.

Do you feel noticeably better? I ask.

'Absolutely, in all aspects,' Harry replies. 'Mentality, athletic performance, not giving in to bad habits. It's the foundation for everything really. It's like a legal steroid.'

Harry claims that semen retention has improved his facial structure and muscle definition. But that's not all. 'Now I can gaze into the sun,' he says, lifting his face up to the sky.

'Don't do that!' Ryan responds.

'My record is seventeen seconds,' Harry says.

He turns to look at me, his eyes pink and streaming with tears. 'The more you look at the sun, the more you can see that it's actually an internal portal rather than an external being,' he explains, his voice cryptic. 'The light caves inward, so there's something more within the sun.'

I don't have a response. There are people who believe the Earth is flat, and there are those who say the Earth is hollow, with secret continents under the planet's crust. I've never heard of anyone who says the same might be true of the sun.

Harry and Jasper are committed to living an alternative lifestyle, and have combined esoteric health practices with far-right politics. Both are worried about catching parasites and together take 'parasite cleanses' by drinking turpentine. 'You shit out loads of worms,' says Harry. I look this up later, and see articles by doctors – real ones – saying parasites are incredibly rare in the UK. The ribbon-like matter excreted after bootleg cleanses is also likely to be intestinal mucus, not parasites.

On the grass, Jasper tells me how to spot parasites. One sign is apparently a sugar craving. Another is 'being more lustful in your behaviour'.

Nathan hasn't heard this, because he murmurs 'Chris', and nods at a woman he's been checking out. Maybe he has parasites.

Harry recommends turpentine as a cure for parasites and much else besides. 'Previous homosexuals who have been massively engaged in batty behaviour, going to orgies and stuff like that . . . they've done a turpentine cleanse and they've gone completely against their old ways, cured.' I'm at a loss, but nod along like the others. Harry has consumed all sorts of parasite cleanses like wormwood, black walnut and cloves.

In the online far right, this type of attention to health

and well-being is sometimes called 'taking the iron pill', in reference to its core message of weightlifting. In its first steps, iron-pilling is inarguably positive: eat healthily, maintain personal hygiene, exercise, stop watching porn, get enough sleep. However, these steps are not really about personal growth. Ryan's friend Kristofer Kearney ran a social media channel called Fascist Fitness, sharing post-workout photos alongside swastikas and comments fantasising about joining the SS. It was part of a programme to turn onanistic layabouts into hardened political activists, associating positive change with a violent ideology. This trend isn't new. Nazi propaganda ascribed a purity to both the health of the Aryan individual and society, which were said to be threatened by weakness and corruption from foreign bodies. Harry and Jasper are worried about parasites in their guts, just as Ryan is worried about parasites – the word he uses to describe Muslims and Jews – in Britain. What would Ryan's equivalent of a turpentine cleanse look like?

It is probably thrilling, and indeed motivating, to believe that actions as simple as lifting weights or avoiding fast food are part of a wider struggle for the white race. It reminds me of the Basketweavers, who say their drunken meet-ups are part of a heroic tradition dating back to *Beowulf*. To listen to Harry and Jasper, however, their health is not just a noble pursuit but something that must be defended from the authorities. 'If you take care of your health, it's something they can never, ever take away from you,' says Jasper. 'Especially if you learn how to fight.'

But the reality of these routines must be exhausting. It's not just about being healthy. Guys like Harry and Jasper believe that every aspect of modern life is part of a conspiracy to make them sick. Sinister elites are pushing pornography, processed food and gut parasites onto the masses to weaken and ultimately control them. Ironically their response is to further risk their health through scorching their retinas by looking at the sun and risking organ failure by drinking turpentine.

We get up from the lawn and walk out of the park over to the Hippodrome casino in Leicester Square, where Ryan has a table booked for dinner. On the way, they talk about a friend of theirs who was doxxed. Yuro, a co-host of Ryan's old podcast, was identified a week earlier by Red Flare, an anti-fascist research collective. What the group wants to know is how. Was Yuro's face revealed in the notes for a criminal trial involving a mutual friend? Was it his girlfriend's public Facebook page? Was it AI facial recognition software?

These guys lead a paranoid existence in which elites, the establishment, the Jews, are out to get them through all sorts of creatively evil schemes. In this fantasy, the police and anti-fascist organisations are two heads of the same hydra. One of them detains or arrests far-right campaigners and the other threatens them with doxxing. 'That's what we're dealing with,' says Ryan, 'and it's why I can't sleep while I'm in this country.' As soon as his European visa situation is sorted, he plans to leave.

We cross Pall Mall, go past the giant M&M's store, and reach the back entrance of the casino. I have a small panic when a security guard searches us one by one – my rucksack contains spare shirt-camera batteries. I hang back, and after barely a glance in my bag, the guard lets me through. We pass roulette tables and slot machines and reach the steak-house upstairs. Ryan takes the seat at the head of the table, and I notice that each of us angles our seats to face him. He picks the wine and recommends we order the cheapest, biggest steak on the menu, which all but one of us chooses.

The conversation turns to other activists they know who are facing trial, and the group speculates whether they have been set up or targeted by the state. Their main concern is a piece of legislation called Schedule 7 of the Terrorism Act. It gives police officers the power to stop, search and question people entering or leaving the UK. Crucially, this law forces travellers to hand over their electronic devices for inspection or else face a terrorism conviction. Ryan was stopped under Schedule 7 returning from the Tallinn conference, and the others listen enrapt to his encounter with the police.

'I anticipated it,' he sniffs. 'I had a burner phone with 150 dumb photos.' This is what he handed over to the police to scan. He says he returned to the UK with no memory cards in his camera or incriminating material on his phone. I don't ask what he did with his real phone. Maybe his story about outfoxing the police has been embellished?

Ryan suggests the state deliberately sent a police officer who would appeal to him. 'There was a chad Anglo,' he says, chad being a nickname for alpha male. 'About six-two, Anglo-Saxon phenotype. His sidekick was a fat Celtic guy, a beta basically.' The Anglo-Saxon and the Celt asked him about his politics, but, Ryan says, 'I had an answer for everything.' The reason for the stop was to get hold of his phone. 'They scan your devices, and if you've got something, you're going down.'

In far-right social media channels, that 'something' is often a bomb-making manual or a shooter manifesto, which the PA activists Kristofer Kearney and Ashley Podsiad-Sharp had. Distributing terrorist publications with the intention of encouraging terrorist acts is a crime. There is also talk about another friend facing charges of assault and harassment. His case hasn't been helped by a police raid on his house. Apparently cops found a load of old banners and pamphlets from Mosley's British Union of Fascists in his bedroom. 'He is smart, he had a lot of potential, but he's fucked,' says Ryan.

The conversation turns to infiltrators, and here the group's paranoia may, in part, be justified. Channel 4 has broadcast an undercover report on Patriotic Alternative, and they start talking about how to spot rats. Harry looks around the table. 'You see those exposés and the camera's down here,' he says, tapping his sternum. 'I'm always looking. If I think someone's filming me, I have a look at their third or fourth button down.' He scans the chests of those sat around the table, and looks directly into my hidden camera. I hold my breath. How has he not seen it?

We are thankfully distracted by the arrival of Leo. His poor timekeeping is legendary in Basketweaving circles and tonight he is four hours late. He's brought with him a friend, an uninvited man called Dennis.*

Ryan looks angry. He wants them to leave. 'It'll be too late for you to join us on the food, we'll just have to meet you in Leicester Square,' he says.

'Yeah, yeah,' Leo replies obliviously, taking a seat. Dennis lingers by the table, his anorak still on.

Ryan stares at Leo. 'We'll meet you outside in, like,

forty-five minutes,' he says more forcefully, nodding his head at the door. 'You can't just turn up here with someone you didn't ask about.'

'Yeah, yeah,' Leo repeats, adding that the three of them met at a far-right conference last year. He seems oblivious to Ryan's indignation.

'It doesn't matter. You didn't ask. You turn up in a place where I come every week. You show me no respect. So I'll see you outside in forty-five minutes.'

Leo finally understands and gets up to leave, taking Dennis with him.

I can't be the only person to find this uncomfortable. I look around the table and see the others glance at Ryan, who is silently cutting into his steak with a frown on his face. Nobody talks about it. Ryan makes the rules.

Five minutes pass before Leo returns alone. 'Oh my God,' I hear myself murmur.

'We got off on the wrong foot,' says Leo. 'I'm sorry.'

Ryan points to the empty seat furthest away from him. 'Just sit over there,' he snaps.

I am cringing for Leo, the recipient of Ryan's lecture on respect, like a victim of some Mafia godfather. At the table, Leo tries to join in the conversation. Nathan shuts him up. 'Don't talk,' he hisses at him. 'You need to listen.' The others ignore him for the rest of the dinner.

We pay the bill, and outside on Leicester Square, Harry and Jasper ask for a photo with Ryan. He stands in the middle with his two fans flanking him, fists raised to the camera like prizefighters. We say goodbye. It's the last time I see him.

Ryan belongs to a new breed on the right, straddling

the two worlds of street activism and the more cerebral environment of conferences and podcasts. He is trying to glamorise both. The effort he puts into maintaining his own image makes him a much more formidable influencer than the ageing, comb-overed speakers I met in Tallinn. It works for Andrew Tate, and it works for Ryan. As I walk away from the casino, Dennis, Leo's anorak-wearing friend, reappears. He must have waited on his own for over an hour just for the chance of meeting Ryan. He was too late.

3

Charlie Fox leans over the dirty pub table, points a big finger at me, and locks eyes. 'You better not turn out to be an infiltrator for HOPE not hate,' he says, deadpan. I freeze. He's flanked by several of his lieutenants, who watch, waiting for my response. Charlie's face softens into a smile. He starts laughing and yanks down his collar, pretending to talk into a shirt mic. 'Abort! Abort!' he shouts. I play along, lifting up my wrist like I have a microphone hidden in my cuff. 'Get me out of here!' I yell. 'They've discovered me!'

In early March, I meet Identity England, a small white nationalist organisation. A lot depends on being accepted by Charlie and his activists, not least my safety. Patrik has devised a plan to infiltrate a much more dangerous and extreme group called Britain First, using Identity England as a stepping stone. We have learned that Nick Scanlon, a senior member of Britain First, also belongs to Identity England. The best way to join a secretive, paranoid group is through the recommendation of a trusted contact. If I can befriend Nick in Identity England, I might be able to secure an invitation to Britain First, which in early 2023 is gearing up for its council elections campaign.

Identity England is an offshoot of a more dynamic, large-scale operation called Generation Identity, which still exists in Europe. GI emerged from the French far-right scene in 2012 and grew to at least sixty regional branches in thirteen countries, peaking in the late 2010s. In the UK, GI had dozens of hardcore activists and many more supporters belonging to chapters across the country, all energised by their connections to the Continent and the sense of belonging to an exciting new movement. Also key to its success was fostering an image of far-right activism that was a few notches less extreme than violent skinhead gangs of the past.

GI members were told to be neat and respectable – they wore smart jeans and polo shirts instead of leather jackets and combat boots. Martin Sellner, a GI leader from Austria who is now the movement's de facto boss, embodied this shift towards respectability. As a teenager, he admitted to the Austrian police that he defaced a synagogue with a swastika poster. Now in his mid-thirties, he wants to give off a sophisticated impression. In reality, his focus has merely shifted from wanting to rid Europe of Jews to purging it of Muslims. Sellner believes the Great Replacement is under way, which will lead 'to the almost complete destruction of European societies within a matter of decades'. He calls for a policy of 'de-Islamisation'.

Identitarianism is based on deeply racist beliefs. One of the movement's most treasured thinkers, the late French writer Guillaume Faye, claimed that people from 'low-IQ Africa' imperil European society as they tend to be 'generally delinquent, criminal, hostile, provocative and parasitic'. Although he did not tell his identitarian followers they should learn how to strip AK-47s and make pipe bombs from household objects, Faye nonetheless anticipated civil war. In his sensitively titled book, *Guerre Civile Raciale*, he said inter-ethnic conflict in which white Europe emerged victorious would be the only way to save civilisation:

> Day by day, things take a turn for the worse, as migration and demographic colonisation progress further and Islam gains ground. Our only hope of awakening will thus unfortunately be embodied by this civil war; provided, of course, that ethnic Europeans dare to defend themselves against the attacks.

Some of the most violent, racist people in the Anglo-sphere were thrilled by Generation Identity. Before Brenton Tarrant shot dead fifty-one Muslims in Christchurch, New Zealand, in 2019, he donated €1,500 to the Austrian branch of GI. He also exchanged friendly emails the year before with Martin Sellner (although not about the attack he was planning).

Identitarians believe that the way to achieve their goals is not through electoral politics but metapolitics. This is activism that influences the culture that ultimately influences politics. They hand out leaflets, drop large banners over bridges, pump out high-quality images and videos on social media, and plan ambitious publicity stunts called 'breakthrough actions'. In the summer of 2017, GI activists chartered a ship to prevent refugee-rescue operations in the Mediterranean. The *C-Star*, a forty-metre-long vessel, had been hired with €200,000 in donations from identitarian supporters. Joe and his team at HOPE not hate assisted the successful international effort to get the ship banned from European ports, grinding the operation to a halt.

In Britain, GI's strength depended on its connections to

European brothers and the fiction that it was less extreme than traditional far-right groups. Both did not last. In 2018, HOPE not hate revealed that a leading figure of GI in the UK had previously belonged to a violent neo-Nazi group. Members concerned with respectability quit in the ensuing scandal. An infiltration the following year revealed that two GI members were serving in the Royal Navy, one of them an engineer on a nuclear submarine.

The final blow was self-inflicted. GI's conference in 2019 invited Colin Robertson, the far-right influencer known by his online handle Millennial Woes. Describing himself as 'sceptical' of the Holocaust, Robertson has also spoken against 'race-mixing' and the importance of killing African migrants in the Mediterranean: 'We need to bomb them, we need to just torpedo them.' The Continental branches of GI disowned their British counterpart, saying it had become too extreme. The more level-headed members departed, and a fraction of those who remained in activism formed Identity England. In January 2023, I fill out an application to join them.

Identity England's website has a questionnaire for prospective activists. The page asks me, like a job interview, why I would make a good fit for the group. I borrow a phrase from my CV: I am motivated, hard-working and enthusiastic. I also say I want to raise awareness about the catastrophic decline in birth rates and enormous rise in mass immigration.

'What do you know about identitarianism?' the form asks. I quote a French author key to the identitarian movement, Alain de Benoist, who writes that if 'everything is equal to everything' then society will feel lonely, oppressive and valueless. I am worried, I add, about the future of Europe and its legacy of scientific, cultural and artistic achievements.

A contact in the Basketweavers also belongs to Identity England, and he says he'll put in a good word. A fretful month passes before my application is processed and I finally hear from Charlie Fox. He is the founder and leader of Identity England, a south Londoner in his early thirties. Charlie has the short-back-and-sides haircut favoured by identitarians, and, historically speaking, the Hitler Youth. He was a former organiser in Generation Identity, where he headed up the London branch, emerging relatively unscathed from internal squabbling when the group imploded in late 2019.

We talk in February. Charlie makes a video call from his sofa, his laptop perched on a coffee table. He says my application was 'really impressive', and that he has heard good things about me from my Basketweaver contact.

Charlie asks me to introduce myself, and I give him my spiel, now well practised, about growing up in the countryside in a Tory family, becoming disillusioned with the lack of conserving the Conservative Party is doing. I talk about working a tedious corporate job in London, and feeling worried about the decline of Britain. Charlie says he set up Identity England to combat multiculturalism. 'We are becoming a minority in our own country, a view that was not considered extreme that long ago,' he says, adding that the 'silent majority' can be tapped into and awakened. He says he wants an Identity England branch in every region of the country by the end of the year.

He asks if I have done any activism before. Patrik had

warned me against lying if this question came up, in case I say I was at a demonstration that Charlie also attended. I say no and instead mention a recent news story about schoolgirls in Dover protesting immigrants.† If teenage girls are willing to commit themselves to activism then everyone else has no excuse, I say.

Charlie roars with laughter. 'I'm stealing that,' he says, and searches for a pen to write it down.

That line may have helped to ingratiate myself with Charlie but I feel dirty for feeding him propaganda lines. I'm relieved that it never appears on Identity England's social media pages.

Charlie says he has a question for me that has no right or wrong answer. I take this to mean there is a wrong answer, and I should think carefully about how to respond.

'What is the most pressing issue facing Europe today,' he asks, 'and who is responsible for it?'

I think he's asking me: what do you think about the Jews? Are they the main villains or not? My mind races with options. Does he want a full-throttle antisemitic answer? Or something a bit subtler? I think back to Identity England's website. I hadn't spotted any reference to Jews on there. Would Charlie accept me if I didn't at least nod to them?

Taking my time, I answer the first part of his question. I quote from *Colonisation of Europe*, another book by

---

† In February 2023, Kent Police arrested four Afghan boys after a report of a sexual offence at a school, leading to protests outside the gates. The story circulated in far-right social media groups at the time. After an investigation, the police released the boys without charge, saying in a statement that there was 'no evidence of a criminal offence'.

Guillaume Faye, which is the foundational text of the identitarian movement. I say there is a grand-scale 'occupation strategy' under way to bring Africans and Asians into Europe to subvert it, weaken it and make it easier to control.

Charlie grins and picks up a copy of the same book from his coffee table. 'Great answer,' he says, motioning for me to continue my answer.

I equivocate. Maybe when we meet in person we can really get into this, I say, stalling. I decide to tread softly. There are some people within our movement who say there are lots of *hidden forces* at work, I add. But there is enough evidence pointing at real targets that we know of, like top politicians, before we need to think about anyone else.

Charlie, to my great relief, nods enthusiastically. He says rival groups such as Patriotic Alternative are likely to reach a ceiling in their appeal because they 'go down the conspiracy theory rabbit hole'. He does, however, leave some room for interpretation. 'When we get into power,' he explains to me in the pub the following month, 'we can attend to things that need attending but before then it's a losing strategy.' I wonder what he means, but given the riskiness of asking him directly, I never find out.

My first action begins in a tourist pub near the British Museum in March. It's barely noon, but Charlie is already making swift work of his pint. 'I don't normally drink this early,' he says sheepishly, handing me one. I really don't want it – I can still taste this morning's toothpaste – but thank him. Annoyingly, Nick Scanlon, my potential bridge to Britain First, isn't here today.

Charlie passes me a large brown envelope with my name

on it. It is full of stickers about Identity England and the Great Replacement. 'You can put those up in your local area,' he says, swigging his beer. Instead, I stick them in the bin when I get home. The envelope also contains a booklet titled 'We are GENERATION IDENTITY'. I open the cover, and see it was printed in 2013. Charlie apologises for not having a more recent publication.

He shows me the secret identitarian handshake, a forearm grip. Over fish and chips with half a dozen of his activists, I notice the conversation is dominated by nostalgia for the days of Generation Identity. The activists say that until 2019, they could travel around France, Germany and Austria meeting fellow identitarians without having to buy a beer or pay for a hotel room. Today, the remaining Identity England campaigners have to spend £7 per pint in a tourist trap off Tottenham Court Road.

They also kvetch about HOPE not hate and the threat of infiltration. 'They'll keep doing it, but I've never let it get to me,' says Charlie. I am unsure what to say when the prospect of an undercover informant comes up. If I say nothing, will that be suspicious? If I join in too loudly, will that also draw attention? I aim for the middle ground, grumbling and shaking my head in disgust whenever the subject arises. Charlie thinks a rival English identitarian group is a set-up. 'It only has two members on Telegram, and one of them is probably Joe Mulhall,' he says. 'They spend every minute of every hour of every day trying to get us, and there is no limit that they won't stoop to.'

Three pints deep on a chilly Sunday afternoon, we leave the pub for the nearby School of Oriental and African Studies. It has a reputation as one of London's most progressive universities, and is thus a target of Identity England.

We reach the campus, and Charlie hands me a sheaf of stickers. He points out lamp posts he wants me to put them on. 'This is a micro action,' he says. 'It's just a bit of fun.' He takes a photo of my hands affixing red stickers that declare 'DEFEND ENGLAND' and 'STOP THE GREAT REPLACE-MENT'. It feels a little dirty, especially when the pictures are posted on social media alongside a caption by Dominique Venner, a French racist who belonged to the Organisation Armée Secrète, a 1960s far-right terrorist group. 'We do not need followers but activists who are defined by their doctrine,' is the quote used.†

Charlie tears down anti-racism posters on our walk through the neighbouring university campuses. 'The students will have a meltdown,' he says gleefully. Later, I try to look for articles about us in the university news-papers, but don't find anything. Charlie points out the Wiesenthal Centre for Holocaust Studies, and tells us to avoid stickering it – that would be asking for trouble. By now, his lunchtime beer is wearing off and he tells us to look for another pub. We walk around in no certain direc-tion, unable to find anywhere in the university village. 'My bladder is bursting,' Charlie moans. We finally find a bar near Euston Station, and while he dashes off in search of the urinal, I get a round in.

Charlie sends the photos of the micro-action to a secret Telegram channel for members. I see an opportunity to ask

† Venner shot himself in Notre-Dame cathedral in 2013, his final blog post complaining about the legalisation of gay marriage.

to join, and he mulls it over. 'We normally only let members join our Telegram after two actions, but you seem like a solid guy and so it makes sense to let you in,' he says, before pointing his finger, teasingly asking me if I am an infiltrator for HOPE not hate. How we laugh.

The secret group on Telegram is not that different to its public-facing channel. Members – who tend to be in their thirties – are not considerably more racist in private than they already are in public, where they talk openly about the decline and replacement of the white race. I keep quiet in the group: I don't want to be any more racist than I have to. When asked about why I don't say much, I tell them I am pursuing a digital detox. I watch with curiosity as an argument takes place in the channel about the ethics of looking for an attractive white bride in war-torn Ukraine, taking advantage of the desperation of local women and the absence of men, away on the front lines.

During the time I spend with Identity England, Charlie talks about wanting to organise a breakthrough action in Dover. He's got hold of an enormous banner he wants to lay on the grass above the white cliffs, film it with a drone, and pack the camera frame with as many activists as he can find. The action gets continually pushed back, and over the course of the year never happens. Meanwhile, Charlie busies himself with AI software to make propaganda posters. They are unintentionally farcical. One computer-generated drawing shows a strong blond dad and a pretty blonde mum gazing down on a village. For some inexplicable reason, each of their three blonde children is depicted holding a foaming pint of beer.

Membership of Identity England makes much less

sense to me than the Basketweavers. I can understand and sympathise with the lonely young men who want to find friendship. Campaigners in Identity England, however, do not describe the social isolation endured by the Basketweavers, and talk about their partners and children and mates outside activism. Charlie's disorganisation – I hear hints about his messy personal life and hectic work schedule – is the main cause of events being postponed. His members are frequently peeved with him. He organises a summer social meeting at a pub in Oxford, but turns up several hours late because he decided to run errands first and then got stuck in motorway traffic.

Why do his members stand for it? Left-wing campaigners are sometimes accused of performative activism, holding demonstrations that make their participants feel important but ultimately achieve little. Is Identity England any different? Sure, the time commitment is low, and they still find pleasure in seeing old friends, using their secret handshake, and talking about the good old days in GI back when their movement was destined for greatness. But some of them are dissatisfied with the lack of action and of new members, though not enough to oust Charlie. The membership of Identity England is moribund, with approximately a dozen activists. A branch in every region by the end of the year? Not likely. Charlie and his team have spent the last five years searching for their lost momentum at the bottom of a thousand pint glasses.

The nostalgia must be potent enough for members to keep showing up because they face an unusually high social cost for belonging to Identity England. This is what I understand the least about why someone would belong to the group. Despite their inactivity and inebriety, Charlie and his team are heavily monitored. Members complain that they are visited by police officers referring them to the Prevent counter-radicalisation programme. Charlie says Identity England even appears on anti-extremism presentations given to new recruits in the army, depicting his face, telling them to watch out for him. I wonder, when the Identity England website crashes because Charlie forgot to pay the server charges, if the army needs to update their training materials.†

Charlie does his group no favours with the actions he plans. In March, he says we're going to hold a demonstration outside the MI5 office in London. He makes a giant plastic banner emblazoned with the words 'BLOOD ON THEIR HANDS', and wants to tie it to a fence opposite the security service's Westminster building. Charlie has been reading the press coverage of the 2017 Manchester Arena bombing inquiry, particularly evidence that MI5 missed an opportunity to investigate the terrorist, Salman Abedi, before he struck. As distressing as the failure to catch him was, I wonder whether a protest against MI5 will really be the breakthrough action that Charlie hopes for. The more I think about it, the worse an idea it seems. However, after feeding him the propaganda line about the Dover schoolgirls, I don't want to give Charlie any more tips on improving his operation, so I don't tell them that his action is unlikely to succeed in generating mass attention. Will his audience be angry about the failure of the security services to prevent an attack that took place six years ago?

† The Ministry of Defence did not answer a request for comment.

On the day of the demo, six of us meet in a Pimlico Pret A Manger. Everyone seems a little nervous, quietly sipping their morning lattes. Charlie has forgotten cable ties for the banner and asks someone else to bring them. I'm happy to see Nick Scanlon, his friend since their days in GI. This is Identity England's first event since the SOAS action a month earlier, and the first opportunity I have had to talk to him. Like the others, Nick seems preoccupied. Stickering the lamp posts of a university is one thing, but holding an action outside the security service is serious business. Now, I sense, is not the time to ask him about joining Britain First.

We hurry in silence to the MI5 offices nearby. The other activists pose with the banner under the enormous grey arch of Thames House, hoping the doors remain shut. It's 10 a.m. on Sunday, and nobody comes in or out. Charlie says I don't have to appear in the photo as it's my first big action and he wants to ease me in. Instead, I take the picture. The other activists scowl at the camera. We cross the road, tie the banner to the railings, and set off sighing with relief that no government hoods have bundled us inside to zap our genitals with a car battery. We deserve a drink. There are no pubs open this early except a gay bar, but Charlie says we can't go there. We eventually find a pub on Whitehall, a mile away, and sit there for the next four hours, getting very drunk. Charlie posts the photo of our protest on Telegram, where it gets a measly eighty-nine likes, and no new membership applications.

I'm not sitting next to Nick, so I don't hear how the conversation begins, but when I catch his mention of Britain First, I focus all my attention on him. He says he is running in the council elections in a suburb of Kent, and has been spending his Saturdays knocking on doors. 'We need all the help we can get with leafleting,' he says.

Do you need a hand? I ask casually.

'Yeah,' he replies. 'That would be great.'

He says he'll get in touch over Telegram to arrange the details for the following week. The group finally disperses, and I tipsily stumble to Euston Station to get my train home. I can't believe my luck. Patrik congratulates me – he thought the invitation to Britain First would only come after weeks, if not months. I feel victorious. The buzz vanishes once I start reading about the leader of Britain First.

There is a curious postscript to Identity England's story, and it happens long after I last see them. In October 2024, the group announces a merger with the Homeland Party, itself a splinter of Patriotic Alternative. Homeland is a political party, seeking to get its members elected at the local level. This marks an end to Identity England's facade of respectability, and its attempts to work on metapolitics instead of regular politics. Senior figures in Homeland are extreme: some have performed Hitler salutes, praised Nazi Germany and denied the Holocaust. The gloves are off.

4

The first time I meet Paul Golding, the leader of Britain First, he swings at me. He swings at me the second time I meet him too. On both occasions he avoids actually making contact, but enjoys seeing me flinch as he sends his fist towards me. 'Go on then, you cunt, let's see what you've got,' he says. Paul is a trained cage fighter who likes to re-enact street fights he has had, using me to demonstrate on.

For twenty years, Paul Golding has terrorised Muslim communities and political opponents. He has been sent to prison multiple times and has criminal convictions for race hate and terrorism. (The terror charge came after one of his trips to Moscow when police detained him at Heathrow. He refused to hand over his electrical devices, breaking a counter-terrorism law.)

Like the far-right parties of the post-war period, such as Oswald Mosley's Union Movement in the 1950s, or A. K. Chesterton's National Front in the 1970s, Britain First sees immigrants as an invading army threatening to ruin the UK. Their language has barely changed, portraying immigrants today – like seventy years ago – as violent, dirty and sexually immoral. In the 1950s, Mosley's newspapers railed against the 'negro invasion' of 'dope peddlers' and 'pimps' who 'debauch British girls'. Today, Paul Golding tells his

240,000 followers on X/Twitter that 'a full-on invasion of Europe' by Muslims is taking place, who come to sexually harass 'local/native girls'.

After a stint in the British National Party, Paul co-founded Britain First in 2011. Inspired by the loyalist para-military organisations of Northern Ireland, Paul believes in 'the boot and the ballot box'. Combining, as he puts it, 'conventional politics and militancy', Britain First is a party with an activist wing, contesting elections and holding public demonstrations. For more than a decade, the party has represented one of the biggest far-right electoral threats while undertaking belligerent street actions. Britain First pickets refugee centres with flash mobs and holds 'mosque invasions', descending on Muslims at prayer to put cameras in people's faces and yell about the evils of Islam. Rumours of Paul's connections to the Kremlin, prompted by his several trips to Russia, where he once spoke in the Duma, have made the party and its volatile leader a priority of anti-extremism research.

I want to understand what Paul Golding is like. How has he stayed in far-right extremism for two decades having enjoyed so few victories and suffered so many defeats? What motivates him – genuine conviction or the pursuit of his members' cash? From an outsider's perspective, he seems dangerous and unhinged – would that be the case up close? And how does he manage to inspire activists to follow him? What do they get out of it? What kind of person reads about Paul's latest arrest in the papers and thinks, 'That's the guy for me'?

Before joining, I read old news stories about Paul with rising alarm. In 2016, he became notorious for 'Christian patrols' where he drove around London's East End in an armoured Land Rover to confront Muslims. Around the same time, he recruited a cadre of thugs trained in hand-to-hand combat to protect him. After 'invading' so many mosques, Paul was banned by the High Court from entering them. He did so anyway and was given an eight-week prison sentence. Upon his release in 2017, he posted a frightening video online, pledging to 'confront and oppose every traitor in this country'. Addressing his enemies – politicians, the media – he said: 'You will all meet your miserable ends at the hands of the Britain First movement. Every last one of you.'

A roster of fearsome criminals have come and gone through Britain First. Members and supporters have been convicted of disseminating terrorist publications and inciting racial hatred. One assaulted a security guard at a hotel housing asylum seekers. Another was convicted for stamping on the head of his ex-girlfriend, choking her with a shower hose, and threatening to kill her. A third tried to run down the owner of a curry restaurant, shouting that he wanted to kill a Muslim.

It takes six months for me to pass through the Basketweavers and Identity England before I am finally able to secure an invitation to team up with Britain First. The more I learn, the more frightened I become. What kind of people would I be spending time with?

I join Britain First during their local elections campaign. Nick Scanlon, who recruits me from Identity England, is standing for Britain First in Darenth, a ward on the south-eastern edge of London near Dartford. There are seven other candidates dotted around the country. I am somewhat reassured that Riley,* another member of Identity England, also offers to help knock on doors for Nick. Safety in numbers, I think.

Patrik and I plan this meet-up with trepidation. Given the well-known paranoia of Britain First's leaders, it seems mad to wear the hidden camera for my first encounter with the party. What if they search my pockets? Instead, I turn on a tracking app on my phone so Patrik can follow me remotely. He tells me to scram if I get into trouble. It's only on the day, when I get to the Essex town of Hockley and see its long, wide cul-de-sacs, that I realise there is nowhere to scram to.

I get off the train feeling short of breath. A handful of tough guys are in the car park staring me out. Are they from Britain First? I don't approach until a janky minibus rumbles into view, and Nick jumps out, waving me over. Riley also pulls up in his car. The tough guys look at us with uncertainty, but soften up when Nick introduces me and Riley. I shake their hands and realise how well Patrik planned our slow method of infiltration. As a friend of Nick and a member of Identity England, a group familiar to many of them, my presence now goes unquestioned. We're simply mates here to help. My relief is compounded when I learn that Paul Golding is away this afternoon, helping out the north-western candidates in Salford. Today feels like a dry run, a chance to befriend the members without the boss's scrutiny.

A middle-aged man with a scrap of ginger hair and an eyebrow piercing hands me a stack of leaflets. He introduces himself as Paul Harding, the party's candidate in the ward of Hockley and Ashingdon, and teaches me the script we're to use when we knock on doors. 'What do you think about illegal immigration?' is what I am told to say. If the person at the door does not seem amenable to us, I am to leave and mark their address on our clipboard as a 'no'. If, however, they say that they are worried about immigration I am to listen to their concerns – perhaps mentioning how hotels are being used as expensive temporary accommodation – and ask for their support come the election in May. That household then gets marked down as a 'yes', meaning they will be sent promotional leaflets and reminders to vote for Britain First. Half joking, Paul Harding provides one last piece of advice: 'Stand a few paces back from the door, so you can leg it if they get mad.'

Paul shadows me to see that I'm canvassing correctly. In order to keep my cover, I have to do as he says. I start knocking on doors, asking about illegal immigration, adding at his suggestion that asylum-seeker accommodation costs the taxpayer around £7 million a day. With him standing behind me, I can't do a bad job, or else I won't be invited back. I feel grubby, but at that moment I have no choice but to get on with it.

It's Saturday afternoon, and most people aren't home. We notice a lack of interest – council elections are hardly thrilling – and get the occasional 'fuck off' from residents, but I am surprised at the positive responses. These people haven't necessarily heard of Britain First, but are happy to chat on the doorstep about immigration and promise to vote for us. I meet a smiley widow who says she moved to Hockley forty-five years ago with her husband, but now there are too many people trying to come here. She points at her garden, manicured and colourful, plus the raked gravel and clean statues and varnished fences. 'I am worried about illegal immigration,' she says sweetly. 'They come here thinking this is the land of milk and honey, but what about us?'

I wonder if this smiley woman would vote for us if she could hear the conversations taking place on our battle bus. Behind the wheel is Warren.* He likes to jeer at other cars. 'Bet she's a Paki,' he says, pointing out a slow driver ahead of us. 'I knew it!' he shouts as we overtake. 'A fucking Paki!' He uses rhyming slang to pepper his conversation with racial slurs, saying 'Feargal Sharkey' for 'darkie' and 'office dog' for 'wog'. Warren says he likes to drive into puddles to splash black people, and cracks up recounting a time he did it. I sit at the back of the bus, quietly typing notes on my phone. If this is my first meet-up, I think, imagine what they'll be like once they feel more comfortable around me.

The campaign session ends without my exposure. I've secured a repeat invitation for the following weekend. This time, I know Paul Golding will be there. It's all I can think about in the intervening days. As an extra precaution, both Patrik and Joe plan to follow me by car, at a safe distance, to provide an escape route if needed.

When I finally meet Paul, he assesses what I say for a beat or two before responding. I feel like he tests me by dropping into conversation UAF (the United Against Fascism campaigners) and HOPE not hate. I plead ignorance to the first and dislike of the second.

Paul's presence today changes the atmosphere. He orders us around, telling us which houses to knock on, which streets to target. We move faster, we talk less. We laugh less. There's a pause in our afternoon of canvassing, and this is when Paul swings at me – using me as the dummy to re-enact his street fight. It's bullying, but I have to bottle up my anger if I am to continue. As Chris, I am supposed to be an affable, dependable guy, and that means doing what Paul says and laughing at his aggressive behaviour. I will not be able to advance if I complain.

For six consecutive weekends in April and May, I show up to help his campaign. I even become a paid-up member of the party. A lifetime activist membership costs £20 – like the campaigning, I tell myself this is the price of infiltration. (There are around forty inner-circle activists, and at the time of writing, Paul says he has 20,000 members, which seems rather high.) My attendance pays off. Soon Paul trusts me enough to share his campaign tactics. He says he learned them from the BNP's elections officer more than a decade ago. Registered political parties are provided with the electoral roll for their target wards, and Paul describes how he goes through the list, crossing off any names that sound non-white. Then he will send his activists to canvas only the houses with 'white names'.

So keen are they to avoid interacting with people of colour that if an activist knocks on the door and a non-white person answers, Paul tells us to lie. 'Tell them you've got the wrong house and leave.' This happens to me. While campaigning in Darenth, I knock on a door with a stack of leaflets in hand, and a black woman answers. Paul, who is on the front step of the house next door, hisses at me to go, so I repeat the line he taught me, and scuttle off, feeling mortified. Other activists, when they accidentally ring the doorbell of a black or brown person, ask to speak to

'Mr O'Dwyer' or 'Mr Bennett' and then have an excuse to leave when told he doesn't live there.

I ask Paul if there would be any merit in knocking on non-white doors. After all, the leaflets we're handing out say we're not a racist organisation and we have mixed-race candidates (in reality, just one candidate, who has a Colombian father). 'Nah,' he says, looking at me quizzically. In party messages, Paul is fond of saying 'it's about space, not race' – meaning his opposition to immigration is based in material arguments and not racial animosity. His ban on us speaking to anyone who isn't white makes me doubt his honesty.

Paul seems to rule by fear. He frightens many of his inner circle, who refer to their leader simply as 'he' or 'him', rarely 'Paul', and shut up when he speaks. He demands we volunteer each Saturday, and some week nights, to canvas prospective voters or protest asylum-seeker accommodation. He hounds us with phone calls and ALL CAPS texts asking us to show up. He praises some members and insults others at random, leaving us unsure whether we'll be spending the day by his side or in his sights. Why do the other activists put up with this? Do they believe in the political mission of Britain First so much they are willing to overlook Paul's aggression? Often he'll make threats that sound like they might be jokes – but might not. Describing what would happen if anyone gets too drunk at an upcoming meeting, Paul says his security team will 'grab them, cable-tie their hands and feet behind their back, and put tape over their mouth and just leave them in one of the minibuses until they sober up'. I worry about what he would do if he unmasked me as an infiltrator.

The fear rubs off on me. It is hardest to deal with in between meet-ups. Every text I receive from Paul is like a mini defibrillator shock, and I can barely bring myself to answer the phone when he calls unexpectedly. Before events, I am convinced that this is the one where I'll make an incorrigible slip-up. We usually meet at Dartford train station and drive out to actions from there. The walk from the platform to the car park feels interminable. Each time, I think that he has clocked me and is planning to expose me in front of the others. When I reach the end of a meet-up without blowing my cover, I convince myself that I'm safe, even thrilled that I'm getting away with it. But then in the following days, I become worried again that my luck has run out.

It is an uncharitable comparison, but Paul Golding bears a resemblance to the Tyneside murderer Raoul Moat, with his scowl, brick-red skin and close-cropped hair. Short but burly, Paul is always agitated. Fuelled by sugar-free Red Bull – he claims to limit himself to two a day but I frequently count four or five – Paul charges around electoral wards, forever ordering his activists to keep up. He drinks so much Red Bull that he needs sleeping pills. It's a small relief that he is now teetotal. 'You don't want me drinking,' he says. 'I'd end up assembling a mob, putting on the war paint, going into the nearest town and smashing the place up.' Paul says that he is off booze but still 'addicted to far-right extremism'.

I often think about where his political addiction comes from. Paul seems to recognise that being involved in the far right is unusual.

'I just wonder what normal people think when they

see us pass,' one party activist says while preparing for an action.

'What do you mean, normal? We're normal,' replies another activist.

'We're not!' says Paul.

How could someone devote so much of their life to something they think is so weird? Paul has been in activism for a quarter-century, mostly uninterrupted. In his autobiography, he describes taking a break from the BNP in his twenties 'due to youthful burnout' (in reality, he was expelled for drunkenly attacking a member of Turkish descent). During his hiatus from politics, he says he lived a normal life, working a regular job and learning Thai boxing in his spare time. But he came back, contesting and winning a council seat for the BNP in 2009. Despite prison sentences and social media bans and membership crises, Paul has never truly quit far-right politics. Could he ever?

The accusation of 'grifting' comes up a lot among the far right, and normally gets thrown at leaders and content creators who claim the most expedient way to save the white race is via their wallets. Paul is certainly after his members' cash (more on this later), but for him, activism is serious business. In his autobiography, he writes about being inspired by Richard the Lionheart and Charles Martel, both of whom went to battle for Christianity in the Middle Ages. Paul believes that society is about to collapse, which will precipitate an apocalyptic showdown between white Christians and brown Muslims for the control of Europe. When he waves a Union Jack outside refugee facilities or gets into shouting matches with women on suburban council estates, Paul is in fact waging a holy war to save the

West. 'I consider it an honour and a privilege to be able to devote my life to the survival and future of my people,' he says in his book.

At first, I'm unsure if his faith is merely a signifier of Britishness, a cudgel against Islam. But he does seem devout. He signs off private texts with the acronym 'OCS', meaning 'Onward Christian Soldiers'. Every day he posts a prayer to the Britain First social media accounts. He tells me he attends his local church in Salford, where he lives with his girlfriend Ashlea Simon, now co-leader of the party. He also tells me about his admiration for Oliver Cromwell, a Protestant hero, and is fond of joking that he is powered by 'Jesus Christ and Red Bull'.

Paul's conviction in the righteousness of his cause justifies all manner of misbehaviour, including his habit of exaggeration and obfuscation. In his autobiography, he fondly writes about growing up in the south-east London suburb of Slade Green, a tight-knit community 'completely free of social ills such as drugs, knives and antisocial behaviour'. His neighbourhood, however, would have been much safer were it not for his brother Jamie Golding, part of the Slade Green Massive gang that committed hundreds of burglaries, car thefts and assaults in the early noughties. Jamie spent his youth in and out of prison and was once sentenced for committing 171 burglaries in the autumn of 2005 alone. Three years earlier, Paul's mother Christine was evicted from her home for antisocial behaviour. A local paper reported neighbours of the Golding family suffered a great deal: their cars were smashed, their children attacked, their houses burgled. These details were conveniently omitted from Paul's book.

While Paul considers himself a modern-day Crusader, he also likes to draw a line between himself and yet more extreme far-right activists. When the teenage Paul joined the BNP in the 1990s, having left school with no qualifications, the party's hardliners and (relative) moderates were battling over strategy. One faction was openly neo-Nazi, raving at every opportunity about the malevolence of international Jewry. The leader of this radical faction was John Tyndall, who in his youth campaigned for the release of Nazi war criminals like Adolf Eichmann and Rudolf Hess. 'The Jew is like a poisonous maggot feeding on a body in an advanced state of decay,' Tyndall once said.

The other faction, led by the Cambridge-educated Nick Griffin, saw themselves as modernisers, more restrained in their language, focusing, for example, on the evils of multiculturalism instead of the glories of the Third Reich. The modernisers scored a victory when Griffin was appointed leader of the BNP in 1999. He took Paul under his wing – dubbing him 'the human photocopier' for his expansive memory – and appointed him the editor of various youth publications, ultimately making him the head of party communications.

While Griffin publicly disavowed racism, in private he said there was a difference between 'selling out your ideas and selling your ideas'. He was, in effect, telling his followers who might think he had gone soft to read between the lines. 'Instead of talking about racial purity,' Griffin said at an American conference in 2000, 'you talk about identity.' Once in power, the semblance of moderation could be dispensed with. As if to prove that Griffin cared only about branding, the audience in front of which he made these remarks included David Duke, the former leader of the Ku Klux Klan, and James W. Von Brunn, a white supremacist who later shot dead the security guard of a Holocaust museum.

Nick Griffin stood down from the BNP in 2014 and has long since abandoned the pretence of moderation. He has returned to his roots as the publisher of explicitly antisemitic diatribes for small audiences. But his protégé Paul Golding remains dedicated to his lesson in marketing. Knowing that his politics aren't normal, he must tone down his party's messaging if he hopes to grow his membership and vote share.

Britain First is not the only party to lie to the electorate, but the agenda it conceals is much more dangerous than that of mainstream political parties. On the website outlining his policies, Paul pledges to create a 'repatriation' system whereby 'citizens of overseas origins' will be paid to return to 'their country of origin'. While he says this system will be 'voluntary', he jokes to me in private that his manifesto can in fact be distilled into three words: 'Deport the lot.' As worried as they are about public finances being spent on housing immigrants in hotels, the cost of a repatriation scheme, which would surely be ruinously expensive, doesn't seem to occur to them. We never discuss it.

Britain First's website includes a statement saying the party rejects racial hatred in all its forms. Members of all ethnic backgrounds are welcome, it says. However, this is contradicted by the party's desire to repatriate British citizens of foreign descent. It is also at odds with Britain First's belief in the Great Replacement and the sinister elites responsible. Who are these sinister elites? Publicly, the party blames the nebulous 'Westminster political elite', but in private members are more specific. They say George Soros, the Jewish philanthropist, and Klaus Schwab, leader of the World Economic Forum conference – both bogeymen of the conspiratorial right – are coordinating the Great Replacement.

Sometimes conversations in Britain First are explicitly antisemitic, for instance during a day of election campaigning when members tell each other Jewish jokes ('What's the difference between a pork pie and a Jew? A pork pie doesn't scream when it's in the oven'). Sometimes they are subtler. Ashlea Simon explains to me that 'politics is the art of the possible'. Patriotic Alternative, the rival organisation that is explicitly white nationalist, 'go straight after Jews', she says, which alienates many followers. 'What I say in public is very different to what I believe in private, but to go after mainstream support you have to watch what you say.'

Paul is even more careful. Indeed, after the 7 October attacks and the beginning of the Israel–Hamas conflict, some have complained that his public statements have been too pro-Israel. He has been emailing followers about the 'slaughter' of 'innocent people', comparing Britain First to the Israelis, believing them to share a common enemy – 'a vast Islamist infestation'.

On a day of campaigning in the Tamworth by-election in mid-October 2023, Ashlea teasingly accuses him of 'taking shekels'. Paul, behind the wheel of the battle bus, plays up to this. 'Principles, schminciples,' he says, then sings 'shekels, lots of shekels' to the tune of 'Hava Nagila'. He tries his hardest to stretch out the syllables of his parody version to match the original. 'Where's my kippah gone!' he jokes. Ashlea retorts: 'If I wasn't an antisemite before . . .'

Paul, in public, has tried to distance himself from the part of the far right that is openly antisemitic. Jews are not targeted in the campaign literature or social media posts of Britain First, even though many of the members think, on balance, that Jews cause more harm to Western society than Muslims. During the May local elections campaign, we leaflet the terraces of Swanscombe in Dartford and I listen to two veteran members tell me about how Auschwitz was fake. 'It's all made up,' one canvasser says as we walk between houses, stuffing party flyers through letter boxes. 'And the gas chambers? For delousing.' The other member nods. 'For typhus. That's all it was.' The first member recommends the works of Holocaust deniers like David Irving, from whom he has a signed and dedicated book. People did die in Auschwitz, but from disease 'not in the gas', he insists.

Paul interjects. 'Not so loud on this topic while we're in public, please,' he says.

His reaction puzzles me. Does it mean that Paul disagrees, and is politely getting us to shut up? Or does it mean he agrees, but is more careful than his loudmouth followers? Given Paul's own preoccupation with marketing himself as mainstream, I want to pin him down.

In November, I ask Nick Scanlon, a close confidant of Paul, where he thinks our leader stands on Jews. Patrik has cautioned me to avoid doing this in conversation. It's such an extreme topic it risks making me seem like a rat, but after six months I know Nick well enough to try. The two of us are drinking in an Irish pub, and emboldened by a couple of Guinnesses, I ask him. 'If Paul was a Zionist,' he replies, 'half of us would have been expelled.' Nick says he has been embarrassed by Britain First's pro-Israel pronouncements – he has no truck with 'our friends in small caps', as he terms them. At the same time, he recognises that talking too much about the evils of Jewry in public is a 'dead end', consigning you to the Nazi end of politics where mainstream success will be forever out of reach.

I join Britain First when the party seems to be briefly experimenting with a less extreme message. In the 2010s, Paul spoke of banning Islam. The year after I leave, he returns to discussing 'native white British' people being demographically replaced, and brags that his is the only political party to believe in replacement theory. While I'm with Britain First, Paul attempts to tone it down. The promotional sheets I stuff through letter boxes focus on the familiar messages about illegal immigration and the high cost of accommodating refugees in hotels. Like a stage director, he tells us to be energetic, demonstrating a theatrical grin to present on the doorstep.

Paul has a limited number of activists to draw on, and not all of them are good at delivering this relatively softer message. Alfie,* a middle-aged activist from Kent, joins us for a day of canvassing in Hockley in late April. His technique is particularly aggressive. Where the rest of us will say something like 'Excuse me, sorry to bother you, we're from the Britain First Party, what do you think about illegal immigration?', Alfie will hammer on the door and snarl: 'Do you like migrants?' In one afternoon, he fails to get a single positive response. He jokes that instead of knocking for votes we should appeal for donations so Britain First can purchase guns to shoot migrants. Alfie, who is tall and doesn't have all of his teeth, occasionally disappears round a corner to apparently knock on a door. He returns, sniffing arrhythmically.

We finish canvassing and head to a pub. Paul Golding normally cuts our socials short before everyone's finished their first pint, but as he's up north canvassing with the Salford team today, we can take our time. There's Paul Harding, Max* – a member of a year's standing – and Alfie sat on the outdoor bench. Several times during the afternoon, Alfie goes to his car and comes back sniffing.

Do you have hay fever? I ask.

'Colombian hay fever,' he says, cackling.

Finally, I understand. I ask him how much cocaine he takes.

'Two grams a week,' he says.

Every day?

'Two or three times a week.'

Paul Harding and Max glance at each other. Alfie goes to his car again, and returns, this time smelling of weed. He asks if we 'like smoke'. Alfie tells Paul to hold out his hand, and drops something in it. It's two little baggies of weed. Paul hands them back, saying he's not interested. He looks a little disturbed.

We've all been nursing one pint in the time it takes Alfie to drink two. He heads to the bar for a third, and I try to stop him. Alfie is slurring his words and repeating himself. I beg him not to order another pint. He's got a ninety-minute drive home ahead of him and could so easily crash.

Alfie thinks it's funny that I'm trying to intervene. 'I don't care,' he says, going up to get his lager.

'If he has three, he's really asking for it,' says Max.

Alfie talks about what he likes to do in his car. 'Whenever I see a puddle and a burka walking past, I drive into it to splash them,' he says, miming his hands on the wheel and yanking them to the side. This is the second member of Britain First to describe splashing ethnic minorities. But he goes further than Warren. 'If I see a coon and her children, I want to go straight for them.' Alfie thinks this is hilarious, but it's too much for Max and Paul. 'I'm a little unsure about him,' Max says later. 'I'm not that comfortable.' One of them must have had a word with Paul Golding because Alfie isn't invited back. He drives away from the pub with a mad grin on his face while I wonder if I should call the police.

There are fewer first-time activists in Britain First than in the Basketweavers or Identity England. Most of Paul's team are a bit older, and some have belonged to far-right groups going as far back as the National Front in the 1970s. They are all obsessed with the idea that too many immigrants live in the UK and are ruining society.

I get to know them on our long battle-bus journeys between Kent and Essex. We spend hours chatting as we wait in traffic over the Dartford Crossing. They tell me about their exercise routines, their plans for the garden, their custody battles, the price of train tickets and the merits of Iron Maiden tribute bands. 'Yes, Chris!' they say when I show up on Saturday mornings, hugging me and shaking my hand. I am able to avoid too much scrutiny by giving vague answers and instead asking questions back at them.

I need them to like me, because then they will be less

suspicious of me. Before long, I feel the beginnings of affection for them – it's hard to listen to them vent about their broken relationships without feeling a grain of sympathy. These feelings confuse me. The fact that some of them have busy lives beyond Britain First makes me hope that one day they might quit far-right activism entirely.

I wonder about how easy it is to leave, particularly for more senior members with a public profile. In 2024, Jayda Fransen – Paul's ex-girlfriend and a deputy of Britain First before my time – gives a candid interview to a podcaster. In it, she talks about feeling trapped in far-right activism. She says she found it difficult to quit because she perceived herself to be 'toxic, totally toxic'. Jayda says that ditching her comfortable office job for a life of extremism made her a 'marked woman'. She remembers thinking dejectedly, some months into her new career, that she would be unable to return. 'You're done with any sort of normality,' she recalls saying to herself.

Jayda is still active in the far right, though, frequently posting about which of her enemies she believes are controlled by Jews. Still, her comments make me think about who else might want to leave the movement but feels stuck. It sounds like members have a bunker mentality where establishment forces have marked them out for persecution. Will they – quite reasonably, perhaps – see me as part of those establishment forces who sent an infiltrator in to befriend and betray them? When they find out who I am, will they quit or feel justified in their views and stay put?

These guilty thoughts are easier to ignore when the conversation on the bus goes in a racist direction, which it inevitably does. One member says she doesn't like modern

TV shows because they feature too many black people. I learn from another about the perils of race-mixing. 'Indians are herd animals but Europeans have creative minds,' says another. When the bus radio plays Classic FM, an activist shouts out: 'You don't get many niggers making music like this!'

One day in April, an activist named Louis starts talking about how political rulers are out of touch with the country. This sounds different to the racism I tend to hear. Researchers often say that grievances fuel extremism, some perceived, some real. It sounds like Louis is talking about a real grievance. 'Eton-educated billionaires like Rishi Sunak [sic] don't have to worry about feeding the kids and paying the bills and buying a house,' he says. 'They shouldn't be allowed to represent the people.'

I'm about to ask him more when Frank* butts in, eager to talk about his pet theory that Stonehenge is fake. 'It's probably no older than Victorian in origin,' he says. Then he launches into a long description – I think I've got this right – of how cancel culture emerged from the fox-hunting ban of 2003, when anti-hunt activists got bored with nothing to protest and started 'hunting humans' instead.

At each campaign session, a member of the Britain First Defence team follows us to provide security. Paul sees the BFD as elite soldiers on the 'front line of the struggle to save our people', and in a recruitment advert shows grizzled blokes sparring in a gym or standing arms folded, wearing sunglasses and black baseball caps, looking tough. In public, Paul wants 'disciplined, heterosexual Christian men' to join the BFD. In private, Paul's recruitment criteria are a little less strict. Someone with 'criminal records, quite severe ones' are ideal, he says. In the pub after a day of campaigning, he acts out a conversation between himself and a BFD recruit. "'Oh, by the way, I've got twenty-five GBH convictions," he says. "Great, you're my personal bodyguard," I say.'

When I join, the head of the BFD is Andy Frain. Nicknamed 'Nightmare', he is a notorious football hooligan, belonging to the Chelsea Headhunters. Andy has a barrel chest and cannonball hands. I watch a video of him laying into rival fans in Glasgow Central train station and feel sick at the thought of being within range of those massive fists. He is a former member of the neo-Nazi terror group Combat 18, and has close ties to the loyalist paramilitary scene in Northern Ireland. There is a photo online of him somewhere in Belfast, sitting in front of a Red Hand of Ulster flag. On the table next to him are two pistols. Andy has a decades-long reputation for violence: he has attacked friends for perceived slights, carved up rivals with a Stanley knife, and once stabbed a police officer, for which he was sentenced to seven years in prison.

I try to avoid Andy. He's cagey, even when his beloved bulldog Hugo seems to take an interest in me. The first time I meet him, I hear his ringtone go off. It's a recording of Hitler screeching 'Sieg Heil! Sieg Heil!' Even the other activists seem a bit nervous of him. Andy is a key figure in the party. Paul invites him to attend the Dartford election-night count, a reward reserved for only the most senior members. It defies understanding that a party seeking mainstream respectability puts a man known as Nightmare front and centre of the organisation, and explains what Britain First is truly like.

There are eight council seats that we are contesting: two in Kent, one in Essex, two around Manchester, one in the New Forest and another two in Devon. If we can succeed in local elections, the thinking goes, we can build up a supporter base to one day win at a parliamentary level. The last day of campaigning – 4 May, election day – we tramp around Darenth once again, reminding households who have accepted our leaflets to go out and vote. The activists are tentatively optimistic. There's a feeling like we might have pulled off a great political upset. We have enough yeses on our lists – people who said they would vote for us – to win a majority. Paul Harding, standing in Hockley, is convinced that he and a handful of others are about to make international headlines and start a new life in power. First local councils, then Parliament, then Downing Street. The private group chat for activists is popping off with exuberant messages:

- 'They'll be crapping themselves.'
- 'If the results were based on who put in the most work, we'd win hands down.'
- 'I do have a sneaky feeling we will do very well tomorrow with multiple candidates being elected.'
- 'Tomorrow is the dawn of something new, something big.'

I feign enthusiasm but am secretly very agitated. What if we actually win? And – oh God – what if I am responsible for giving Britain First a tiny edge that brings the party into office? I knew this undercover project would dirty my hands, but now I imagine the history books of the British far right including a trenchant footnote about how some cretin in 2023 had a bright idea to infiltrate Britain First and ended up helping them.

The morning after polling day, I pick up the phone lying by my bed to look at the overnight results, and a hidden vice squeezes the air out of my chest. Paul Golding has posted a photo of Paul Harding giving the V for Victory sign, listing all the parties he has beaten in his ward of Hockley and Ashingdon. The activist chat group is filled with champagne emojis. 'Well done, you go down in the history of Britain First, being the first to take a seat,' says a fellow campaigner. No! I keep scrolling, sitting up now, my face hot, my heart pounding. Did he really win?

We are all mistaken. Paul Golding – unable to utter the words 'we lost' – merely mentioned the other parties that Paul Harding beat in his ward. He couldn't bring himself to name the actual winner. In response to the congratulatory messages, he now clarifies that Paul Harding only got 13 per cent of the vote, losing heavily to the Conservatives. Misunderstanding cleared up, I am able to breathe again. Results from the other wards trickle in over the weekend. It is a clean sweep of eight losses. In Darenth, where we spent so much time, we only get 10 per cent. In our eight target seats, we receive 1,252 votes, barely 8 per cent of the total turnout in our wards.

The group chat is despondent. 'I'm so disappointed,' says one activist. 'Was really hoping for a breakthrough.' One activist quits. Others don't come to our actions for months. Even Paul Golding takes a fortnight off due to fatigue, saying he has been 'driven to the edge of insanity' by the campaign.

Why did Britain First fail? There are cries of voter apathy and media bias – although not fraud, as Paul sent activists to watch the votes being counted and secured with plastic tags. Later, members will say they think we were too aggressive and single-minded on the doorstep. It's hard to convince voters you are going to fix their potholes and improve their bus timetables when the first thing you talk about is immigration. There's also a big difference between agreeing with a canvasser that the daily government expenditure on temporary asylum-seeker housing is too high and actually voting for them.

Ultimately, most voters do not see Britain First as a credible party. Even Nick Griffin recognised this when he was the head of the BNP, citing the failure of inexperienced or hardline activists to connect with mainstream voters. He said the reaction of ordinary people to BNP canvassers was 'oh my God, this bloke is barking mad'. Griffin, during elections, would think 'How many of these fools are going to cock things up?' I think about Alfie, high on cocaine, and Frank, peddling conspiracy theories. Would you vote for their party, if they knocked on your door?

So much for Paul's strategy of the ballot. What about the boot? We take a break following the local elections and return in June for what Paul promises to be a summer in 'turbo activism mode'. He hopes to organise eye-grabbing actions that bring the party new members and financial support.

For Paul, activism isn't just righteous but fun. It offers him the chance to play soldiers. He plans our actions as part military operation, part James Bond mission. In July, we meet once again at Dartford train station for a trip to Kent's south coast. The target? Napier, a former army barracks now used as a refugee camp.

We drive to a motorway McDonald's outside Folkestone to get ready for today's action, tying banners on the bus opposing the Napier camp. Despite the heat, Paul wears a pinstripe suit and tie, and sprays himself with gusts of sickly aftershave. He becomes fidgety and excited, ordering us around like an officer before going out on patrol. He is fond of reminding us that his great-grandparents were World War II veterans. 'When I pull up outside the gates and say "go go go!", everyone run around and go behind the banner.'

We climb back onto the minibus and drive five minutes to the barracks, as Paul bounces up and down in the driver's seat. He gives himself another spray of aftershave – 'I want to smell good for these migrants,' he says – and scans the street. 'There's one of 'em,' he snarls, as we approach the barracks, thinking he's spotted an asylum seeker. 'Oh, he's English.' It's just a white man in a tracksuit, unaware of how close he came to being accosted. We arrive and rush out of the bus to raise our Union Jack flags. The battle bus has a megaphone sound system that blares out 'Jerusalem' and a tape of Paul repeating the words 'close the borders' and 'say no to the dinghy invasion'.

Fired up and grinning, Paul aims his camcorder – 'my weapon', he calls it – at refugees coming in and out of the camp. They try to ignore him.

Paul looks over to the field on the other side of the road. 'Migrants, just sitting in that park there,' he snaps. 'There's a children's play area right there. There'll be a disaster here soon.' Paul likes to offer his senior members the chance to speak on camera, and asks Nick about what he's seen today. Nick complains that the only refugees inside are all men – and thus undeserving. 'They're the least vulnerable people in their countries. Young, healthy men.'

Later, we go leafleting around an estate down the road from the camp. I'm stuffing pamphlets about migrants into letter boxes when I hear the escalating volume of an argument between Paul and a local woman. 'You are not welcome inciting hatred,' she says. 'You need to stop filming me. Leave our streets.' Paul has his camcorder close up on her, talking about his democratic right to film her. He calls her 'darling'. She says: 'Don't condescend me.' Other residents are opening their windows and front doors to peer out at the commotion. 'She supports all the migrants,' Paul jeers. 'No one's on your side, darling! You've got no support.' The woman says Paul is intimidating her.

Nobody hears me when I say we should leave. The other activists think this is hilarious: a deluded woke woman in favour of migrants. As much as Patrik and I prepare for undercover meet-ups by practising conversations, there's no way to plan for a shouting match. It's agonising. The whole point about infiltration is to disrupt far-right activists from dividing communities. And here I am, with far-right activists in the process of dividing a community. I don't do anything. I tell myself that as an infiltrator, I can't intervene or I might break my cover. I just feel guilt. Guilt and fear of standing up to Paul.

The woman turns away, and we climb aboard our minibus. Paul films the woman as she goes back to her home. Then we return to Dartford and hit the pub – lagers for us, sugar-free Red Bull for Paul. In the garden, he expands on his political philosophy. 'I want this country to become a shithole,' he says. Only when Britain is 'a fucking nightmare' – caused by a precipitous decline in living standards and community cohesion with violence on the streets – will people finally wake up and support Britain First.

Oswald Mosley said the same thing. He hoped for – even depended on – the immiseration of ordinary Brits, who, when faced with empty wallets and hungry children, would support his fascist movement. 'If things aren't bad, people aren't taking notice,' he wrote. It is deeply cynical and unpatriotic to wish suffering upon your supporters, and yet Paul considers himself a proud Brit. In reality, he is obsessed with power and not his people.

We're sitting on a pub bench outside, talking about the war in Ukraine, and Paul reminds us he has been to Russia. He thinks of it as a strong, nationalist, Christian society. In 2019, he spoke in the Duma against 'globalist policies of multiculturalism and mass immigration' leading to the 'extinction and replacement' of European people. Paul's links to Moscow, where he has been three times, are the subject of much speculation. Just how deep is the connection? He was hosted by the Liberal Democratic Party (LDP), an anti-immigrant party nominally opposed to the state. Russia experts say the party is in fact in the Kremlin's pocket and rarely disagrees with Vladimir Putin. Patrik has briefed me to listen out for any mention of Russia, but warns me not to ask anything directly to avoid scrutiny.

In the pub, I focus on Paul. He says his speech in the Duma was one of the highlights of his career, and laments that the Ukraine invasion prevents him from returning. Paul talks about visiting Red Square and watching Putin's motorcade – I ask if he met him, but Paul says no. I struggle to think of a natural-sounding way to ask more. Paul talks about other trips he's been on, and the moment frustratingly slips away. If there is more to Britain First and Russia, I never hear about it.

Paul wants the support of the system, but he also wants revenge on it. Most of the time he appears in the press, he is painted as racist or incompetent (in the London mayoral election of 2024, his party received fewer votes than a comedy candidate named Count Binface, a fact gleefully reported by the media). When Paul was released from one of his prison stints in 2017, he wrote in his autobiography: 'I live and breathe purely to fight for my country and I despise and hate every last politician and journalist who has contributed during their careers to the dismemberment of Britain.' One day, he promised, 'the boot will be on the other foot'.

This vindictive streak is at odds with the family-friendly, approachable image that Paul also wants for the party. To make this charade seem plausible, Paul tries to prevent the conspiratorial, aggressive contingent of Britain First slipping through. He is not always successful.

In August, we go to Finchingfield, a village in Essex. Few countryside communities are as gorgeous as this. The cottages look like delicious macaroons, painted in sugary blues and yellows and pinks. An eighteenth-century windmill looms over the thatched roofs, and a pond in the centre of the village glitters in the summer sun. Jamie Oliver, the TV chef, lives in the Elizabethan mansion nearby. When I was a newspaper reporter in 2020, I came to Finchingfield to interview a local landowner who was rewilding his estate with beavers. Everyone I met, from the beaver owner to the staff of the pub where I wrote my article, greeted me with smiles.

I am told to fuck off on my return visit to Finchingfield three years later, although this is understandable. We are here to protest an asylum-seeker camp that has been set up nearby in Wethersfield to eventually house up to 1,800 refugees. The members of Britain First believe they are about to unleash a wave of sexual violence upon Essex.

The problem is nobody in the village wants us here. The battle bus plays patriotic tunes through the sound system. 'Land of Hope and Glory' is booming as a dozen far-right campaigners climb out of the vehicles and ruin a lovely Saturday afternoon. The drinkers in the pub, the diners in the tea room, and every dog walker and picnicker look at us like we're manure salesmen.

Joining us today is Sylvia,* who says she joined Britain First because of immigration. She was already a supporter and donor to Britain First, and answered an email from Paul asking for help with this action. 'There are so many moaning Minnies on Facebook who don't want to get off their arses and do anything,' she says, explaining why she joined.

Paul tells us to start handing out leaflets. Even the veteran activists wonder if we've picked the right place. We're getting a lot of funny looks. We start putting Britain First leaflets under the windscreen wipers of parked cars and into letter boxes. It does not go well. A woman leans out of the first-floor window of her cottage as I approach and shouts: 'Fuck off with your Nazi propaganda!' I can't help laughing. The other activists don't find it so funny. 'I just want to slap these filthy idiots,' mutters an activist.

Sylvia looks a bit confused by the reception we're getting. She approaches families on the green, and her opening line is 'We're not the National Front!' It does nothing to assuage their concerns, and the other members tell her to stop.

It is strange, feeling this unwelcome. We weren't prepared for confrontation, and Alex feels uncomfortable at the attention we're getting. 'We're getting stared out here,' he says. 'It's creepy.' Paul's encouragement to be aggressive and charismatic isn't enough. The landlady of the pub asks us to leave when we try to leaflet her customers, and we get heckled by a few blokes hanging out on the green. Paul shouts back at them and condescendingly waves goodbye.

We head to our cars, nervously looking around for the atmosphere to snap. Paul gets behind the wheel of the battle bus and drives off, turning 'Pomp and Circumstance' on the sound system up to max volume. The brass, usually so rousing, sounds pathetic.

I sit in Paul Harding's car with Alex, Sylvia and Max, who is fuming.

'Let's hope they rape your daughters,' he shouts as we speed away, so I'm not sure anyone hears us.

'Oh, don't say that,' Sylvia responds.

'Why not?'

'It's not the kids' fault,' Paul says.

'I don't want right-wing kids touched,' Max says.

'If you're talking preference, then obviously yeah,' Paul says. 'I'd rather their fucking kids got raped than mine. But I'd rather no kids got raped.'

This conversation is cut short when we notice Paul Golding is parking the battle bus on the other side of the village green. He signals for us to get out. The other activists don't want to. 'No,' says Alex, despair in his voice. 'No!'

Paul makes us leaflet the other half of the village. We spend five minutes slipping our pamphlets into the remaining houses grumbling about Paul. He finally calls us back to the cars, just in time for a young woman to shout at us for bringing racist leaflets to her village. We drive off, 'Pomp and Circumstance' on the speakers again, while the activists continue to bellow at her.

'Let's hope they fuck her up the arse,' Max yells.

'Jesus Christ,' says Paul Harding.

'Fucking right,' says Max. 'If she loves them so much, let her fucking have a bit of 'em.'

Alex joins in. 'That's probably what she wants. She probably wants 1,800 boyfriends.'

'When they're fucking pinning her down and raping her,' Max says, 'let her say then we're racist.'

Sylvia is silent. So am I. We reach the next village along – Wethersfield itself. It is much quieter, there's no one about. We get out and find Paul complaining that his camcorder footage is unusable because his activists were screaming and shouting behind him. I wonder if it's more because we were almost chased out of the village and if Paul released any video evidence of this action we would look like losers. After we're done leafleting, an activist whispers to me: 'I don't know if we did a lot of good this week.'

We head to the pub, and I see Sylvia standing a little bit shaken, smoking a cigarette. 'It's never normally like that,' Nick says apologetically. 'Normally it's 75 per cent supportive.' She looks around at the dozen of us. 'I thought there'd be more people,' she says. Paul replies that he keeps actions small to prevent leaks. Having spent the day with us, Sylvia must know this is not the truth. I don't see her again.

The discontent within Britain First comes to a head. We're demoralised after the election campaign, and during our actions the members complain Paul is a 'slave driver', demanding everyone puts in hour after hour of volunteering. When the camping weekend rolls around in August, the party is at a low ebb. It is about to get much lower.

Far-right organisations are fond of summer camping weekends as annual rewards for their volunteers. For £5, campaigners of Britain First can bring their families to a Peak District campsite and enjoy bouncy castles during the day and drinks by the fire pit at night. There's a tug-of-war between the northerners and southerners, plus an awards ceremony for the hardest-working activists.

During their heyday, the BNP used to hold a similar event on a farm, also in Derbyshire. Known as the Red, White, and Blue Festival, it was an opportunity to present a softer, family-friendly side to the public – one with children running around. This was, of course, a fiction. In 2009, an undercover journalist for the *News of the World* sneaked in and watched as members saluted Hitler, talked about attacking black people in the nearby town, and held a mock trial for a golly that ended in a twelve-year-old girl burning the doll on a fire pit.

In 2023, Paul is keen for the Britain First event to be attended by as many people as possible, for them not to get too drunk, and to post photos showing a busy, active community of all ages. Patrik and I plan how best to infiltrate it. Although I have been using the hidden camera for the last few months, we decide that it is too risky for this campsite. Where would I hide the kit – in my tent? Instead, we buy a watch with an audio recording function. Patrik, meanwhile, will bring a long-lens camera and try to snap the campsite from a distance.

I drive into the Peak District, fretting whether my new audio recorder will work, questioning why I am spending a sunny summer weekend at the racist equivalent of Glastonbury and not with my diminishing circle of friends. In the last nine months, I have spent more time with my new associates than my actual friends and family. I feel guilty about lying to everyone so much. Only my wife knows the truth, and she has to put up with me either being away on weekends and evenings, or pranging out over my next encounter.

Chris mode kicks in once I call Paul at Buxton, where he has set up a redirection point to prevent infiltrators from discovering his location. He cheerfully tells me to come to a campsite up the valley, and along a dirt track I find the Britain First lot setting up marquees. I scout around for drystone walls that Patrik might be able to crouch behind with his long lens, and quietly message him a couple of photos to point out where he could hide. Later, he stealthily approaches the edge of the camp and takes some excellent shots of the senior members.

Vera Lynn is playing on the sound system – Paul says that he should have put 'Horst Wessel Lied' and the works of Skrewdriver on the playlist. The first was the Nazi national anthem, the second is a neo-Nazi punk band.

Given his efforts at keeping a lid on the more extreme members under his command, it's surprising that Paul would make a gag like that. Perhaps he's just excited for the weekend and feeling naughty. He later talks about stripping one of the activists and throwing him on the fire. 'Whatever direction he jumps off at, that's the equivalent of spinning the bottle,' he says, laughing. Nobody else finds it funny.

He gets me busy hammering up Union Jack flags, which form a circle around the marquees and bouncy castles to mask us from outsiders. Paul shows me how he wants the metal flagpoles placed into the earth, and in doing so bashes his fist with a wooden mallet, roaring in pain. We gather round to look at his pink, swollen hand. He denies my offer of painkillers, saying he doesn't need them as he is 'Anglo-Saxon'.

We eat a chicken curry that Ashlea has prepared, and as it's the first night, with more campers arriving tomorrow, everyone heads to their tents early. Except for me. I have to pick up Robert the Basketweaver, who has snagged an invitation to the event. He calls me from the pub next to Stockport train station, drunk, saying his train to Buxton has been cancelled. When he finally arrives around 11.30 p.m., he is smashed, slurring heavily, his conversation circular. He says it's too late to put up his tent and asks to stay in mine. I'm glad I didn't bring my hidden camera equipment with me. I unzip the tent for him. 'I can't be arsed to brush my teeth,' he says, throwing himself down on my air mattress still in his work suit. His breath smells like he has eaten a bushel of raw onions. He listens to a neo-Nazi podcast to drift off, and when he does, snores like a diesel generator. I swallow a dozen melatonin pills to drift off, but the sound and the scent of Robert's breathing keeps me awake. I leave the tent and fold myself into the back seat of my car. In the morning, Robert wakes me up by knocking on the window to tell me a dog has urinated on the tarpaulin entrance to my tent. He wanders off for breakfast, leaving me to wash away a pool of canine piss, reminding myself that I volunteered for this. *I volunteered for this.* So begins the second day of the Britain First camping weekend.

The activist awards ceremony comes up in the afternoon, and this is the best bit for me. We pile into the marquee, and sit down on camping chairs for Paul to hand out prizes. 'The first is for someone who joined six months ago, and proved himself by showing up week after week during the local election campaign,' he says. 'I'd like to welcome to the stage . . . Christopher! Everyone give him a big hand!' I am so stunned that the eyes bug out of my head. I get up, lift up a fist, and hear the crowd cheer. Giddily, I step onto the small stage so Ashlea, the party deputy, can put a medal over my head. She and Paul shake my hand and we pose for a picture. 'Well done, son,' says another activist, patting my back as I sit down.

Later, when Paul sends the photo of me winning the award, he also shares a snap of the elite activist plaque. 'This one next,' he says. It's an exhilarating moment – it feels like a racist Oscar – and shows just how well the infiltration has worked. Far-right organisations typically try to minimise the impact of an undercover sting by saying the journalist was peripheral, only joining for a session or two. This feels like a victory, and I cheer on the other award winners. It's only later, when I get home, that I think about what I had to do to earn it.

This weekend, I get to know Ashlea. Of all the senior figures in Britain First, she is the most unknowable. Ashlea commands the north-west division and so I haven't spent much time with her until now. She is friendly and curious about me in a way that the other activists are not. Ashlea wants to know about my family, where I grew up, and my wife. Her questions are inquisitive, not interrogative, and she dispenses motherly advice, telling me to have two children instead of one, so they each have someone to play with.

There's a hubbub outside the kitchen tent. The campers are talking about Alice, who has been necking prosecco since sunrise. After a drunken argument with her boyfriend, she speeds away in her car. I find her abandoned partner by the fire pit wearing a hat that says 'COCAINE AND HOOKERS' on it. I ask if he is OK – if his partner is OK. 'She's tapped,' he says. Tapped? 'Mental,' he replies, tapping his head. He can't call her because he passed out on the grass the night before and his phone short-circuited in the rain.

The mood begins to sour. Paul, who was so amped up on Friday, mutters that a lot of expected guests haven't shown up. One of the veteran activists leaves in a huff when asked to put up Ashlea's tent. A party member has been following Paul around, trying to tell him about the Earth being flat. 'It makes sense for a thousand reasons,' he says. 'If you have the time I'll explain it to you.' Paul looks agitated.

It's dinner time, and an activist goes around dosing people's food with a hot sauce called 'Da Bomb: Beyond Insanity'. It has a radioactive danger sign on the bottle, and when the football hooligan Andy Frain – aka

Nightmare – eats some of the sauce sprinkled on a paper plate of chilli con carne, he careens around the kitchen tent like a bull. 'Ahhh!' he screams. 'Faaak! Ahhhhhh!' A little later, word spreads around the camp that Andy has shat himself. This, apparently, has been a common occurrence since the 1990s, when an Irish gangster stabbed him in the butthole. Andy will be sitting in the pub and suddenly curse and run to the toilet to deal with soiled underwear.

I see him as I get into my car to drive down into Buxton. Paul has asked me to refill the jerry cans of petrol that power the bouncy castle generators. This offers me a much-needed break from the campsite. Seeing me get into my Golf, Andy asks for a lift to a nearby pub. Twenty years ago, Andy got into the car of an undercover BBC journalist and confessed to slashing the throat of a police officer. What terrible secrets will he reveal this time? He heaves himself in with a groan. 'I had a curry Thursday night, and I've been continuously pooing,' he tells me. The chilli doused with hot sauce only made it worse. Andy's caravan toilet is broken, so he had to shit into an Asda bag for life. 'Then I just had to go for it, *boom boom boom.* Oh, it was horrendous.' We arrive at the pub. He gets out of my car, and heads off inside. I watch him go, a little stunned, and look down at the passenger seat he has vacated.

After another errand in the village later on, I come back to find a strangely tense atmosphere. There is a nastiness in the air. I learn that a fight broke out, and hear the story from other activists, who whisper the details to me. A drunken member, many pints deep, accosted Paul and Ashlea about their repeated requests for donations. 'You can shove that hundred quid I gave you up your arse,' he said. Paul grabbed the man by the collar – a scuffle kicked off and suddenly broke up. Andy Frain was somehow involved in the beef, disagreeing with Paul's aggressive reaction. It takes me a while to piece this together from snatched conversations with the senior activists who stop talking when Paul comes within earshot. He is in a rage, and paces around the campsite cursing his members. 'He's a fucking lying bastard,' he says of one. 'They're all fucking wankers,' he says of the rest. The next day, Andy and four other members are kicked out of the party.

Many of the activists are annoyed with Paul's controlling behaviour. Lots of people didn't show up this weekend. Maybe it was the bad weather, or maybe they just didn't want to be around Paul. Every two hours, he texts us with a place to be. That place is normally around him, where we are expected to listen to his stories and laugh at his jokes. Paul's big weekend to promote the party has been a failure.

Paul claims that he is motivated by 'genuine conviction' and not money. But I listen to a revealing exchange on the final night of the camping weekend as drizzle spits onto the fire pit. I'm not meant to hear this, but his muttered voice travels across the empty camp chairs. 'I've come to a big realisation,' Paul mutters to Ashlea. 'The thing is, there is no money any more. Everyone's skint these days. Half the people have got on with their life, people haven't turned up . . . We just spent seven grand on sitting round a fire.' Seven grand of his members' money.

Some of the activists clearly feel ripped off. Paul sees his members as cashpoints but they ultimately want a return on their donations. Activists already have to volunteer their free time to follow Paul's orders during campaigns. They are also expected to give him whatever spare money they have. Britain First members are not rich and are asked to give him money they can barely afford. 'Tenners and fivers, when I have them,' is how one activist puts it to me.

Where do these tenners and fivers go? In July, Paul sent us three emails demanding £2,000 to buy video cameras so local branches could film their actions. We never got the cameras, but interestingly that same month Paul took Ashlea to Thailand for a ten-day holiday. Looking over Paul's shoulder while he's on his phone, I saw a message come in from her. 'Just one more wage till Thailand,' it said. Nobody dares confront Paul about their money being spent on tropical holidays.

The average life cycle of a Britain First member is short. They might initially be taken in by Paul's charisma, but his abrasive, demanding attitude soon puts them off. For a while, his urgent emails and hounding text messages might work to mobilise activists, but it's an unsustainable strategy. Members can only take so many weeks of his demands before dropping out. Newcomers are disappointed by low turnout for actions, which are often arduous and time-consuming. Paul frequently springs upon activists campaigning in Kent in the morning that we will also head to Essex for the afternoon, sucking up an entire day of tedious leafleting. It is so common for people to quit that when I eventually stop attending events at the end of 2023, nobody questions it, and I simply fade away from the party.

The long-serving members of Britain First find themselves in a weird position, disliking Paul, even fearing him, and yet regularly volunteering for him. Despite its history of failure, Britain First is one of the most recognisable far-right organisations in the country. There are few alternatives for extremists who believe in replacement theory and want to campaign against it, using legal means.

Paul might believe he is saving Western civilisation with his own holy army but sitting around the campfire embers, listening to the story of his fight with drunken activists, it is hard to believe that we are charging towards anything except a hangover.

The end of the year approaches, and with it my time at Britain First. Being with them is straining my nerves. I spend an afternoon at Paul's house in Dartford, and when he looks at my chest, I am convinced that he has spotted my camera, and I start sweating. I've become as frightened of him as his members, the ones who say 'him' instead of 'Paul'. I find myself shutting up when he speaks. The thought of helping out on yet another immigrant-obsessed protest or electoral campaign fills me with dread.

There's one last trip I want to make with Britain First. As a trusted member, I am invited to Warsaw for a parade on 11 November. For some people, this event celebrates Polish independence, but for far-right groups it is an opportunity to crudely re-enact the menace that once tyrannised Poland under Nazi occupation.

The local mayor has tried to shut down the march, which begins in Warsaw's main square and proceeds east, over the River Vistula, and ends in a park where far-right organisations from across Europe light flares, explode firecrackers and show off their banners promising a whites-only continent.

The far-right Polish MEP, Dominik Tarczyński – famous for his speeches and media appearances promising 'not even one' Muslim will be allowed to live in his country – has offered to host Britain First at the event. Paul, Ashlea, Alex, Nick and his friend Charlie Fox, head of Identity England, all fly in the day before. None of them have previously been to the march, and they are all fired up at the thought of joining in with such a spectacle.

Paul maintains that Britain First is not a racist party, that it campaigns for what ordinary Britons want. Knowing that the 11 November march is the biggest far-right event in the European calendar, I want to watch the party's senior figures when they're around like-minded extremists. How will they react when they see neo-Nazis walking by?

There's also a more personal reason for going to Poland. The Shukman family – then called Szuchman – were Polish. My great-grandfather David came to London in 1913, leaving his parents Aron and Chana and sister Fayga behind in eastern Poland. There is no record of what happened to Fayga beyond the 1930s. An uncle of mine is working with a Polish archivist to find out her fate, but has yet to turn up any conclusive documentation. She is believed to have died in 1942, perhaps in Majdanek, but possibly in one of the many concentration or death camps in eastern Poland. The Szuchmans were a poor family, unable to read until my grandfather's generation, so there are no letters or diaries that hint at the fate of our family's Polish left-behinds. Witnessing the return of Nazis in Poland is deeply unsettling, and seeing how the Britain First delegation interacts with them feels, in some small way, retributive.

I get to Warsaw before any of the Britain First activists

arrive and head to a Holiday Inn outside the city centre where Patrik and I can plan our coverage. Joe's here too, having previously reported on this march. We wonder how much networking there will be with other far-right groups. Paul says he has secured a pre-rally meeting with Dominik inside the Polish parliament.

Contact-making aside, it becomes clear that on this trip, a key objective for the members of Britain First is to get as pissed as possible. Nick texts me the location of a themed bar called the British Bulldog and asks me to come over. I can see why the members of Britain First chose to drink in the British Bulldog, but the only British signifiers in this place are a gimmicky red phone box and fish and chips on the menu.

Nick, Alex and Charlie are here. The last gleefully says he has heard about a strip club 'where for eighty euros they'll nosh you off'. He then describes how many drinks he has had. Three pints at the airport, two cans on the plane, two pints in the pub by the time I join them. He'll have two more while I'm there, then a shot of frozen petrol he claims is vodka, and, after he nips to his hotel to check in, two double whiskies in the bar. He passes out on his bed, and Nick is unable to shake him awake for the evening.

With Charlie unconscious and Alex tired, it's just me and Nick. I'm still quite drunk from the afternoon, but he seems fine. Over whiskies in a cocktail bar, he tells me that what he'd really like to do is move to Dubai, where he has friends and likes the weather and fancies a girl there. I encourage him to go, hoping there is a version of Nick who isn't involved in Britain First – but he says he is committed to contesting the London mayoral election in the spring.

We talk about how to bring up our politics with romantic partners, and Nick tells a story about taking a girl out in Shoreditch, a trendy area of east London, and being unsure about how to check if her racial politics aligned with his.

'There's a lot of niggers in Shoreditch,' he says. 'I wouldn't say nothing straight away, of course. I'd give it time before I started dropping stuff. And she said to me, out of nowhere, "Fucking black people, I can't fucking stand black people."' He laughs. 'So you could say we share a hatred for coons.' Nick describes what he looks for in a girl, and says he wouldn't go out with anyone who has 'slept with a Negro'.

Nick uses these slurs as punchlines, and it is gross to laugh along with him. He finishes his story and pulls out his phone to look at Twitter. It's almost midnight and we've been boozing for hours. I'm in an unpleasant no man's land between smashed and hungover, and tell Nick that I'm going to rest before the march tomorrow.

I stumble into a taxi and find Patrik and Joe back at my hotel. I show them my tapes of the night. When I press play on the laptop, we don't straight away hear Nick talking about black people in east London, but instead listen to me telling a sexist joke (Nick asked for a vodka lemonade from the bar, and I asked if he would like a tampon with his drink). It's embarrassing. But Patrik and Joe say it's different, that it's part of my cover, and only by befriending far-right activists is it possible to learn what they are really like. But it sounds like the chauvinism trips off my tongue pretty fluently. As I show them the video of me high-fiving Nick when he talks about 'coons', I think we look and sound depressingly similar.

The next morning, my head feels like it has been silted with nauseating powders: chalk in my mouth, sand in my sinuses, cement mix in my brain. My hangover is displaced quickly by fear. Patrik and I meet before the march, and learn that at past events, police have arrested participants en masse. There have also been cases of demonstrators macing journalists. I write Patrik's number on my arm in permanent marker in case I lose my phone and can't contact him. Next to his, I scrawl the number of a lawyer if I'm arrested.

The Britain First crew, including Paul and Ashlea who arrived late last night, meet in the lobby of the Sheraton Grand, a fancy central Warsaw hotel. Much of the city is blocked off by riot police barricades, and everyone is late to get there. An immaculately coiffed Polish man walks in, and greets Paul warmly. It's Dominik Tarczyński, the MEP belonging to the right-wing Law and Justice Party. He ushers us past the police barriers to the front of the march just in time for kick-off.

We're in a giant crowd, around 100,000 roaring, chanting people. Some of them are families with small children and old grandmas, but most are young men waving red-and-white flags. A lot of them are dressed in black, balaclavas over their faces, banners in their hands bearing neo-Nazi iconography and demands for a white ethnostate. There are a few LGBT flags on the ground, and demonstrators stamp on them.

The theme of this year's march is 'Poland is not yet lost', and begins with speeches before the procession east through the city. We set off along Solidarności Avenue. The noise is overwhelming, not just from all the people yelling but the firecrackers which explode with disorientating bangs.

I spot Patrik through the crowd, and something profoundly weird happens. He's been trying to follow us and take pictures with a long-lens camera, but the poor phone signal means my location tracker isn't working properly. I see him scanning the demonstrators, and just as we're metres away, about to pass him, we make eye contact. Ten thousand volts zap into me, and my skin crackles. Despite the November chill, I am suddenly sweaty and hot. My two personalities, Chris and Harry, collide in that strange, panicky moment. Patrik raises his camera, and snaps us walking by. The photos show a look of total bewilderment on my face.

We pause halfway over the Poniatowski Bridge, and watch the hardliners advance. Their flags and armbands indicate they have come from across Europe, some as far as the US. They are clad in black, and are eerily quiet as they pass, waving banners depicting aborted foetuses, plus Celtic crosses and other neo-Nazi insignia. The Britain First members watch with approval. Alex is amazed by their discipline: they are marching in formation, none of them drinking or smoking. Paul trains his camera on the ones with anti-abortion banners. 'This is what a real country looks like,' he says.

Dominik, who has been getting stopped by selfie-seeking fans every minute, says the march's destination isn't that interesting, and suggests we return to our hotel for an early dinner. I wonder why he wants to leave before the climax, and later find out that on the other side of the bridge, neo-Nazi groups light flares and pose for photos, and that Dominik would probably rather limit the time he spends with them.

In the pan-Asian restaurant of the Sheraton Grand, we slump over the table, looking at our phones. Dominik asks Paul and Ashlea how he can help their organisation. Paul invites him to an upcoming Britain First conference. Dominik asks how many members he has, and Paul says 16,000, a figure that is clearly a massive exaggeration.

I sense that Paul and Ashlea are losing an opportunity to impress Dominik, especially when they say Poles are coming to England to steal jobs and commit crimes. Dominik seems unsure how to respond. Not only are his guests insulting his people, but now Paul is praising Vladimir Putin and talking fondly about his visits to Russia. Does he not realise this is the wrong way to butter up Dominik, a Polish nationalist who despises Russia? They are on firmer ground in talking about non-white immigration into Europe.

'They are taking over, trying to push this fucking bullshit on our society, on Christian society,' says Dominik. 'Our culture, movies, food, everything. We don't want that. It's not enrichment any more, we are becoming slaves.' Nobody forced us to eat in an Asian restaurant, I think to myself.

We say goodbye to Dominik, thanking him for joining us. His presence will have made our attendance at the rally look much more professional. I'm not sure what, if anything, he got out of it. Paul and Alex say they're tired, and the rest of us head out for a drink without them. By popular demand, we head to the British Bulldog. In the taxi there, I ask Ashlea what happened to our trip to the Polish parliament, and she laughingly says Paul made that up.

In the pub, we find Warren slumped on the sofa with two friends of his, former National Front members. Warren didn't join the Britain First delegation because he wanted to get in with the hardliners. He tells me he brought two flags with him. One had the words 'Millwall' and '14 words' on it, a reference to the fourteen-word slogan of white nationalists: 'We must secure the existence of our people and a future for white children.'

What was the other flag?

'Can't tell ya,' he says.

It can't be worse than the fourteen words, I say.

'Can't tell ya.'

When Warren is in the loo, I ask his friends what was on the other flag. It turns out Warren was also carrying a flag for the British Movement, a neo-Nazi organisation set up in the late 1960s. He must have thought it would get him booted out of Britain First. Warren, who says he has been trying to buy cocaine from the pub's waitress, returns and points out a sticker on the wall that he put up. It says 'WHITE PRIDE WORLDWIDE'.

I've been wired for hours. A convoy of riot police zooms past, filling the bar with flashing lights and the sound of sirens. At first, the frozen vodka we knock back has a soothing effect. But the shots keep coming, and I can feel my thoughts losing their form like wet toilet paper. I listen to Warren and Nick talk about politicians they believe are on the payroll of Jews. Warren asks if anyone is going to Auschwitz while in Poland.

Has he been?

'Don't want to go,' he says. 'Listen, there was no gassing there. That gas chamber has no Zyklon B in the walls.' He recommends a film by a Holocaust denier called David Cole. 'He proved to no end that it was absolutely fake. It was all bollocks. They had a day centre for the children where they used to do plays, they had a Disney character painted on the wall.'

I feel queasy. Ashlea is looking at her phone, scrolling through social media. Charlie and Nick say they're going to a strip club, and I say my goodbyes. I tell them I'm leaving early in the morning.

The next day, Patrik and I rent a car and drive east to Baranów, the village where the Szuchmans once lived. We arrive after sunset, and park outside the local church. There's no one around, no movement except the spasmodic flickering of the supermarket's busted neon sign. The winter quiet is broken only by barking dogs and cars speeding by somewhere in the distance.

There used to be a Jewish community here, but the only trace we know of is in a dirty field at the edge of the village, where a few broken gravestones are hidden in the weeds. There are photos of them on Google Maps, and we spend half an hour searching for them in the dark, trying to pinpoint their location based on the surrounding landmarks visible online. It feels important to find these gravestones, proving to the Britain First members – not that they can hear me – that the erasure of European Jewry was real. We finally find the graves. I dig with my bare hands, yanking out moss and grass and weeds until a weathered Star of David pokes through the dirt. Brushing off the mud, I try to make out the inscriptions in Hebrew. We stand over these three or four broken headstones, shivering in the dark, listening to the dogs. I think of one far-right content creator who has a habit of saying 'six million' in a voice of panto surprise, wailing and waving his hands, and what I'd say to him if he were here now. I can't think of anything.

The next day, we tour Auschwitz and see the piles of shaved hair and smashed spectacles that my far-right friends say are fake. We see the crematoria ovens that Andy Frain once tried to climb into for a joke. We look at the hallway of prisoner photographs showing the faces of teenagers wizened by hunger and horror. Are all these photos meant to be forgeries?

Waiting in the departure hall at Kraków Airport, a Polish man in a camouflage baseball cap sits down next to us, and strikes up a conversation. Within a minute, he's talking about the Jewish Rothschild family. 'They control everything,' he says. 'Everything.'

5

Alison Chabloz is preparing dishes for a barbecue in the cramped kitchen of a north London terrace. 'She runs the place,' says her friend Allen by way of introduction. 'She's the *Obersturmbannführer* of the house.' Alison smiles. Adolf Eichmann, organiser of the Holocaust, had the same SS rank. Alison teases Allen for loudly singing 'Horst Wessel Lied' earlier in the day. 'With all the windows open, my God!'

She shakes my hand and points to the stove, where a mucky pan is filled with a thick yellow liquid. It's home-made lemonade. I politely decline, and instead offer to take dishes up to the roof terrace where her friends are grilling and then burning lamb sausages, venison burgers and halloumi. They call her 'the queen of British antisemitism'. A former cruise ship singer now in her early sixties, for the last decade she has been a prominent Holocaust denier. When I meet her in June 2023, she has returned from a 22-week prison sentence for communications offences, her second time locked up. Her friends, far-right campaigners like her, sit in the afternoon sun, drinking beer, smoking weed, and eating passionfruit mochi balls.

I was invited a few days before by Allen, a middle-aged habitué of London's intellectual far-right scene. In May, we met at a tedious lecture held above a Marylebone pub on fascist philosophy, and exchanged Telegram details. He owns a ramshackle terrace in St John's Wood, renting out rooms to other activists. One of them is Colin Robertson, aka Millennial Woes (and away today). Another is Alison Chabloz.

After the Tallinn conference, I learned to my horror that one of the British guests didn't like the look of me, and has been spreading his suspicions that I am a 'fed'. Patrik tried to allay my fears, saying that the occasional allegation of being an infiltrator is to be expected from insular paranoiacs. During his undercover stint, he was accused of being a rat multiple times without being exposed. When Allen texted me that he was organising a Sunday-afternoon hangout at his place, Patrik and I thought it could help to make new friends who might vouch for me if the rumour about me continues to circulate.

I fret in a corner shop near Allen's house beforehand, wondering what to bring with me. Do the odd beliefs of Holocaust deniers extend to food and drink? I buy two packs of San Miguel lager. A barefooted Allen lets me into his house, pointing out the rooms he rents out as we go upstairs. He introduces me to Emma, a pagan painter tattooed with a *Sonnenrad*, the black sun used in Nazi iconography. I nip to the loo. It is stained and smelly.

We head up a rickety staircase to the roof terrace, where I meet Alison's friends and supporters. There is Brian,* involved in anti-drag-queen demonstrations, and Jonothon Boulter, formerly chairman of New Right, an intellectual far-right group that emerged in the mid-2000s, incorporating elements of the BNP. Allen jokes that my black shirt is 'ideologically correct' but a bad choice for June. He's right, the sweat is running off my face. After an hour of use, the hidden camera heats up and sizzles against my chest like a miniature clothes iron.

Alison shows me her azaleas, sunflowers and cherry tomatoes, clarifying that although certain varieties of the last were developed in Israel, hers are not Jewish. 'Mine are British,' she insists.

Holocaust denial is the blending of far-right politics with conspiratorial fantasy. It attracts a strange crowd. Alison and her friends seem even less stable than the Basket-weavers, Identity England and Britain First.

One of her pals is Claire Khaw, a former activist in the BNP. I have seen photos of Claire, who is of Chinese descent, posing with a rifle in front of a shrine to Adolf Hitler. She collars me over the barbecue to talk about the liberals in charge of the education system. 'We want to sacrifice our children to Moloch,' she says, referring to the ancient Canaanite god. 'Fornication, sodomy, bestiality. Educational standards are being lowered all the time, and we don't notice.'

Claire has invented the concept of 'secular koranism', which she believes will restore patriarchy and nationalism to the West by borrowing concepts from Islam. I smile to think that any of the Islamophobes I have met would ever decide to beat Muslims by converting to Islam. Alison jokes that Claire has become fixated by secular koranism, repeating it at every opportunity to anyone who will listen. She puts on a pantomime parrot voice, squawking: 'Pretty Polly! Pretty Polly! Secular koranism! Secular koranism!'

The conversation turns to flat earth – which, according to Alison, can be witnessed with high-powered zoom telescopes – and then time travel. I've not met anyone yet who thinks we can go back in time, but Alison's friends believe a machine has been invented that can allow users to witness past events. Naturally, shadowy elites have suppressed this incredible technology, known as a Kozyrev mirror, named after a Soviet scientist.

'People have been making their own,' Brian says enthusiastically. 'It's an aluminium tube that you lie in, you stay there for seven hours, you start feeling uncomfortable and then things start happening.'

'An aluminium tube?' his friend Jonothon asks, perking up.

I imagine after seven hours in any tube, you'd start feeling a little uncomfortable, I say. Brian and I have been getting along, so it feels OK to tease him a tiny bit. Is it easy to build your own?

'No,' he says. 'It's a big pipe. If you read the information, it's fascinating.'

You can time travel if you get into this?

'It does something they're hiding from people,' he responds cryptically.

What are they seeing?

'Well, that's it. Bloody Twitter keeps on taking it down. But they're seeing stuff.' Brian looks at me with a grin. 'He thinks we're making it up! I can see in your face you think it sounds fantastical.'

I smile back at him. Can you choose where to go?

'No, it's not like that. Once they get past the seven-hour thing, they start to realise that whatever they think of, they can not only picture it like a TV screen, some of them have been able to see themselves in childhood and even communicate with their younger selves. Do you know what the possibility of that is? If you were to go to yourself when you were seven . . .'

Jonothon says a Catholic priest called Father Ernetti developed a similar time machine in the 1960s. It was called the Chronovisor, he says, but the Vatican terminated Ernetti's research and impounded his device. I look this up later – Ernetti says he used the Chronovisor to watch the speeches of Cicero and the crucifixion of Jesus. He told an Italian magazine in 1972 that he took a photo of the Last Supper as it happened. Actually he had pilfered this image from a postcard of a church painting.

I eat a plate of incinerated kebab and notice Alison rolling a joint. She passes it around the circle. I say no, and luckily she doesn't insist. I don't need to be any more anxious than I am now. 'HARRY!' yells one of the guests. I jump, my hands involuntarily jerking up in alarm. Everyone turns to look. Not at me, thank God, but the neighbour's cat who has jumped over the wall. He shares my name. While they coo over him, I try to catch my breath.

Everyone wants to hear about Alison's time in prison. 'It was a significant case,' she says weightily. 'There's no free speech here. The Israel lobby has used me in a prosecution to try and make a law here. It's made me into a free-speech hero.'

Holocaust denial is illegal in most European countries and can lead to prison sentences. In the UK, there is no law against it, and Alison was instead prosecuted under communications legislation, in which she was judged to have been 'grossly offensive'. One of her songs, shared online, described Auschwitz as a 'theme park' and repeated other antisemitic slurs about Jews being liars and unfair moneylenders.

During her first trial for communications offences in 2018, Alison said she faced a 'win–win' situation. Either she would be found not guilty and emerge triumphant, or she would be convicted as a free-speech martyr, a champion of the Holocaust denial movement. If anything, she actually looked forward to a prison sentence. 'There is no doubt in my mind that a guilty verdict as far as my music is concerned will have been worth every note, every bar, right down to the final chord,' she said.

Five years and three convictions later, rolling yet another joint up on the roof, Alison doesn't seem quite so bullish. 'I got banged up for twenty-two weeks,' she says wearily. 'Surreal, completely surreal . . . So the result is where I am today. Unemployable.'

The movement that she hoped would coalesce around her never materialised, much to Alison's disappointment. She has a handful of friends, but few fans. 'When I lost my case, all the support from the quote-unquote British far right dropped,' she complains. 'I couldn't go to meetings.'

She names former associates who, she believes, were informants working with an organisation called the Campaign Against Antisemitism (CAA), which launched a private prosecution against her that ultimately saw her jailed. 'They wine and dine judges and lords and all the rest, they have funny handshakes,' she mutters conspiratorially to me.

Alison may be regretful, but she is unrepentant. A little

glassy-eyed after several joints, she describes one of her songs. It is called '(((Survivors)))'. The triple parentheses are an antisemitic convention to indicate Jews. Her song mocks Anne Frank, Elie Wiesel and Irene Zisblatt, all Jewish victims or survivors of the Holocaust. I listen to it later, and it talks about faking Holocaust evidence.

Alison says she should have come out of prison with greater recognition from the British far right. I wonder why she hasn't. Perhaps because her songs aren't very good. They don't rhyme, they're very long, and the audio is low-quality.

As I scroll back through Alison's website and Telegram channel, another factor emerges. I see pages and pages of her spats with other far-right personalities. Alison was once briefly in the inner circle of Patriotic Alternative, but was kicked out after getting into a fight with its leader, Mark Collett. She regularly beefs with him and the other PA leaders, calling them 'grifters' and 'frauds' belonging to 'a state-run honeytrap black-op'.

During her first trial, she called just one defence witness: Peter Rushton, assistant editor of *Heritage & Destiny*, a far-right magazine. According to a CAA report, Alison made the unusual decision to berate him on the stand. She also posted online an eight-minute song about Michele Renouf, a fellow denier and former housemate. 'Sophisticated or spasticated?' it went. 'Actually just a cunt, good for any stunt.' Her friends on the rooftop are the only ones left.

I don't know at what point Alison began to publicly deny the Holocaust or why. Born in Charlesworth, a village on the Manchester side of the Peak District, she moved to Geneva for music school. Alison stayed in Switzerland, teaching music, working on a newspaper in Gstaad, and living with her husband Pierre, who runs a flooring business. Their marriage broke down after twenty-two years. None of the family members I contacted wished to talk to me. Alison's daughter Carmel was interviewed by the *Daily Mail* in 2018, and said she had not spoken to her mother for three years, around the time she started blogging about the Holocaust. 'I'm not in contact with my mother at the moment and I don't know anything she's doing,' she said. Other family members in the UK said they had broken off contact with her.

In 2015, Alison first appeared in the press for giving the *quenelle* (a kind of Nazi salute with the arm pointing down) outside Edinburgh Castle. The following year, her Fringe Festival show was pulled. *Tell Me More Lies* was going to be a 45-minute performance featuring some of her Holocaust denial songs. Her appearance at the London Forum in 2016, in which she sang her antisemitic ditties and received a standing ovation, cemented her status as one of the far right's most controversial figures.

Within months, Alison's activism detached her from what could be considered normal life. She was sacked from the job she had singing on a cruise ship and kicked out of her folk band. On her blog, she continued to rail against Jews and their control of media, politics and finance, using the Holocaust as a fraudulent guilt narrative for leverage over society. 'Auschwitz,' she huffed, 'where everything is fake.'

Many, perhaps most, of the far-right activists I have met so far think the Holocaust is a hoax to some degree. But

Alison and her associates are a different breed. They have made their disbelief of the Holocaust into a career. There is something deeply depressing about the lives of committed Holocaust deniers. However, Gerard Menuhin, Alison's songwriting partner, stands out among them. He is the son of Yehudi Menuhin, the celebrated violinist, who, bafflingly, is Jewish.† Yehudi, whose name means 'Jew', played for survivors of the Bergen-Belsen concentration camp shortly after it was liberated in 1945. His son Gerard became a Holocaust denier in the 1990s after years of false starts in acting and writing. He wrote for far-right publications and published books claiming the Holocaust was fake, spurred on by a 'lurking mental itch' that the history of World War II had somehow been concocted by deceitful Jews. His family was distraught with his new hobby, his brother telling him: 'I would have far preferred you to have committed murder than espouse those views.'

Gerard's autobiography has a heartbreaking title: *Lived It Wrong*. 'I tried quite hard to enjoy life,' he writes. 'I failed. I simply don't know how to have a good time.' He describes his household rule of 'no shoes, no dogs, no ethnics' and his habit of listening to Hitler's speeches while cooking. He recounts a difficult childhood, with his parents' love being 'absolutely conditional'. In trying to pinpoint where his troubles began, he reaches a sad conclusion. 'From the perspective of a seventy-year-old, one essentially minor

---

† The number of far-right antisemites who are Jewish is, surprisingly, not zero. David Cole, an American Jewish activist who made a Holocaust denial movie, has been celebrated by the far right for being, in their eyes, a heretical truth-teller.

detail stands out as having perhaps been instrumental in setting me on the wrong path: the late loss of my virginity.'

On the rooftop, Alison, by now slurring her words and slumped in her chair, says she no longer thinks of prison as an exciting career opportunity. During her last sentence, she didn't get on with the guards or any of the black prisoners, and had to listen to an inmate above her working out in her cell, 'jumping up and down on the ceiling, *dun dun dun dun*, that's like torture going on'.

Alison is part of a long line of Holocaust deniers. The white-washing or rejection of Nazi crimes began soon after Hitler came to power. Oswald Mosley's newspapers ran articles that repeated Third Reich propaganda. 'The concentration camps which the gullible British people imagines to be crammed with people who cannot accept National Socialist principles do not exist,' claimed a *Blackshirt* article. It was not until the 1970s that attempts to deny the Holocaust professionalised. Academics and historians like David Irving began to write books, publish pamphlets and produce films that sought to undermine what they considered Jewish power and rehabilitate Nazi Germany by whitewashing its greatest crime.

In the 1980s and 90s the fact of the Holocaust was debated on mainstream TV shows and radio programmes. Today the Holocaust denial movement has run out of steam. Mark Weber, head of a denial organisation called the Institute for Historical Review (and Tallinn speaker), came to the realisation that after decades of trying, he and his colleagues have failed to cut through. Their movement, he wrote in 2009, has a 'discouraging record of achievement'.

If the goal is to oppose 'Jewish Zionist power' then denying the Holocaust 'has proved to be as much a hindrance as a help'.

In 2024, HOPE not hate polled 25,000 British people about conspiracy theories, asking them if they thought the official account of the Holocaust was a lie and the number of Jews killed purposely exaggerated. Five per cent thought this statement was definitely true, a further 7 per cent thought it was probably true. Almost a quarter said they didn't know.

Holocaust denial remains a common belief of far-right groups, just not part of their core activism. It is as historically distant today as the Boer War was to David Irving when he began writing about World War II. Most see it as a topic to occasionally post memes in the hope of annoying enemies. Few recognise obsessive Holocaust denial as a likely path to success. Few, but not all.

6

Back at the Tallinn conference, I met another group that would change the course of the undercover project. It began with a lecture by a racist Danish academic called Helmuth Nyborg, a former professor of psychology at Aarhus University. Wearing an odd pink shirt with two collars that folded into each other like the ice-cream swirls on a Viennetta cake, he told us about a looming disaster. According to Nyborg, Muslims of low intelligence are coming to Europe and having lots of babies, threatening smarter, low-fertility Europeans.

'This is a biological fight for being on national territory,' he rasped, staring into the audience. 'And we are about to lose it.'

What he proposed instead was unclear. But it didn't sound good.

'We have to realise that the great immigration problem that is currently overwhelming the West can neither be solved by cultural, social, nor legal engineering.'

Did he mean forced deportations? Ethnic cleansing? He didn't say.

He showed us a presentation slide with a chart that purportedly told us the IQ of people in the fourteenth century, some six hundred years before the invention of the IQ test. The slide implausibly claimed that Europeans in the medieval period were twice as clever as Africans.

Although the content of Nyborg's speech was objectionable, after the final round of applause concluded, I wasn't too worried about his impact in the real world. Race science – the misuse of science to promote racist ideology – may be popular among the far right but people like Nyborg tend to be ridiculed in the mainstream press as weird conspiracy theorists. His idea to stop poor women having babies to 'avoid degenerates in the population' was criticised by the *Daily Mail* as a Nazi idea. Anyone who believes that races or nations can be categorised and ranked by intelligence is surely a crank, I thought.

By the end of the Tallinn conference, I realised that I was horribly mistaken. The race-science movement is not composed of fringe oddballs with risible ideas. As Patrik and I discovered, it is well funded and sophisticated, reaching the ears of the world's most powerful people.

Our journey into the world of race science began on the main square of Tallinn's old town. While conference guests were drunkenly milling around after dinner, I heard an English accent. I turned to see a sharp-looking man in his early thirties, wearing the tech entrepreneur's outfit of a tight blazer and a dark blue T-shirt. I introduced myself, saying it was nice to meet a fellow countryman. He shook my hand, and said his name was Matt Archer. Unlike the inebriated revellers around us, he was focused and alert.

Matt described running a remarkable operation. It's called Aporia, he said, an online magazine that publishes stories about 'HBD'. HBD stands for human biodiversity, the concept that races, sexes and socio-economic classes can be ranked by traits like intelligence. Advocates of HBD believe that differences between these groups are principally caused by genetic factors rather than environmental ones, the result of nature rather than nurture. HBD appeals to far-right activists, believing it justifies their hatred of other races and desire to live separately from them.

Aporia had built an audience eager to read HBD stories, Matt said. In his measured voice, he told me that he adopted a subtle editorial line in order to be as persuasive as possible. 'Less spicy' is how he described it, presumably in relation to some of the speakers at this conference.

Matt, I was electrified to hear, said he had secured thousands of dollars in funding from a Silicon Valley investor.

Congratulations, I replied. Was it Peter Thiel?

Thiel, the billionaire co-founder of PayPal and early investor in Facebook, is frequently whispered about as a funder of far-right projects. Activists joke that they are trying to get their hands on 'Thielbucks'.

Matt laughed. 'Not him,' he said, refusing to be drawn on a name.

I was intrigued. My impression of race science was that it was not a dynamic field. I thought its main characters were ageing obsessives like Helmuth Nyborg. Matt, conversely, was young, articulate and business-minded. What attracted him to race science? And, more importantly, who was funding him?

HBD, or race science, underpins eugenics, the idea that desirable traits can be bred. Notions of racial purity were integral to the Holocaust and the Nazi euthanasia programme that murdered 250,000 people and forcibly sterilised a further 360,000. Eugenics were not confined to the Third Reich, however. The US castrated 70,000 people in the twentieth century, hoping to remove those deemed 'mentally deficient' from the gene pool.

In the UK, support for eugenics was once surprisingly prevalent, even among progressives. D. H. Lawrence fantasised about gassing 'the sick, the halt, and the maimed' while Virginia Woolf wrote about killing 'imbeciles'. For years, Winston Churchill fretted about the 'feeble-minded', and on becoming home secretary in 1910, he wrote to the prime minister about the need to protect 'thrifty, energetic and superior stocks'. When the Mental Deficiency Act was being drafted in the 1910s, Churchill initially advocated that it should enforce the castration of people who fell under the undesirable categories of idiot, imbecile, feeble-minded and morally defective. The law, passed in 1913, ultimately enforced incarceration instead, not that this was necessarily less cruel. By the time the Act was repealed in 1959, 65,000 people had been locked away with no right to petition for release. Criminals and alcoholics were deemed defectives, as were poor women who had given birth out of wedlock.

Eugenics advocacy dwindled after the horrors of Nazi Germany became fully known, but the desire to protect racial or national health through selective breeding, forced sterilisations and murder has never gone away. 'This is normal science,' Nyborg has written, 'but it all changed radically around the mid-20th century.' He has done his best to keep the flame of this brutal discipline alive.

In the post-war era, eugenics lingered in obscure journals and conferences like the Scandza Forum. Today, eugenicists are obsessed with IQ scores. IQ (standing for intelligence quotient) tests feature a battery of questions on abstract reasoning, vocabulary and arithmetic. They are an attempt to put a number on intelligence, a psychological construct that is not as easily observable or measurable as other traits like height. Most people score between 85 and 115, the average IQ being 100. Scores are not immutable, and can vary over lifetimes.

IQ, it is worth saying, is not the same as intelligence. An IQ test measures a narrow range of cognitive abilities. Because education systems in different countries have their own teaching materials and styles, IQ scores cannot usefully be applied across cultural contexts. This is, of course, what race scientists want to do: point to IQ tests in the West and say the reason they are higher than ones overseas is due to genetics.

The history of the IQ test is deeply troubling. Although its inventor, a Frenchman named Alfred Binet, said that his test was not a perfect measure of intelligence, in the early twentieth century it was used to advance eugenic goals. Henry Goddard, an American psychologist, translated Binet's test into English and used it to grade immigrants arriving at Ellis Island. 'We are getting the poorest of each race,' he concluded, advocating for low scorers to be prevented from breeding with wider society.

The IQ test has developed since its inauspicious beginnings, and today is correlated with life outcomes, like high income or good health. It is a useful tool in scientific research, and can help to identify students struggling in school who might need extra support. It is also useful to far-right activists looking to justify their very obvious hatred of other races.

Real geneticists say IQ is not merely the result of genetic heritage and that the impact of your environment is enormously important. The results of an IQ test can be greatly improved by access to clean air, good diet, whether you grew up with books at home or among chaos and trauma, plus countless other factors.

This likely accounts for cases when IQ scores have dramatically risen in short spaces of time. One study of IQs in rural Kenya, for instance, reported that over the course of fourteen years – not enough time for a generational change to have occurred – the IQ scores of participants rose by an average of 26 points. The researchers of this 2003 paper believe improvements in child nutrition, health and schooling were likely responsible. Dutch IQs similarly rose by 20 points between 1962 and 1982. The IQ scores of West Germans were on average higher than East Germans on the other side of the Iron Curtain.

Race science, as the name suggests, insists that races are meaningful biological categories, particularly where intelligence is concerned: that white is different from black, and black different from Asian. But geneticists disagree. 'We can state unequivocally that race is a fluid social, historical and political construct with no biological or genetic basis,' write Bill Newman, president of the European Society of Human Genetics, and Demetra Georgiou, chair of the British Society for Genetic Medicine. 'There is convincing evidence that there is more genetic variation within self-identified racial groups than there is between them.' Traits like skin colour and hair type give a false impression that race is a box you can assign people to, when in reality genetic variation is highly complex and on a continuum.

Following my introduction to Matt Archer, I take a look at Aporia. It looks slick and has well-produced podcasts. 'We're the world's only sociobiology magazine,' runs the tagline. Perhaps this is what Matt means by less spicy. 'We're the world's only race-science magazine' might attract fewer readers.

'Aporia magazine is an attempt to widen the Overton Window through social science, philosophy, and cultural commentary,' says the 'about' page. The Overton Window describes the range of ideas deemed acceptable by mainstream society. The far right is fond of the term, believing that if the Overton Window can be widened to include things like race science, then a concept such as repatriation might also be shoved through the gap.

What would Aporia like society to accept? 'There is no possibility of blacks and whites living peacefully together,' says the white nationalist Jared Taylor, who was billed to speak at the Tallinn conference. He appears on Aporia's podcast and later writes an article for the magazine. 'And all the places in which you find blacks and whites living together, whether it's in Great Britain, Canada, France, it's a failure.' He added that black people are less intelligent, are violently hostile towards white people, and are unable to plan for the future.

The magazine's executive editor is Bo Winegard. He was fired from his American university job amid a race-science scandal and had his last paper retracted because it cited dodgy data. He repeatedly writes about the need for his audience to attain a sense of white racial consciousness. 'Without white identity, European culture, the unique manifestation of the European temperament, will decay and its fragments will either be absorbed into a vast, insipid cultural porridge or they will disappear.'

The website has a podcast, and has invited on well-known authors like the linguistics professor Noam Chomsky, the *Mail on Sunday* journalist Peter Hitchens, and the historian Nigel Biggar – none of whom has endorsed race science. Helmuth Nyborg, who also features in the podcast archive, presumably knows what Aporia's agenda is. But do the others?

In between lectures at Tallinn, a tantalising rumour flits around. I hear it during the coffee break, and then later in the smoking area outside a bar. Guests tell me about it like they've just spotted a celebrity. The Pioneer Fund, they say, is secretly back in operation.

When I relay this to Patrik in his hotel room, he can't believe it. The Pioneer Fund, based in the US, developed links to Nazi Germany and financially supported British and American race scientists. Their operations are believed to have ground to a halt as their board members have died of old age. As a charity registered in the US, it has to annually publish its accounts. Looking at its recent filings, its multimillion-dollar endowment has shrunk to a few hundred thousand dollars and it has been giving less money to fewer people. Its website is no longer online. For most of the past decade, it has appeared to be effectively dormant.

Is it really up and running again? This rumour is relayed

to me from very drunk conference guests – hardly the most reliable of sources, but they did speak with some certainty.

The Pioneer Fund, potentially in business again. A new race-science publication called Aporia, gaining readers. Might they be connected?

Patrik and I leave Tallinn with new goals. We must substantiate, if we can, these Pioneer Fund rumours, and find out what is happening at Aporia. Does it really have Silicon Valley money? If so, who is involved?

Back in England, I read about Pioneer's long, dark history. Founded in 1937 by an American textile magnate named Wickliffe Draper, Pioneer's first act was to distribute a Nazi propaganda film called *Erbkrank*, or *The Hereditary Defective*, which claimed 'Jews produce an exceptionally high percentage of mentally ill'. It was part of the Third Reich's propaganda strategy to prepare Germany for the euthanasia programme, and Pioneer wanted to bring it to a US audience.

In the 1930s, Nazi Germany and the American board members of the Pioneer Fund became close. Harry Laughlin, a founder member of Pioneer, was awarded an honorary medical degree from the Nazi-controlled University of Heidelberg for his eugenics advocacy. Writing to his colleague at Heidelberg's medical department, Laughlin said the US and Third Reich shared 'a common understanding' about 'racial health'. He separately wrote out a list of 'Jew traits', which included the words 'parasite', 'dishonest', 'lie' and 'steal'.

Pioneer's enthusiasm for race science was undiminished by the fall of the Third Reich. During the civil rights era, the organisation lobbied against desegregation, when white state schools in the American South were ordered to accept black students. Pioneer leaders paid for legal cases aimed at reversing equality legislation. Their money funded committees to prevent the 1964 Civil Rights Act from passing, and created whites-only private schools in Mississippi to circumvent mixed-race state ones. Spending millions of dollars in this period, Pioneer was estimated to be the largest single backer of anti-civil rights agitation.

Race science is about justifying bigotry, giving the illusion that prejudice is not a knee-jerk reaction but an acceptable response to academic findings. Pioneer may have financed university researchers, but the conclusions of their papers were always foregone. It only sought to give racism a respectable gloss.

Wickliffe Draper even approached potential researchers to tell them about the papers he wanted them to write. 'He did not really know any genetics himself and was a racist of the usual type,' said a geneticist who Draper tried to recruit in 1960. 'He wished to prove simply that Negroes were inferior to other people and wished to promote some program to send them all to Africa. We merely told him that his ideas were a lot of nonsense and certainly would not work.'

Henry Garrett, an American academic who chaired the psychology department at Columbia University from 1941 to 1955 – and went on to work as a director at Pioneer – similarly believed black people were 'guests' in the US, a 'white man's civilization'. 'No matter how low (in a socio-economic sense) an American white may be, his ancestors built the civilizations of Europe,' he wrote. But, 'no matter how high . . . a Negro may be, his ancestors were (and his kinsmen still are) savages in an African jungle'.

William Shockley, another Pioneer-backed academic, proposed in 1970 a programme to sterilise anyone who scored less than 100 on an IQ test. By his estimate, this would include 85 per cent of all black people.

Pioneer researchers claimed to be interested in the truth, but they were only ever interested in the simulacrum of scientific endeavour. 'Real scientific journals,' writes William Tucker, a historian critical of the Pioneer Fund, 'do not publish the same conclusions – indeed, sometimes substantially the same article – again and again.'

Pioneer supported some of the most extreme far-right activists of the twentieth century. In the 1970s, a British activist named Roger Pearson ran a Pioneer-backed journal, *Mankind Quarterly*, which published articles claiming black people were 'temperamentally unsuited for citizenship'. Pearson had earlier created an organisation called the Northern League, and filled it with former officers of the Nazi SS. Pioneer personally gave him an estimated $2 million during his career to write and edit their journals.

Although Pioneer sought to influence the academic world, occasionally it scored a victory in the mainstream. In 1984, Roger Pearson received a herogram from the US president, Ronald Reagan. 'You are performing a valuable service,' Reagan wrote, citing another of Pearson's publications, the *Journal of Social, Political and Economic Studies*. The magazine, during its years in operation, published race-science articles. 'I hope that your efforts continue to receive broad interest and support and wish you every success in your future endeavors.' The letter was exposed by HOPE not hate's predecessor organisation, Searchlight. It proved an embarrassment for the White House, which did not deny the letter's existence, but merely asked Pearson to refrain from using it to sell subscriptions to *Mankind Quarterly*.

The Pioneer Fund, until the early 2010s, gave out hundreds of thousands of dollars every year. Some grants went into university research departments, others to segregationists like Jared Taylor.

As a charity, Pioneer's filings are open to the public. I scroll back through their annual reports, amazed at the size of the grants. In 2001, a total of $314,247 was sent out, including $80,000 to a race scientist in England, $75,000 to the University of Texas at Austin, $10,000 to Jared Taylor. At its peak, it had assets of $6.5 million.

In the last decade, Pioneer activity has declined. The conclusion drawn by most researchers who track Pioneer is that its activities have been winding inexorably down.

Patrik and I resolve to find out if Pioneer is truly back in action, influencing academia, the press and politicians to accept race science. It is especially worrying to think that this sinister movement might be enjoying a fresh boost of energy thanks to the younger, image-conscious leadership of Matt Archer and his secret Silicon Valley funder.

After Tallinn, our infiltration stalls. I email Matt, asking to meet up. He is slow to reply, and tells me he is abroad for the next few months. My messages asking to link up with other race scientists from Tallinn are also ignored. When

I ask Basketweavers about the Pioneer Fund, they say they haven't heard anything.

Patrik and I decide to contact Richard Lynn. Although he is in his early nineties, according to Pioneer's filings published that year, he is still its president. We hope that he might be able to tell us about the organisation's current capacity, and its possible connections to Aporia. Matt describes him as one of the most 'important' psychologists of his generation, and publishes a long video interview with him on Aporia. Believing that the white race is being outbred, Lynn was worried about the 'considerable deterioration' of white society. His ambition, he once said, was to 'have a go at the rehabilitation of eugenics'.

'It seems extraordinary,' Lynn wrote, 'that basically sound principles, that we need to find ways to correct genetic deterioration, should have become so widely accepted in the first four decades of the century and subsequently have become lost.'

Among Richard Lynn's legacies is the national IQ data set, first published in 2002. The average IQ in Europe, he claimed, is around 100. In sub-Saharan Africa, Lynn said it is 70. According to the British Psychological Society, this level of IQ would indicate significant impairment in intellectual functioning.

The evidence behind these statistics is highly dubious, to say the least. Compiling IQ tests carried out by other researchers, no matter how poor the data, Lynn determined average scores. He declared the national IQ of Angola was 77 using a sample size of nineteen. Somalia's score (67), was based on interviews with civil war refugees, average age thirteen, in a Kenyan refugee camp where only a quarter of respondents went to school. Included in the Eritrean data set was a test of seventy-two war orphans, aged four to seven. The scientists who conducted the test noted these children were severely traumatised: they lacked proper food and water, and suffered from sleep disturbances. Lynn's conclusion for Eritrea's IQ: 69.

One review of Lynn's research found that he further ignored test results that showed high IQ scores, only citing studies that confirmed his prejudices. His data is considered so poor that academics who rely on it risk their papers being retracted. 'There's probably no such thing as a perfect sample,' Lynn later said in defence of his work.

The conclusions he came to through his research were used to justify something he called 'not genocide':

> The foreign aid which we give to the under-developed world is a mistake, akin to keeping going incompetent species like the dinosaurs which are not fit for the competitive struggle for existing. What is called for here is not genocide, the killing off of the populations of incompetent cultures. But we do need to think realistically in terms of the 'phasing out' of such peoples.

Lynn did not clarify, in this article, what phasing out would actually entail, but he said that 'incompetent societies have to be allowed to go to the wall'.

It was not merely other races that Lynn wanted to eradicate. In the same article, he wrote:

> We are too altruistic in our social welfare policies towards the poor. People are poor largely because they are incompetent and unintelligent. Such people

should not be encouraged to breed. Conversely, we are too harsh to the rich. Progressive taxation, for example, is hard to justify. The rich are rich, broadly speaking, because they are intelligent and competent and we should encourage them to have more children.

Which rich people did Lynn have in mind? I wonder. Robber barons of the nineteenth century? Industrial Revolution-era factory owners putting children to work?

Placing these thoughts aside, I email Richard Lynn on 18 July, introducing myself as a fan. I hope to start a conversation, ideally in person, in which I can ask about what his organisation is up to.

How can someone who is not in academia support this field of research? I ask.

A week passes, and I wonder why he doesn't reply. Then his obituary appears on a far-right website. It says he died on 17 July at the age of ninety-three.

Two months after Tallinn, we have yet to make any progress.

Frustrated, Patrik and I discuss a new approach. I tell him about an article I wrote the year before on a community of conspiracy theorists in Birmingham. Knowing they were intensely paranoid of the media, I told them I was a donor with deep pockets. This granted me a meeting with their leader that would otherwise have been impossible to secure. She invited me to the office she ran out of a council building in the city centre, and spoke unreservedly about her battles to expose the people she believed were murderous, paedophilic satanists.

What if Chris was also a donor? Would race scientists start answering my emails if they knew I had money to spend on them?

Patrik and I start to brainstorm a new backstory for Chris as a philanthropist. We decide that Chris should remain a corporate drone. The only change is that he has come into a substantial inheritance, and wants to become an investor or donor. Chris's money, we hope, can gloss over his lack of race-science knowledge.

In September, I email Matt Archer, telling him I'd like to contribute to Aporia. After about ten tense hours, he replies, suggesting the possibility of meeting in a month's time. He must think I want to contribute articles to Aporia, not money. I send another message, this time making my intentions clearer.

I was hoping for a discussion on how I might be able to fund your mission, I say.

This time, Matt replies within minutes. We set up a Zoom date. I'm thrilled that the ruse has worked so quickly. Might it be possible to find out the identity of his funder just as fast?

I test the camera on my laptop, hoping what he sees on the video will look sufficiently donor-ish. We'll be talking in the bedroom of my flat. Within shot is an attic hatch hanging crookedly on its hinges. If I bend my laptop lid down enough, it is just about off-screen. I take a deep breath, start my tape recorder, and dial in.

To my surprise, Ed Dutton appears on the call. He makes race-science videos on YouTube and writes books claiming black people are less intelligent than white people. I haven't seen him since the Tallinn conference. Matt hadn't told me to expect him. In fact, in an earlier email, Matt had told me he didn't really know Ed. Was he lying?

I ask Ed how he has been since Estonia, and he launches into a story about the latest video he is researching. 'I've just planned a video of this guy in Australia that had sex with forty-two dogs between 2014 and 2022, and I've been looking into the psychological correlates of people who do that,' he says eagerly.

'Anyway,' says Matt, interrupting.

I sense this is the time to explain myself, and I run through the lines I prepared with Patrik, about admiring Aporia, about wanting to help, and putting my recently changed financial situation to good use.

'Thank you very much,' says Matt. 'It's a very, very generous offer.' I'm relieved that the investor persona seems to be working. Matt asks if I would like to fund the Jolly Heretic, Ed's social media page.

Do you two work together? I ask Ed.

'Yeah, I help out occasionally, perhaps,' he replies. His answer sounds oddly vague. Why is he trying to obfuscate his connection to Matt?

'Ed is the only person in this movement who has the right combination of charisma, intellect, work ethic,' says Matt. If they could afford to rent a London office and pay for a videographer and camera equipment, then Ed could be made into the next big social media star. During this conversation, Ed seems to be looking at other things on his computer. I ask what he thinks about these grand plans.

'I personally find that it's best for me to focus on what I'm apparently good at and not think about these things,' he says.

I'm puzzled. Matt is dominating the conversation about Ed's own career. Meanwhile, Ed seems to be mentally elsewhere. Why is he so deferential to Matt?

Funding the Jolly Heretic, I think, is not the best way to find out about Aporia, so I steer the conversation back to the magazine. Ed continues to tune out.

Aporia, says Matt assuredly, is going to be 'read by the elite, people aspiring to the elite, people who accidentally end up becoming the elite because they're so crazy or entrepreneurial they make it big'. This line has the ring of a confident elevator pitch, and I wonder how many times he has used it before.

'In three or four years' time, this will be the destination for controversial social science,' he says. 'We would rather be read by a few billionaires than 10,000 normies. Judging by our email list, this is already happening: I can look down and see academics, entrepreneurs, journalists at the *New York Times*. I'm not going to doxx them but they're very important people, and that's what I want to grow further.' He says 'a friend of ours' just had a three-hour conversation with Elon Musk.

Ed logs off the call to look after his kids. Matt says something that grabs my attention. He describes Ed as his employee, not the other way around. Matt even says Ed's channel is under his 'control'.

It is odd to listen to Matt treat Ed with contempt. 'I don't get excitement or gratitude or any sense of understanding about where he is and where we're going to go,' says Matt. He complains that Ed needs 'micromanagement' and is uninterested in professionalising his channel.

That sounds frustrating, I say.

'It's more frustrating because it's passive. He'll basically do what he's told.'

Matt appears to have a lot more going on besides Aporia and the Jolly Heretic. He tells me that he works with an 'underground research organisation'.

I take a chance, and say that this sounds a bit like the Pioneer Fund.

'Yep,' he says.

Is it me, or is there a pregnant pause in the air? I'm not sure how to fill it. Our call has lasted over an hour, and Matt signs off to get to another meeting.

I slump back in my chair, exhausted from pretending. I think about Matt. His well-rehearsed lines, the way he paused to write down my questions before replying, struck me as very business-minded. Did he use the same speech on his Silicon Valley investor?

When Matt thought my fictional finances would stretch to camera equipment and an office space, he told me all about running Aporia and Edward Dutton's channel. If I made him think I had a much bigger investment to offer, what else might he tell me?

We make a date to meet for dinner in October.

I book a table at a restaurant in Holland Park, where Matt has rented an apartment while visiting London. It's a bougie place, in keeping with my image as a wealthy investor – the menu has potted partridge and £350 burgundies. I arrive early, and spend a while choosing the right table where my camera might best film Matt. When he shows up, he refuses my offer of a drink. 'I got paralytic at university like every-body does but I don't like getting out of control, I don't like the way it makes me feel,' he says. We're both trying hard to remain in control. I order sparkling water.

A waiter arrives, and I ask, hoping to come across like a bon vivant, what he would recommend. Unfortunately, he begins an explanation of every dish on the long menu. Conscious that I have a limited time with Matt, I mentally urge the waiter to stop talking. Matt orders smoked salmon with tiny beetroot and black garlic, I ask for venison with celeriac puree. I barely notice when it arrives, as I am so focused on him. Before we met, I wondered if we would get along, but we bypass pleasantries and talk about business straight away. He must be determined to secure my invest-ment. Both our preparations for this evening must have been pretty similar, rehearsing lines to impress the other.

I ask Matt about the underground research team that he mentioned last time. He tells me it is run by Emil Kir-kegaard, a race scientist I saw in Tallinn but did not meet. Emil, who is Danish and looks to be in his late thirties, has a reputation as perhaps the most active writer in the race-science world today. For a while, he ran *Mankind Quarterly* and was close to Richard Lynn. Am I getting close to the Pioneer Fund? Matt promises to introduce us soon.

In the meantime, Matt describes how the ten-man underground research team publishes articles on race science online and in academic journals, which Aporia will then write about as an interesting new study. Ed Dutton might also promote it through a video on his channel. The links between all three of these operations are kept hidden so the more reputable Aporia isn't tarnished by association with the Jolly Heretic, and the underground research team remains completely secret.

Matt is being open with me, so I decide to take a risk. I want to push him on Pioneer again. I am convinced, from the way our call ended last time, that Matt was holding his tongue.

What you're talking about sounds like a new version of the Pioneer Fund, I say.

'I guess so,' he responds. 'The Pioneer Fund was public. They've appropriated the money, the remaining money, but there's virtually nothing left, 150 grand or something. They just appropriated the remaining money when Richard Lynn died. It was left to Emil and now that becomes part of our organisation.'

One of the hardest things about undercover work is not betraying emotions upon hearing a detail this important. My first instinct is always to shout: 'What? You're joking! That's MENTAL!' Instead, seated in front of Matt, I nod thoughtfully, trying to keep control of my eyes and eyebrows.

I notice that Matt talks about 'our organisation', instead of just Aporia. I ask what the difference is, and he explains that Emil is in charge of an LLC, a limited liability company, registered in the US, in a state with helpful privacy laws. The funder, name still unknown, owns roughly a 10 per cent stake. I name-drop a couple of billionaires known for investing in far-right projects, just to see if it will elicit a response, but Matt stays tight-lipped, except to say that when he met him in Vienna in June to raise more money, the funder was 'in a down period' due to negative press. Matt indicates that he has now received around £1 million from this mystery investor, a serious amount of money. Despite Matt's indiscretion up until now, I sense that this is one detail he is unhappy to divulge, and decide not to press him further.

Instead, I try to discern Matt's interest in running Aporia. At first, he describes himself simply as the pursuer of truth, as many race scientists do. 'You've been telling us for over half a century that it's evil, but it's true,' he says. 'I personally think it's immoral to bury your head in the sand.'

But later, he recounts a conversation he had with his business partner Erik Ahrens, who I've yet to meet. Erik is a communications expert with the Alternative für Deutschland, the German far-right party. Both hope that if the AfD, which is polling well, gets into power, it will enforce a remigration policy. 'Imagine if Germany did that,' Matt says in a hushed, animated voice. He says he told Erik: 'It's your fucking duty to do this.'

Matt fantasises about filling ships with people and man-oeuvring them to Morocco, and forcing the government there to receive a human cargo. 'We're smarter than you, we're bigger than you: you're going to do this.' Matt's eyes are shining with enthusiasm. 'Imagine that this happened in the next ten, fifteen years, what that would do for the West, for Europe.'

The bill arrives, and Matt says he has another meeting to dash off to. Once he's gone, I exhale deeply.

I phone Patrik to relay the details. The Pioneer Fund isn't back, as we heard in Tallinn. It never went away. It has rebranded, re-formed and gone into hiding as a private company, its projects more nimble now they have moved into the dark. Matt sounds part of a highly ambitious, highly motivated race-science project explicitly tied to political goals. We want to find out more about him.

Matt Archer has a sparse presence online, and there is little information about him before he created Aporia. Together, Patrik and I try to find out more. We watch the blurry footage my camera recorded of Matt in Tallinn. Scanning through the tape, we revisit one brief snippet in which his backpack is visible. We didn't think much of it at the time, dismissing it as an old university bag. Now we take another look. The design below the zip looks like the quadrant of a school crest with some text underneath. There are three words. It looks like one of them says 'Kensington', but we can't be sure. Below that are two clear letters: 'MF'. Are those his real initials? In Matt's podcast appearances, he discusses his past career teaching at a secondary school. Is this a bag from his last job?

We try googling different schools with 'Kensington' in the name. Patrik finds the crest of Kensington Park School in west London: the purples, reds and yellows match the colours on Matt's bag. We trawl the school's website for pictures of him. There's nothing. In any case, the man we're searching for must have left at least two years ago, when he started Aporia. We look on the Internet Archive, and by chance, there is a saved version of Kensington Park School's staff page. We scroll through the pictures. There, above a photograph of the man who calls himself Matt Archer, is the name Matthew Frost, teacher of religious studies. There's even a blog on the school website under his name, describing a 2019 Christmas trip to the Natural History Museum ice rink.

Why did a schoolteacher leave his job to become an advocate for race science? Matt tells a story about himself in an article on Aporia's website, and elaborates on it in a now deleted video interview with Ed Dutton. He was the only child in a working-class family somewhere in England, he says. Realising at a young age that there was a 'gulf in intelligence' between him and his parents, he grew distant from them. This 'canyon' was especially noticeable with his mother, whose IQ he estimates to be less than 80, at least 20 points below average. 'I just felt like we spoke different languages and that it was impossible for her to learn very basic things,' he explains in the article. 'All of which is difficult to write, let alone say, without people thinking you're a weird asshole for calling your own mother stupid.'

Skipping breakfast, living on a diet of sweets and chocolate, Matt suffered migraines in school, and scored low marks in his GCSEs. 'My parents were a good example of why a parenting licence should have to be obtained,' he says. There were fights. He describes a physical altercation in which he slapped his father. 'Stir in some child neglect and maternal depression, and you have a recipe for a very odd life.'

He says he had an intellectual awakening in his late teens, encouraged in part by a clever girlfriend. He made it to Loughborough University for an undergraduate degree, then Cambridge for a master's in philosophy. When he became a teacher, he took an interest in gifted students, and claimed at one point to be writing a book about exceptionally smart children. He learned that his parents were unable to conceive, so his mother used a sperm donor. After taking a DNA test in his mid-twenties, he was contacted by a woman claiming to be his half-sister, an Oxford-educated classicist. They hired a DNA detective and tracked down their biological father.

Matt has not publicly identified his father, but hints that he is much smarter than either of the two people who raised him. 'Let's just say it's someone who, in their field, is probably quite famous.'

Ed describes it as 'the triumph of genetics over environment'. Matt's IQ, according to Ed, is likely around 145 – genius level – although this is a guess, as he has not had it tested.

I have no way of confirming what details of the story are true, except that his surname of Archer is a pseudonym (which is fairly common in the far right). What is certain is how neatly Matt's tale fits into the race scientist's view that genes are much more important in educational outcomes than environment.

Matt introduces me to Emil Kirkegaard on a call in October. I feel the need to impress Emil – I'm not sure what Matt has told him, and imagine that as the boss of this secret company, he might be extra cautious. To appear like a serious investor, I offer them both business advice at the start of the call. They need to believe that I am the corporate consultant I claim to be. I tell Matt to improve the headlines on Aporia: instead of the generically titled 'research round-up' stories, I recommend making them more specific about what research the article highlights. (Matt puts this into practice, and I feel grimy when I see his engagement statistics rise: more people hit the like button, more people leave comments.)

Emil now lives in Germany on the property of an AfD official. He has a neat beard and a sweeping fringe of brown hair. He has changed his legal name to William Engman to avoid scrutiny, although continues to go by Emil in his work. He seems amiable and keen to impress. I'm pleased that my investor character seems to be helping me avoid any personal questions from him.

Emil has been blogging for more than a decade. In 2012, he published a piece on his website about paedophilia, suggesting that abusers could be accommodated by 'having sex with a sleeping child without them knowing it (so, using sleeping medicine)'. He added: 'If they don't notice it is difficult to see how they cud [sic] be harmed, even if it is rape.' He later argued he was merely discussing a hypothetical. An ethnonationalist, he advocates for eugenic policies and believes the biggest threat society faces is 'demographics'. Emil is not a geneticist by profession, having completed a bachelor's degree in linguistics. In order to disseminate his work, Emil created OpenPsych, a website that looks like an academic publication. One of his interests is sexual differences between races: who has a bigger penis, who is more interested in breasts or buttocks, and whether a high sex drive is indicative of lower intelligence (white people with smaller penises and a lower sex drive being, apparently, smarter).

On our call, Emil says their organisation has sixteen people – a lot, given most race scientists work alone. They want to create a website in which users submit their DNA profiles from Ancestry.com or 23andMe and, in addition to taking an IQ test and providing information about their ethnicity, will be told what kind of diseases they might be likely to get. Like Matt and Emil's other projects, the connection between this DNA website and its owners will be kept secret.

Why are they doing this? Race scientists like Emil need genetic data sets for their research, but they are hard to access. 'Sometimes private sector people give you stuff under the table,' he says, but they risk being identified and potentially losing their jobs.

Emil says his reach is growing, and provides an example. On 13 October, he blogged about a data set of several hundred Palestinian refugees who sought asylum in Denmark, and the percentage of them who had received criminal convictions since they arrived in the 1990s. The sources he provided were all in Danish. On 19 October, Nigel Farage made a video using the same statistics, giving source links to the same Danish articles that Emil cited on his blog. 'He clearly got them from my blog post,' Emil says gleefully, 'but he didn't mention me. He cites Danish sources that he can't read.'†

I tell Matt that before investing, I would like a full picture of his company, and want to sit in on a research team meeting. Matt says the other researchers are wary, but that he will arrange it nonetheless. The money I am offering him must be too enticing. He sends a link to their weekly call, and I join with my microphone muted. Emil introduces me as a new investor, and I wave to my laptop camera. There are ten researchers here. Their names have all appeared on the website of Aporia, some of them as podcast guests or authors of articles. Some of them used

† Nigel Farage did not answer a request for comment.

to hold bona fide academic positions but have since been fired.

I stay quiet, hoping not to draw attention to myself. Emil runs through the upcoming projects of his team. There are papers on 'international dysgenics', 'income and intelligence' and 'wokeness and mental illness'.

He advises one writer that his paper on dysgenics is unlikely to be published anywhere but *Mankind Quarterly* or OpenPsych. He suggests enlisting Bryan Pesta, a former professor at Cleveland State University in Ohio, to 'make the words soft and sweet', which might help to slip the paper past the editorial board of an academic journal. 'We might be able to get through.'

Pesta is on the call, smoking a cigarette, pouring a glass of mid-afternoon wine. When he was employed by Cleveland State, he published race-science articles in *Mankind Quarterly* for which he received Pioneer Fund money. He was fired after requesting genetic data from the National Institutes of Health, a biomedical agency, without telling them he would use it to write about racial differences and intelligence. Pesta tried to sue his old university, calling the investigators of his case 'bastards'. He lost.

The other researchers run through their projects. One says he has access to data from the UK Biobank, a massive medical database that is supposed to be closely guarded, only given to proper academics. How has he got access? I never find out.

Another researcher is an Italian man named Davide Piffer. His name rings a bell. He tells us that he is working with Emil Kirkegaard on a paper analysing genetic information from Neolithic samples to show Europeans had superior genes to Africans. After the call, I look up Piffer online and see a post on X/Twitter in which he calls African immigrants to Italy 'gorillas'. It takes me a few days before I remember why his name rang a bell.

On 14 May 2022, a white eighteen-year-old entered a supermarket in Buffalo, a city in the state of New York, and shot dead ten people. All of them were black. In a manifesto that he uploaded to the internet before the attack, Payton Gendron included a section that quoted the arguments of race scientists, inserting charts, graphs and screenshots of their published papers. Among the links were two extracts of an article written by Davide Piffer. Published in 2013, it was about educational attainment and IQ, and appeared in *Mankind Quarterly*.

Pioneer-backed scientists like Richard Lynn feature heavily in this section of the Buffalo terrorist's manifesto. Gendron spoke, as they did, of general fluid intelligence factors, bell curves and standard deviations. His conclusion: 'Blacks on average have a lesser IQ due to restrictions of their brain development. They are prone to violence and common criminal activity. We must remove blacks from our western civilizations.' He is serving a life sentence with no chance of parole.

In March 2024, the paper that Piffer discussed on the call appeared in *Twin Research and Human Genetics*, a Cambridge University Press journal.

I tell Matt that I am willing to put up a six-figure investment, perhaps as much as $300,000. He starts telling me much more, revealing the name of the secret organisation he runs with Emil: the Human Diversity Foundation, or HDF. It is registered as a company in Wyoming, a state that allows founders a great deal of secrecy.

HDF, I learn, is divided into two sections. The first consists of the underground research team and *Mankind Quarterly*, headed by Emil. This is similar to the Pioneer Fund's original operation. The second section is more innovative. It manages Aporia, the Jolly Heretic, and a host of projects run by Matt and his colleague Erik Ahrens, the Alternative für Deutschland apparatchik. This section tries much more explicitly to tie race science to policy.

In October, they get Scyldings – the Basketweaver-affiliated conference group – to organise an event for them at the Little Ship Club in central London. Ed Dutton will be the star speaker, preceded by Erik. I meet the latter before he takes the stand. He is a tall, precisely spoken German man, and grasps my hand with an unsettlingly hard stare.

When he takes the stage, Erik introduces himself as 'Mr Schmitt'. I find this weird. He has a public profile – why would he lie? Mr Schmitt asks the audience, which is about a hundred strong, for volunteers willing to build something called 'Neo Byzantium' with him. 'The whole Western world is lacking a truly elite system and so the organisation which Ed and I are working with is taking more concrete steps towards the establishment of such an elite,' he says. 'We're doing this partly through media outreach, partly through showing up to events like this and talking to people on the ground and also partly through networking which is taking place more behind the scenes.' It sounds stirring, if a little obscure.

He invites people to scan a QR code and talk to him

about how they can contribute. What they are meant to contribute is unclear. Some of the Basketweavers attend the event, and I leave early to avoid having to converse with them and the HDF team at the same time.

Matt and Erik explain what they're up to on an internet call in October. Neo Byzantium is going to be a private members' club, connoting a bridgehead of elite Westerners resisting foreign invaders. They want to charge up to $4,000 – a ridiculous amount of money – for the top tier of access to the club, which will host secret events where they can meet and mingle with race scientists. It's for wealthy fans of Aporia and Ed Dutton.

Several weeks after the Little Ship Club speech, Erik tells me the young, male applicants to Neo Byzantium expressed feelings of loneliness. 'I wish I had others to talk to' is the refrain they hear, so common to the Basketweavers. 'I don't recall talking to anyone who didn't say that,' he says. 'Everyone who attends the events is looking for community.'

'They've clearly never been listened to in their life,' adds Matt. 'The journey is different but they all end up in the same place, which is "I want meaning".'

With Neo Byzantium, the HDF team aims to profit from the isolation of these young men by selling them on a membership programme to give them the semblance of a community. Erik cites Andrew Tate, the misogynist influencer, whose 'Hustlers University' scheme attracted more than 100,000 men – many of them teenagers – paying a £40 monthly fee for access to his online community. 'He is not our main source of inspiration but it is a working business model,' says Erik.

He and Matt have put a lot of thought into Neo Byzantium. They are deliberately ambiguous with their applicants. Erik interviews them pretending to be Mr Schmitt – 'a persona', he says, a 'cold' man. He wants to destabilise them, and root out potential infiltrators. During the interviews, applicants are subjected to a litmus test. 'And the litmus test is, obviously, "what do you believe about race",' says Matt. Neither of them elaborates on the answer they expect to hear.

Those who pass the interview round are sent an Android phone, wrapped up in a neat black box. It has been stripped of all apps except one, an encrypted instant messenger, loaded with one contact: 'Org'. After a few days, members receive a call, during which they hear about a private event they can pay to attend. 'You have to work a little bit with smoke and mirrors to get these people engaged so that they pay for it,' says Erik. A dozen phones have so far been sent out.

Where did Erik get the idea for all this? Scientology, in part: the cult that enforces a strict hierarchy requiring members to give increasingly large amounts of money to reach salvation. 'We have to control everything,' Erik says. He is instilling an us-versus-them mentality to foster uncertainty among members of Neo Byzantium. 'We need to keep people on edge and emotionally engaged like this. A little bit of paranoia makes the world more comfy.'

He has begun dividing early recruits by indeterminately rewarding them. One member is coming to a strategy retreat in Spain – another was rejected for that trip, but will instead be invited to an upcoming one in Greece. Erik hopes that when they eventually meet, they will talk to each other, grow jealous, and compete for advancement in Neo Byzantium.

They want to 'separate' one member from an outside friend who believes Neo Byzantium is a scam. Erik has given him an internship with the underground research team. 'This is how we break up that bond,' he explains. Erik wants this member to commit to Neo Byzantium by 'systematically taking away the other options from him'.

He looks at me. 'Some of this stuff, I'm aware, sounds quite manipulative. But who are we fighting against? We're fighting against extremely manipulative systems. It's not us who made these rules.' He insists he is 'acting in good faith'.

Brilliant, I tell them. This is all brilliant. Great work.

Inwardly, I am reeling. Not only are they exploiting the loneliness of these young men, they are also rinsing them of whatever money they have. They describe how one member got his parents to pay for the membership because he couldn't afford it. In order to attend a dinner at a cheap chain pub before Christmas, members of Neo Byzantium will have to pay £245. This is after paying an entry fee of £650 into the club. In exchange, they are being manipulated by people who have studied the secrets of cult management.

The structure of HDF is becoming clearer, although one final detail, perhaps the most important one, is uncertain. We need to know the identity of HDF's secret Silicon Valley investor.

During a call with Emil in early November, he almost lets the name slip. 'Currently we have one main funder,' he says, who has given a total of $1.3 million, a sum of money that other far-right organisations can only dream of.

Is the funder ideologically aligned? I ask.

'I would say he's secure in terms of ideology,' Emil replies. 'I don't know what politics he is into, but he hates woke stuff. I would guess he's fairly typical, somewhere between, you know, white nationalist and libertarian.'

Emil goes on to say that this funder had to deal with 'some adverse publicity of his own creation that I have nothing to do with'. Apparently, he put money behind a similar project 'in a way that could be found out'.

Matt chimes in to say the funder has been 'supporting dissidents for many years'.

'Is there any reason we shouldn't tell him?' says Emil. I'm so thrilled at the possibility that I feel my face burning.

'Probably want to check with the funder first,' says Matt.

'OK, well, let's do that,' Emil agrees.

I can't believe it. I was so close to finding out. For hours afterwards, I rehash the conversation, trying to figure out if there was some perfect combination of words that I could have spoken to convince them otherwise.

With these clues, Patrik and I try to deduce who the investor might be. We identify a few potential names, but can't be certain. By now, securing the investor's identity has become a priority, even an obsession. If major Silicon Valley money is indeed backing a project as nasty as HDF, then we are committed to finding out.

We face a crisis when Matt tells me, shortly after this call, that he is leaving the UK. He's going to Athens for the next two months to take advantage of winter sun and cheap office space. This is disappointing. I feel like the funder's identity is slipping out of reach and I can only maintain my relationship with the HDF team for as long as they think I am about to give them a stack of cash. They have already sent me a contract to sign. Can I stall for another two months in the hope of seeing Matt on his return to London, where he might tell me? Not likely.

Time is running out, I tell Patrik on the phone.

'What if you went to Athens?' he says.

We think for a moment. Is it possible that Chris would fly over on a whim to check in on his investment? If Matt is going to tell me about the source of his funds, the odds of him spilling in the casual atmosphere of a real-life meet-up are better than on another video call. This all makes sense. And yet as I book my ticket to Greece, it feels completely hare-brained.

The sun sets as I land in Athens. I see nothing of the city on the taxi ride to my hotel. I'm mentally preparing lines stuffed with half-understood investor jargon, praying this will convince Matt to divulge the name of his funder. Patrik, who flew in before me, is waiting in the hotel lobby. He booked me a five-star hotel to impress Matt, should I need the option of bringing him back to the bar here. Patrik, meanwhile, has to make do with a hostel.

Patrik's advice before going undercover is usually to listen and not press anyone for information. Tonight, he says I should break that rule. I've met Matt online or in-person on seven different occasions now, building up some social credit that I can spend on pushing him for the name. If necessary, I can demand to know. The plan is to meet at the office Matt has rented in the city centre, then head for dinner at a swanky restaurant that I have promised to pay for. Erik Ahrens will also join us.

Twitchy with nerves, I screw in my hidden camera. I

keep checking the sound on my spare tape recorder, the charge levels on my camera batteries, the angle of the button lens. Matt texts me, asking where I am, so I dash out to find a taxi. On the way over, I think about what would happen if I fail to secure the name, and imagine returning to Patrik empty-handed. Part of what makes HDF so sinister is its connection to powerful, rich people. We need the name to make that case.

Stress grips my chest as the cab pulls up to Matt's office. 'Fancy seeing you here!' he says amiably, shaking my hand. He is much warmer towards me than when we first exchanged emails. Matt thinks he is just a meeting or two away from $300,000. He and Erik usher me upstairs to a glass-panelled meeting room, where they brief me on their plans to add other arms to HDF. They begin a presentation on a laptop. The easiest way of asking about the investor will be over dinner, so for now, I cross my legs, pull out a leather-bound notepad, and write notes in the manner of what I hope is a perceptive business consultant.

Matt and Erik want to launch an app called Liegent that summarises far-right books, and use this to advertise on the social media channels of influencers. Erik says this is 'economics as coercion', and describes a similar version he created in Germany named Blinkist. 'Once you are the ad network, once you are providing them with these product placements, you can basically agenda-set,' he explains. 'Imagine being able to tell ten to fifteen right-wing You-Tubers to talk about topic X, or talk positively about politician Y.' He says his network will be able to 'make or break a politician'.

Curiously, Erik says there is a split within HDF over how to run their other project, their own version of 23andMe. Emil wants to use it for data harvesting, so he can have statistics for his race-science papers. Matt and Erik want to make it more gimmicky, telling white users whether they are descended from Vikings, Celts or Romans.

'Emil is a genius – I like him as a friend,' says Erik. 'But he's not business-minded. Just as you cannot argue with a woman, you cannot argue with someone like that. You cannot convince him that this is a good idea. Do we need more research showing group difference in IQ? No . . . Research needs to go on, but we don't need more "Did you know black people are on average less trustworthy?" No, it's settled science. It's become autistic and repetitive. I don't need more convincing, and neither do the people who watch Ed Dutton.'

I make a mental note of this dispute. I have an idea how to turn it back on them later.

We take a taxi from the office to the restaurant I've booked. On the way over, Matt tells me Neema Parvini will arrive the next day. 'We're flying him to Athens, putting him up in a penthouse apartment, wining and dining him,' he says. 'He thinks he's coming to pitch a think tank.'

'He's delusional,' interjects Erik.

Neema wants to set up a far-right think tank, and believes Matt and Erik will be the guys to make it happen. They have practised a good-cop, bad-cop routine. Erik will 'play the stonewall character' of Mr Schmitt, and discusses sprinting out of the meeting and returning without explanation, just to unsettle Neema. Matt will be more welcoming – he discusses whether to buy an expensive watch for Neema as a gift to reel him in. 'I've befriended him, saying, "I think you could be the man for the job".'

They are going to hoodwink Neema into believing they will fund his think tank. While the bogus plans are being incrementally drawn up, they will meanwhile take advantage of his audience to flog memberships to Neo Byzantium. 'We get his hopes up, and we keep dangling this in front of his eyes,' says Erik. They will have him address their events and accept advertising on his channel, giving them input over the videos he produces. 'We'll say, "It's the one step you need to do, so we can pull this off." And maybe he's gonna get this think tank, just not in the foreseeable future.'

Erik calls Neema 'a comfy boy, a doughy boy'.

Do they think he will be receptive to their scheme?

'He's receptive to money,' replies Matt. He describes a preliminary call in which Neema did not come across well. 'He wasn't asking any questions. I don't like the mumbling. He's not charismatic.' Neema is now demanding an annual salary of $200,000 to run his think tank. 'He has no sense of proportion or what's realistic,' says Matt.

Incredibly, they are using the very same tactic that I am on them. Given what Matt and Erik have planned in their scamming of Neema, are they pulling something on me? Matt is fond of saying that in exchange for my investment, I will be able to put 'rocket boosters' under HDF. They have even offered me a board seat – is that a real position? Matt and Erik show me a breakdown of what they would spend my money on. They want $75,000 to spend on an office, travel, accommodation, software and staff – just for Neo Byzantium. I have a feeling that were the investment to go ahead, I would not be presented with itemised expenditures and receipts.

We reach a swish seafood restaurant near the Acropolis. I text Patrik that we are close – he is going to try and snap us with his long lens. We walk inside and approach the front-of-house staff, announcing our reservation. It's Monday in the off-season, and the place is empty. We are led to a white-linen table by the window, hopefully giving Patrik a view. The waiters take our orders: fish soup to start, then grilled sea bream for me, and octopus for them. Erik and I encourage Matt to have a rare drink when our bottle of white wine arrives.

Now that they have delivered their pitch, it's my turn to direct the conversation. Patrik and I have tried to plan this so I can appear to naturally ask for the name of the funder. The clamp around my heart tightens as I begin.

Having read about nebulous Silicon Valley terminology, I ask Matt and Erik to explain to me their 'theory of change'. In response, Erik tells me his lifelong ambition. 'My vision is to one day run in Germany, in a Trump-like fashion. It hasn't been done for a hundred years, to run a populist movement centred around a person.' I try to figure out if he could possibly be talking about anyone who isn't Hitler.

'I was looking for who can be this, and I probably have to go into that role,' he says. 'In order to do this, I need to build myself obviously, and need to be both financially and politically independent from a party. I want to be in a position where, when the German government inevitably goes after me – because they don't want this to happen – I need to have an international network generating revenue in different countries, so when you take one leg you have five others to stand on, like a spider or octopus.'

Bowls of gluey fish soup arrive. A lounge-music version of Madonna's 'Material Girl' plays on the restaurant sound system. Erik continues with his vision of the future. His inspiration, he says, is 'world Jewry and Israel', adding, 'You have a state, but the benefit of a transnational, stateless organisation . . . This, but run by based people. So Judaism' – here, he lowers his voice – 'for white, Christian people.' He's talking about an ethnostate.

The waiters here are very attentive, distracting Erik. They keep arriving to clip fresh oregano into a bowl of olive oil, to top up our wine glasses, to replace our soup spoons with fish forks.

'All of these people, all across the world, ideally across the white world, need to be connected,' says Erik, resuming his flow. 'This is for them – what we're building is for them. Ideally you have a homeland like Germany, or probably eastern Germany, a state power, which looks out for them, like Israel looks out for the Jews. It's not ideal, but it's the only way to survive.'

Erik says he is so committed to this plan that he broke up with his girlfriend of six years in order to devote more time to HDF and the Neo Byzantium project.

'I put a lot on the line, and I'm all in,' he says, in a firm voice. 'It matters that we are all in to the degree that we say we want to spend the next year travelling from major city to major city, setting up these cells, while we are building the network.'

Cells? I think.

Erik says he told Matt to break up with his girlfriend too.

Will you? I ask him.

'Yeah,' Matt replies. 'It's one of those things where she's being slowly phased out.' He doesn't sound regretful. He sounds determined.

'All in,' says Erik, nodding. 'We live for the race now.'

Our main courses arrive. I'm so tense that my fish tastes dry, drier than kindling. I want to make them think that my pen is poised above the contract, but I have some doubts.

Let's talk numbers, I say.

Both of them straighten up, alert. I try to unsettle them by repeating Erik's line about Emil not being business-minded, that he cannot be convinced of a good idea.

Does this not speak to a cultural problem in the company?

They shift in their chairs. Erik rallies. 'Emil just doesn't want to do business,' he says. 'It's just something that he doesn't want to do, he needs to be forced to do it.'

Now that we're on the subject of my questions about HDF, I take a breath, and look at my notepad as if this is just another item of business.

I have to say that the biggest concern I have is the other funder, I say.

Matt stops eating and puts his fingers to his lips. Erik arches his hands and scowls.

His involvement is integral to the whole operation, I continue.

'He has nothing to do with Neo Byzantium,' Erik shoots back.

If the going got tough, if a cancellation, a targeted campaign, whatever, and he were to get scared – if he decides to pull out, it puts me on the hook.

I'm talking too fast. I can hear the panic in my voice. I

try to slow down, and take a bite of my fish. It tastes revolting. The lines I spent so long preparing continue to tumble from my mouth out of sync.

I've only heard about him in the vaguest of terms, I say.

'If you want I think we could get you a meeting with him,' replies Matt.

I need to know this guy exists, I say. You know I'm discreet. It's very important for us to proceed. I think I know who it is.

'You can say a name,' Matt says, calling my bluff.

I reply with the name of an American investor who seems to fit the description: not a billionaire but not far off, associated with funding far-right projects and embroiled in a scandal this summer about one of them.

Matt shakes his head.

'It's not that we want to keep him secret, but we don't want to bring up his name without his knowing first,' says Erik.

'He has had one leak,' adds Matt. 'He's funded other people.'

Unless I know who it is, it's like we're talking about an imaginary figure here, I say. I like you guys – I believe in your vision – but until I have a clearer idea about the inner workings of this company, it makes me hesitate at the final push.

Matt talks about wanting to ask the funder first. Erik says their desire to keep his identity secret is a good thing – it shows they would protect me.

We've been at this for ages. I hear myself groan, then sigh. I've run out of ways to ask. This whole time, I've been trying to appear nonchalant by eating my fish, which is so dry it feels like placing plain cream crackers into the mouth of a skeleton.

Matt reassures me that the funder is 'fully aligned' and 'ideologically driven'. I'm not really listening. I picture returning to my hotel, telling Patrik I failed.

It's a bad idea, I say, to start a business relationship when there are key facts that I'm not apprised of, because it makes me think: what else are they not telling me? My voice sounds pathetic now.

'We completely agree,' says Erik. 'We want to tell you, we just need to ask him before we give away his identity.' He pauses. Apparently he learned the identity of the funder the first time he met Emil. He looks at Matt and shrugs. 'Hey, can you ask Emil? Maybe Emil has given the green light.'

Every muscle in my body is tensed. I look down at my plate, and spear another forkful of this horrid fish.

Matt picks up his phone. He tries to call Emil. Emil does not pick up.

'I want this to be dealt with swiftly,' says Erik. He digs out his own phone and looks up the number for Emil's girlfriend.

It's late, but she picks up. Erik asks her to put Emil on the line. I wait.

Erik speaks in single words. 'Confirm', 'Good', 'Yes', 'Perfect', 'OK'.

He hangs up. He nods at Matt. Matt looks at me. 'Andrew Conru,' he says. 'He made his money through a service called Adult Friend Finder. One of these people, right place, right time.'

Matt says Conru has been secretly funding Emil Kirkegaard for years, as well as Jared Taylor.

I have pictured this moment for so many weeks. I thought that if it happened, I would feel a rush. I'm so adrenalised that it doesn't make a difference. Now that I have pressured Matt and Erik this hard, I feel like we need to end the conversation on a more convivial note.

Waiters bring us a glass of dessert wine, sweet and refreshing. I ask about Ed Dutton, and if he's got enough capacity, given his life in Finland, to do everything they want him to. 'We're taking care of that too,' says Erik. 'I have quite straightforward ways of dealing with these family issues. We're dealing with something bigger.'

Does this mean divorcing his wife?

'Everyone's got to make a sacrifice,' Erik replies. He says he will encourage Ed to spend longer and longer periods of time away from his family in Finland.

Matt asks Erik to tell me about the activists. 'When I saw this I thought this is so exciting and fantastic,' he says.

Erik pulls out his phone, and opens a channel on the Telegram social media app. He shows me a video of muscular young men fighting. Their faces are blurred. It looks like an active club of far-right campaigners learning combat skills. He says this is a Swiss organisation called Junge Tat.

He describes his desire to select an inner circle from the Neo Byzantium club and send them for 'elite preparation training' with this group, which he is friendly with. Erik wants to rent a house in Slovenia, or Croatia, or Serbia, and run a fight camp.

'These are the groups I associate with,' he says. 'When you have young guys, to put them through something like this, it is very formative. This is how you build a certain wing of an organisation.' He chuckles at this. Is this what he means by 'cells'?

'Imagine. Fifty guys, in Serbia. Boxing. Shooting.'

He lets the last word hang in the air, and we all laugh.

'The opportunities are endless,' he says. 'I am so dedicated I would die for this. I will die for this, or I will live to be successful. It's one of the two for me.'

I let Erik continue. He is leaning forward, fired up, chopping with his hands for emphasis. He wants to create an elite, he says. 'That's what the SS was. Do you know the history of the SS?'

Yeah, I reply.

'The SA was thugs,' Erik says. 'Guys who were veterans or unemployed. The SS was elites. They didn't have IQ tests but physiognomy requirements, and certain outward characteristics. The principle is the same. You know who won? The SS won over the SA, because they're elites, so they win. Elites can't be doughy boys, soft boys.'

Erik mentions one of the Neo Byzantium candidates who he thinks could benefit from this course, a 'week-long struggle session'. 'Maybe he could be set straight,' he wonders. 'I could really brainwash this guy.'

All this time, Erik and Matt have been drip-feeding me details about what they want to achieve within HDF. Now it feels like their masks have slipped. Brainwashing, remaking the SS, manipulating their employees into breaking up their families. What chills me is that they are building this with or without my fictional investment.

A waiter brings the bill. I pay. Both of them thank me for coming to Athens. The difficult atmosphere has eased, and we seem to leave on good terms. I say they will hear from me in a couple of weeks, once I'm finished with a work trip. We shake hands warmly, and I turn and walk away.

Patrik meets me back in the hotel. It's past midnight, but I'm still cranked up. Pulling off my hidden camera, I plug in the memory card. I skip ahead to the part where Matt names Andrew Conru, and am exhilarated to see the shaky camera, for once, reach its target. This crucial moment is plainly audible, clearly visible. Patrik congratulates me on getting Conru's name. He leaves for his own hotel, exhausted from waiting outside the restaurant in the cold, trying to take photographs from a distance.

I am so alert that I am unable to sleep. The next morning, worried about bumping into Matt and Erik, I catch the first available flight out of Athens. On the journey home, I read about Andrew Conru.

He is not hungry for publicity. A tech entrepreneur who made his fortune during the early days of Silicon Valley, he created Adult Friend Finder, a hook-up service that became one of the most popular websites in America. In 2007, he sold it for $500 million, although he has since regained control of it. Conru maintains a sparse presence on X/Twitter, mainly posting about the benefits of artificial intelligence. He also has a personal website where he shares his oil paintings of fruit and flowers, and, more recently, AI-generated drawings of naked women with huge breasts.

Matt had said over dinner that Conru suffered negative publicity in the summer. A journalist had spotted that the Conru Foundation – the charitable organisation he runs – gave $200,000 to the Center for the Study of Partisanship & Ideology. It was founded by an American academic named Richard Hanania, formerly a research fellow at the University of Texas at Austin. After news of the donation circulated in the American press, Hanania was exposed for blogs he had written on far-right websites about miscegenation and the forced sterilisation of low-IQ people. 'Race mixing is like destroying a unique species or piece of art,' Hanania said. 'It's shameful.' When he was later confronted with these posts by reporters, he said he now found the posts 'repulsive'.

Matt had told me Conru was 'burned once', and is now worried about being linked to far-right projects. Given how many extremist ventures Conru has supported, it is surprising he has not been burned more often. His charitable donations through the Conru Foundation are public, and reveal a surprising history that has mostly escaped journalistic scrutiny. In 2021 – the year he gave the six-figure donation to Richard Hanania – Conru also gave $25,000 to the Center for Immigration Studies, founded by the white nationalist John Tanton, another recipient of Pioneer Fund money.

Between 2019 and 2021, he gave $150,000 to Turning Point USA, run by Charlie Kirk, who said the LGBT pride flag is 'an insult to all of us', and sent $5,000 to the Unz Review, a viciously racist website run by the Holocaust denier Ron Unz.

Strangely, however, Conru has also sent money to charities that are decidedly at odds with these far-right organisations. He has donated:

- $5,400 to Books For Africa
- $10,000 to Girls Who Code
- $25,000 to Doctors Without Borders
- $25,000 to the Trevor Project, which works in suicide prevention for LGBT youth

Why would Conru donate to a charity defending LGBT youth while also funding a charity that is waging a campaign against them?

Before we publish our reports at HOPE not hate about HDF in October 2024, Patrik and I approach Conru for comment. His representative says he cut ties with HDF and ordered a review of his philanthropic activities. 'Mr Conru helped to fund the HDF project at the beginning,' says a statement. 'It unfortunately now appears that it has deviated from its initial objective, and the motivation for his funding, which was to promote free and non-partisan academic research.' We ask Conru whether he also privately funded Jared Taylor. The statement sent on his behalf did not deny it.

HDF marks a frightening new moment in race science. Because of its company structure, it is able to fund its activists in secret. As a charity, Pioneer is at least subject to some degree of public scrutiny. As a company, HDF can allocate grants unchecked. There are ten HDF-backed researchers who we can identify. However, this is not a complete picture of the company's operations. There are likely other researchers, as yet unknown, who benefit from it.

HDF has picked up where Pioneer left off, and seemingly enjoys more success. During our WhatsApp conversations, Matt sends me a screenshot of Neil O'Brien, a Conservative MP, sharing an Aporia article about Western birth rates. He is overjoyed, and sends an image of a hand manipulating a marionette.

Marc Andreessen, the billionaire co-founder of the Silicon Valley venture capital company Andreessen

Horowitz, is a fan of Ed Dutton. A top-tier subscriber to the Jolly Heretic, Andreessen pays the maximum fee of £500 per year.

In 2019, Emil Kirkegaard was flown out to meet Peter Thiel to talk about his work. He calls it 'the Thiel treatment'.

The number of followers giving money to HDF is sizeable. Aporia currently has 12,000 subscribers, earning approximately $50,000 in annual revenue. Ed Dutton's channel pulls in around $110,000 a year.

HDF has access to the pockets of tycoons and the ears of policymakers. Compared to the speech I saw in Tallinn by the elderly Helmuth Nyborg, HDF represents a new generation of race scientists, one that is considerably more dynamic and image-conscious. The greatest worry about race science is not that a group of obscure bloggers is posting racist bilge into the internet, but that it is cutting through with people in positions of power. By going underground, they have perversely become more powerful. They used to lobby in plain sight. What they are building in the shadows now seems much more sinister.

My last contact with anyone on the HDF team was in January 2024, when I told Matt and Erik I would not be investing in their organisation. I then ghosted them, ignoring their texts. In October of that year, when HOPE not hate and the *Guardian* were preparing reports about the race science movement, Patrik contacted Emil, Matt, and Erik with the opportunity to comment.

Emil did not reply.

Matt said: 'I intended to establish the "Apple" of British gentlemen's clubs, entirely independent from HDF, which was focused solely on academic research. During this process, a fraudulent investor increased his potential commitment every time he heard something that aligned with his own agenda. His dishonesty, combined with the false information he provided, led me to suspect he was a fantasist. I tested these suspicions and confirmed them when he tacitly endorsed outlandish views, which I reject.'

Erik was less concerned about specific details: 'Mr Shukman and Hope not Hate are complete losers with nothing interesting to say.'

In a comment sent to HOPE not hate in October, Matt says he left Aporia and no longer has any affiliation with HDF. In a leaving article on Aporia he does, however, state that he will 'still write the occasional piece and host meetups'. Matt remains the administrator of Aporia's official Telegram chat as of October 2024.

7

During a coffee break at the Tallinn conference, I spotted Matthew Frost talking to Ryan Williams, the neo-Nazi influencer. They were both speaking too quietly for me to overhear their conversation, but I did catch three words: 'pronatal', 'eugenics' and 'Collins'. This meant nothing to me until a week later, when Ed Dutton posts a new video interview on his website. It is a ninety-minute conversation with an American woman named Simone Collins. 'Elite Super-Breeder Simone Collins Aims to Rebuild Civilization By Having Lots of Genius Babies' is the title.

Simone wants to talk to Ed about a very scary topic. She says there will be a 'demographic collapse' because women are having fewer babies. According to her, society as we know it will only endure in small pockets: 'I do kind of see there being protected zones – Noah's Ark style – that carry through the type of civilisation that we think is most viable, that we think is most optimal. It's probably going to happen in pockets that protect themselves.'

Optimal types of civilisation? In pockets that protect themselves? It sounds like an apocalyptic scenario from a movie like *Mad Max*.

Simone Collins and her husband Malcolm call themselves pronatalists. They want women to have more children and reverse downward trends in fertility. Despite sharing a platform with someone as extreme as Ed Dutton, the Collinses say they have nothing to do with the far right and publicly disavow racism. They do, however, have an idea in common with the far right: society is tumbling towards catastrophe and the way to fix it is by returning to a simpler, purer past when birth rates were higher. 'There are going to be countries of old people starving to death,' Malcolm tells the *Guardian* in May 2024.

The trouble with pronatalism is that its main champions, historically speaking, have been far-right activists. Oswald Mosley's newspapers ran articles about white women having fewer babies as far back as the 1930s. 'This will begin the decline of the race, which, if carried to such lengths, will result in our ultimate extinction,' wrote a female writer for *Action*, one of his newspapers.

A handful of terrorists have taken this message to heart. Brenton Tarrant, the gunman who shot fifty-one people in a mosque in Christchurch in 2019, began his manifesto with the words: 'It's the birthrates. It's the birthrates. It's the birthrates.' Payton Gendron, the Buffalo attacker mentioned in the previous chapter, likewise said: 'If there's one thing I want you to get from these writings, it's that White birth rates must change.' Dennis Mahon, who in 2004 blew up a government building in Scottsdale, Arizona, wrote that the survival of the Aryan race depends on having 'as many babies as we can'. 'Our racial battle is in reality a battle of the groin.'

While extremists have long been worried about the quantity of white births, they also express fears about their quality. 'BREED OR DIE!' was a headline printed by *Spearhead*, a far-right magazine in 1983. The article said:

People of genetic merit have to be encouraged to produce more off-spring and those with genetic defects must be prevented from passing them on to future generations, if need be by compulsory sterilisation.

Mainstream conservatives have begun to discuss their anxieties about birth rates. 'We wanna produce babies in this country,' announced Donald Trump in August 2024. He has elsewhere complained that illegal immigration, especially from Asia and Africa, is 'poisoning the blood of our country', leading critics to wonder if the desire to produce American babies is meant to counteract the rate of immigrant births. Meanwhile, J. D. Vance, Trump's choice of vice president, opposes 'anti-family and anti-child' policies, claiming that women who prioritise their careers over motherhood 'choose a path to misery'.

Elon Musk, the world's richest man, is also interested in fertility. He has repeatedly posted on X in support of large families, and has had at least twelve children by three women. 'If the alarming collapse in birth rate continues, civilization will indeed die with a whimper in adult diapers,' he wrote online. However, he isn't just concerned about an ageing society. 'If each successive generation of smart people has fewer kids, that's probably bad,' he has said. It has an unfortunate echo of the *Spearhead* article calling for babies from 'people of genetic merit'.

Right-wing politicians on the Continent have framed their falling birth rates as a 'struggle for the future of Europe', as the Hungarian prime minister Viktor Orbán put it. Curbing migration and boosting what he calls 'natural reproduction' are thus seen as part of the same objective.

The German party Alternative für Deutschland, which won the state election in Thuringia for the first time in September 2024, has called in its manifesto for an end to 'undesirable demographic development' in Germany, adding as a slogan: 'Larger Families instead of Mass Immigration'.

The British press began writing about immigration and birth rates in the early 2000s, perturbed by the rise of the former and decline of the latter. In the 1960s, mothers in the UK had an average of three babies, and by the new millennium, they had 1.6 (today it is 1.4). Newspapers chastised women for delaying motherhood. 'All around is the siren voice of the feminist argument,' a *Daily Mail* article said in 2002. 'Self-fulfilment lies less in being a wife and mother than in independence and a job which delivers a fat pay packet.' In a discomfiting reminder of *Spearhead*'s editorial line, a 2001 piece in *The Times* written by Michael Gove, the future Conservative Cabinet minister, was headlined 'Breed or die out'. He wrote: 'The main factor driving this population spiral downward is the failure of the British to breed.' Gove's article questioned whether the combination of immigration and low birth rates would mean the loss of Britain's 'original identity'.

Fertility has become a minor issue in the Conservative Party. 'A low birth rate is not just a problem in itself, it's also a symptom of serious societal malaise,' said the former Conservative MP Miriam Cates. Her fellow Tory MP Neil O'Brien, who shared an Aporia article on social media headlined 'The West's Fertility Crisis', has said 'there are large numbers of people who would like children (or more children) but feel they are held back', mainly by economic factors. Further to the right, Nigel Farage, leader of the

Reform Party, has similarly said: 'We should be encouraging people to have children, we should even perhaps through the tax system be encouraging marriage, as well.'

Clearly not everyone who talks about birth rates is a *Spearhead*-subscribing far-right extremist. There are indeed financial obstacles to starting a family, like the exorbitant cost of nursery (for a child under two, it costs an average of £8,194 per year for twenty-five hours a week of care). Parents are also disincentivised from having large families. For example, the government provides a benefit for the first and second child, but not the third. There are also discussions to be had on what happens when an elderly society has fewer young workers whose taxes pay for schools, hospitals and pensions.†

People who want to encourage reproduction call themselves pronatalists. Many of them deny they are racist or eugenicists, and say pronatalism is perfectly compatible with feminism. However, some pronatalists have rather distressing ideas. An article in Aporia, for instance, argues that the solution to solving 'demographic collapse' is by restricting women's access to education and work, which would apparently encourage them to stay home and have more children. Among Aporia's policy recommendations are a ban on scholarships for women, the stigmatisation of extramarital sex, and an end to no-fault divorce, to keep

---

† The degrowth movement says, on the other hand, that population decline might not be so bad, that an economy dependent on growth has exploited vulnerable workers and wrecked the environment. Others say immigration from higher fertility countries can supplement the number of young people needed to fill important jobs.

wives in marriages and pumping out children. 'Roll back the Sexual Revolution,' concludes the article.

The most famous pronatalists today are Malcolm and Simone Collins, who feature regularly in the international media. Piers Morgan has interviewed them, as has the *Guardian*, the *Telegraph*, Bloomberg, Business Insider (twice), the *Wall Street Journal*, NBC, *VICE,* and a slew of other big-name outlets in Britain, the US, Canada and France. Malcolm and Simone are highly educated: she has a master's degree from Cambridge, he has one from Stanford. They have worked in venture capital funds, private equity firms and neuroscience start-ups. According to public records, they have received half a million dollars in funding from Jaan Tallinn, the billionaire co-founder of Skype, to lobby for pronatalism. In addition to their media hits, they organise private networking dinners, inviting entrepreneurs and inventors. In November 2024, Simone ran in a state election in Pennsylvania for the Republican Party and lost to the Democrat.

The Collinses have an eccentric appearance, wearing the large glasses and black turtlenecks of Silicon Valley inventors. Both speak quickly in memorable sound bites. Simone, who has had four children, jokes that she will keep having babies until her uterus is 'forcibly removed'. They clearly put a lot of thought into how they will be perceived. When they appear on Piers Morgan's TV programme, Malcolm moves his lips silently while Simone speaks, perhaps checking that his wife is sticking to their script.

Together, they make the case in their frequent press appearances that we should all start addressing the topic of birth rates. Malcolm says when he worked for a South

Korean venture capital fund, he was asked to plan for the long-term future, and saw a population collapse just over the horizon. The birth rate in South Korea is currently around 0.7. 'This means that, for every 100 Koreans living, there will be only 4.3 grandchildren,' he wrote in the *New York Post*. 'Neither an economy nor a culture can survive with that kind of population decline.'

Critics of pronatalism say the movement doesn't actually care about encouraging reproduction worldwide, just among specific ethnic or national groups. The Collinses disagree, and say on the website of their non-profit organisation, Pronatalist.org, that they are worried about declining birth rates across the whole world, not just majority-white nations. 'We work to protect and expand human diversity,' their website says.

What makes Malcolm and Simone especially controversial is their interest in reproductive technology to screen embryos for desirable traits. As they were unable to conceive naturally, their children were born through IVF. They used a private screening service that analysed the DNA of their embryos to determine what kind of traits they were likely to have. In 2022, when they first spoke about this in interviews, they said they chose embryos based on health factors – Simone's mother died young of cancer, and they wanted to give their children the best chance in life. Over the course of 2023, however, they began talking about how they also selected embryos based on their predicted IQ, although they are curiously guarded over what company offers this science-fiction-type service.

This is where critics of pronatalism identify something wrong about the Collinses' movement. Implanting embryos with the highest IQ sounds like a form of eugenics – selective breeding for desirable traits. So is pronatalism just about quantity or is it actually about quality?

In one media interview, Simone dismisses the idea that she and her husband are prejudiced. 'People assume that we're Nazi, racist, eugenicist monsters,' she says with a laugh. They both mock far-right opinions in their videos. 'The Pronatalist Immigration Position (and Why White Nationalism is Stupid)' is the title of one clip. Another is called 'Scientific Racism is for Midwits as is Ethno-Nationalism', a midwit being someone who believes they are smarter than they really are. In the video, Malcolm calls racism 'dumb', 'stupid' and 'insane'.

Despite these public anti-racist statements, the Collinses have on occasion promoted racist narratives. In an interview with a conservative news site, Malcolm says the Great Replacement conspiracy theory is useful for attracting support. 'If you have daily reminders that people who look, act, and think like you might be "replaced", that is a strong motivation to have kids.'

On another occasion, the Collinses invite Ed Dutton onto their internet show, where he receives an effusive welcome. Malcolm tells his audience to read *The Naked Classroom*, Ed's latest book. It is 150 pages long and claims black people and South Asians are less intelligent than white people.

Here is an extract:

You will likely have noticed that many of the Black children, whose parents or grandparents are from Jamaica, don't do very well academically and don't behave very well either. In fact, they may actively disrupt the class.

If Malcolm really rejects race science, why would he endorse a book on it? 'I really would encourage people to check out this book if you like some of the topics we were talking about and dissident science, the last real science that's left,' he says. (Malcolm later explains that he hadn't read it and regrets promoting it.)

The Collinses' connection to the far right is not merely ideological. In 2023, they go to the Natalism conference, a gathering of pronatalists and far-right activists in Austin, Texas. The event is organised by the Mormon campaigner Kevin Dolan. Jared Taylor, the white nationalist, is also a guest at the conference. Speakers include conspiracy theorists who have called for the deportation of legal migrants.

In September 2023, the first time I speak to Matt Frost, aka Archer, I learn there are connections between him and the Collinses. He says he knows Malcolm and Simone, telling me: 'We help each other out.' He adds they are 'very calculated' in their media appearances. It seems that way to me: there are things they say to their podcast audience, but won't tell to mainstream news outlets. What else might they say in private?

Patrik and I want to know about what other connections the Collinses might have to the race-science movement. What are they trying to achieve in their frequent press appearances? One *Guardian* article accuses them of practising 'hipster eugenics'. Hipsterness aside, is the charge of eugenics justified? I'm also curious about where they sprang from. It seems like they suddenly appeared fully formed in 2022 to promote pronatalism. How did they come to this very specific niche?

On their website, the Collinses invite anyone with an interest in pronatalism to get in touch, so in September I send them an email, introducing myself as Chris, a rich Brit curious about their work.

I was wondering if you would be open to a discussion on funding, I say.

Within ten minutes, Simone replies, enthusiastically arranging a Zoom call a week later.

Malcolm and Simone dial in from their home in Valley Forge, Pennsylvania, appearing on their own devices from separate rooms. All smiles, full of energy, they say they have just returned from a trip to Silicon Valley.

Right at the start of the call, I mention that I have been speaking to Matt Archer of Aporia. I want to gauge their response, as well as break the ice by identifying myself as a friend of his.

'Oh yeah!' exclaims Simone.

'Oh, we know Matt. We like Matt,' adds Malcolm. He says Matt came to stay with them in the summer – they both love Aporia. They considered 'officially' tying themselves to Aporia, but decided against it due to its open support of race science.

Simone asks me to introduce myself and to say why I'm interested in pronatalism. I give them my prepared lines about growing up in a Conservative household, feeling unfamiliar and unsafe in London, while also worried about birth rates and demographic change. I say my wife and I will soon start a family, and I'm interested in pronatalism.

Now I'd like to fund projects in this space. As they are both so loquacious – Malcolm especially – I don't have to talk much before they want to interrupt.

Malcolm is fired up on our call, just as he is during his public appearances. He speaks quickly at a high pitch, rocking back and forth. His monologues frequently last longer than two minutes. I time one that goes on for eight. Simone listens attentively while he talks, but when she opens her mouth, Malcolm's attention seems to wander. As she answers one of my questions, he gets up, walks into the kitchen and peers into the fridge.

I need to build a rapport with the Collinses, so during a rare pause in one of Malcolm's speeches, I praise them both for securing so much press coverage. Malcolm smiles, thanks me, then mentions an upcoming profile in a major American newspaper.

Then he tells me something I never would have expected within just forty minutes of meeting me.

'When we talk to reporters we're very, "Oh this isn't just for the elites," but, in truth, we do target the elites unfortunately,' he says, laughing.

Perhaps it was the mention that I'm in cahoots with Matt Archer, perhaps it was the prospect of money – although we haven't yet spoken about what I might fund. I can't believe that Malcolm is being this open with me. Their website, the carefully worded statements about declining fertility around the world – this is all apparently a cover for their secret goal: maintaining the birth rates of the elite. It is a remarkable thing to admit.

'A lot of this is about ensuring our kids grow up around families who we feel model a lifestyle that is one we would want to model,' Malcolm explains. What the Collinses are building is a network of ideologically aligned friends who they can make their own community with. 'We want our kids to know other kids [their] age. As we're worried about the same things you're worried about, I hate to say it, but the only path forward is likely to be speciation, even though we're never going to get everyone on board. That means I need to know lots of people who my kids can marry.'

This knocks me back for a second. Speciation is when a new species with different characteristics splits from an existing species, like horses and donkeys evolving from a single common ancestor.

A species is defined as a group that is 'reproductively isolated' from other populations. This means that one species can't breed with another to produce fertile offspring (donkeys and horses can make mules, but mules are usually infertile and can't produce foals of their own). When Malcolm says speciation is the only path forward, it seems like he is not just talking about creating a community of elites who are culturally different but one that is biologically distinct from other humans.

'What I'm really trying to do is make sure my kids have an isolated and differential breeding network. And that's what we're really trying to build to an extent, and that has the highest source of value going into the future.'

Malcolm's phrase 'isolated and differential breeding network' rings in my head for days. I catch myself saying it in the shower, walking the dog, buying toilet paper in the supermarket. I picture the Habsburg family of medieval Europe, fond of intermarriage, and their protuberant jaws.

What genetic abnormalities might find their way into the Collinses' isolated and differential breeding network?

Malcolm and Simone say that if they can produce eight children, and if each descendant has a further eight children, within eleven generations they will number 8.5 billion people, and their descendants will outnumber the current global population.

This is going to be difficult. Within a generation, Elon Musk's experiment with pronatalism has already resulted in the ostracisation of one of his children. He accused his daughter Vivian, who is trans, of being 'dead, killed by the woke mind virus'. Vivian responded that her father is 'uncaring' and 'cruel'.

The Collinses believe they can create an original inter-generationally durable culture that prizes high fertility. Their culture teaches children to look towards the future, they say. Malcolm and Simone tell reporters that they do not celebrate Christmas with their kids but Future Day, in which their children receive presents from the Future Police, based on contracts they draw up pledging to complete certain objectives over the course of the year. Malcolm also wants to offer arranged marriages so young people can remain in his isolated and differential breeding network.

On their website and in their self-help books, Malcolm and Simone call their new culture 'techno puritanism' or 'secular Calvinism'. In practice, it means viewing central heating and fun as unnecessary indulgences, while advocating for smacking children as a form of discipline. The most important aspect of techno puritanism seems to be a belief in predestination. Religious Calvinists believe that certain individuals are part of the 'elect'. Unlike, say, in Protestantism, where anyone who repents can receive salvation, theological Calvinists think the everlasting joys of heaven are reserved just for the predetermined few.

What does predetermination mean in the Collinses' secular version of Calvinism? In one of their books, they write that 'some people's lives do not matter in the grand scheme of the universe . . . Whether you matter and manage to become a virtuous, productive person is predetermined.'

Race scientists say something discomfitingly similar, that success in life is almost entirely a matter of genetics. Some people are predestined to a life of genius and prosperity, while others are condemned to a life of vice and indolence.

Predestination, elites, quality, isolated and differential breeding networks – the ideas that make up the Collinses' culture are rather unnerving. What makes them especially interesting is that they seem to be a reaction to both Simone's and Malcolm's upbringing, which they describe in their five self-help books, called *The Pragmatist's Guide* series, and countless podcasts.

Simone is less interested in publicly discussing her childhood, so hers can be explained more briefly. She was born in Japan to American hippies who had moved there to study aikido, the martial art. They returned to the San Francisco Bay Area to raise her and moved in woo-woo circles. Simone says on one podcast that the weddings of family friends typically involved 'a naked sweat lodge and putting on masks in the forest'. She rebelled by doing homework, and went to George Washington University for her undergraduate degree, then Cambridge for a master's.

Aged twenty-four, she came to a strange decision. Having not dated before, she resolved to live alone, but first wanted to know what it felt like to be dumped by a boyfriend. She thought it would help her fit better into society. 'I need to fall in love and have my heart broken – I need to experience that, otherwise people will say I'm pathetic and sad,' she says in one video, recalling her mindset at the time. She met Malcolm as he was headed to Stanford, and instead decided to build a life with him.

Malcolm, on the other hand, has a lot more to say in their books and podcasts about his upbringing. He comes from a powerful Texan dynasty. His great-grandfather, Carr P. Collins, born in 1892, sold a laxative powder that claimed to have healing powers. It was called Crazy Crystals. 'Every home needs Crazy Crystals because they help remove waste and impurities from the system,' the 1930s radio ad used to say, accompanied by a five-piece hillbilly band that hooted and hollered and shouted 'yahoo!' Carr inspired the huckster politicians of the Coen brothers' movie, *O Brother, Where Art Thou?*.

James Collins, Malcolm's grandfather, was a Republican congressman elected in 1968. He opposed efforts to desegregate white schools, and was accused (but never charged) of masterminding a kickback scam, taking a chunk of his staff's salary. Malcolm's father, Michael, was an insurance executive. Intriguingly, his godfather ran the Bohemian Grove, a secret male-only club of business tycoons and politicians who meet every year in the forests of northern California to schmooze and get drunk. Bohemian Grove is the source of many conspiracy theories about shadowy elites engaging in arcane rituals and ruling the world. Malcolm, when we meet, says he is not a member but has attended as a guest (Simone is also familiar with elite secret societies and used to run Dialog, a networking group set up by the billionaire Peter Thiel).

Although Malcolm was born into Dallas high society – living in the fancy Highland Park neighbourhood, enjoying holidays on a private island in the Bahamas – his childhood sounds tough. 'If you don't learn to fix your lisp,' his mother warned him, 'you will sound effeminate and even fat chicks won't fuck you.'† Malcolm recalls this experience in one of his self-help books to describe how parents can motivate their kids.

Aged eleven, Malcolm's childhood took an appalling turn when he was sent to a prison school in the desert. He writes that it was like a more brutal version of *Holes*, the Louis Sachar novel in which boys locked up in a Texan work camp are forced to dig.

US prison schools, sometimes called 'troubled teen' camps, can be hellish, sadistic places where parents, and sometimes courts, dispatch children to be disciplined. Children have been known to take their own lives in prison schools; they have also died from physical abuse and medical neglect.

Malcolm doesn't explain exactly why he was sent to prison school. In a podcast, he vaguely says that he was 'expelled' from his family, elsewhere clarifying that it was not for any 'remarkable offence'. He speculates in one of his books that his parents thought their lives would be easier

---

† When Malcolm's mother, Wynnell, passed away in July 2023, he wrote on Facebook that he missed her: 'She lives on through us – through the wisdom she gave us and the thousands of hours of shared life-well-lived.'

with him 'out of the picture for a while'. An alternative explanation, which speaks to the upsetting dysfunction of his family, is that he was merely a pawn in their break-up. 'It could be that my parents thought they could get better terms in a highly contentious and litigious divorce if they could convince a judge that I had behavioural problems caused by the other parent,' he writes.

Whatever the reason, Malcolm was packed off, still a child. The food was so bad, he lost more than half of his body weight and had to subsist on insects. His mail was censored, so he couldn't alert his parents. He recounts a story in his book about another child who threatened to kill him one night. Malcolm stuffed clothes into the plastic sheets they were made to sleep in, creating the outline of a sleeping child. Then he hid and watched his aggressor repeatedly strike that spot with a shovel.

Unsurprisingly, he was deeply affected by his experience in the camp. 'I spent all my formative years navigating corrupt governance structures as my only source of basic necessities like housing, food, etc,' he writes. The details are hazy, but he says he managed to transfer to another school, one that allowed students to read books. By accessing a family trust fund, Malcolm was able to move again to a boarding school. Even there, he struggled. Most of his friends were people he spoke to on the internet. He never returned to live with his family because they told him he would not be welcome.

Malcolm says he does not wish to present this as a 'sob story', more of a lesson. 'Instead of fighting the system, I have been able to improve my lot by increasing my value to that system.' He appears to have taken this transactional mentality into adult life. One of his books advises readers to rank their friends by utility, and cut out the ones at the bottom of the list if they are 'not optimal for your objective function'. Society, he writes, has 'delusions about the magic of friendship'. Now he wants to send children in his isolated and differential breeding network to a wilderness camp of his own design and teach them how to cope with hardship.

Simone says that when they met, before Malcolm was due to begin studying at Stanford, she 'wasn't good enough for him'. She won him round by pledging to follow his advice: she got a new wardrobe, changed her diet, ditched her old friends, and altered her accent from a Kardashian vocal fry to a deeper, more measured tone. She even started to wear prescriptionless glasses to 'increase perception of competence and intelligence', as she puts it on a podcast.

Dismissing the suggestion that Malcolm's advice was 'hostile and possibly even abusive', she tells her readers that because of him, her social anxiety abated and she was able to become the CEO of a multimillion-dollar business, lecturing at Ivy League universities.

'As with all marketplaces, every item in stock has a value, and that value is determined by its desirability,' they write in their book on relationships. Reading this, I am reminded of the Basketweavers, especially the lonely members looking for love and friendship. It may have helped Malcolm navigate the violent, dangerous world of prison school, but it is bleak to think that human beings can and should be ranked by value or utility. Is it that different to the world race scientists want?

Malcolm and Simone recommend developing a public

persona, separate to one's own identity, to succeed. 'This character should be intentionally created to maximise your ability to achieve your objective function,' they write. Being yourself will make you 'bland and forgettable'. They suggest identifying an idol, watching their speeches, learning their mannerisms and the sound of their voice. 'Will some people tease you? Maybe.' But only by altering your image is success in life possible.

When Malcolm and Simone speak to me over Zoom, they explain how they lobby for pronatalism, and I get an extraordinary glimpse of their 'mechanistic, clockwork understanding of reality'.

'It's easy to forget how small the population of people in the world who actually impacts anything or matters is,' says Malcolm, riffing on the idea that only a fraction of the world's eight billion humans are interesting. 'When we do our campaigns, we work really aggressively on how we spread ideas within that narrow network, because they are also the people we want having kids.'

Key to reaching these elites, he says, is arranging for media coverage with a specific slant. It can't be positive, or else they will look like 'shills'. It can't be neutral, because then the article about them will be too dull to share on social media. The Goldilocks result is when an article about them is a little bit negative. 'We really intentionally court negative media,' Malcolm explains. 'They' – the elite readers he wants – 'will engage if someone is being unjustly attacked.'

I notice that Malcolm seems to push his luck in one interview. The *National Post*, a big Canadian newspaper, asks Malcolm about the pronatalist agenda, and if it really applies to all populations or just the ones he cares about.

His response is to indignantly reject the accusation and mock the reporter. 'Imagine if there really were some secret cabals of rich dudes trying to just make more of themselves,' he says. 'Wouldn't that be outrageous and wild?'

On other occasions, I wonder if Malcolm and Simone rely on the incuriosity of the reporters interviewing them, hoping that they won't have the time or energy to check their claims. A *Guardian* journalist in May 2024 asks about the Collinses' connection to racists. Malcolm replies: 'People are like, "Why do you allow the racists to come to your events?" and I'm like, "Because we convert them." It's actually really easy when you show them the data.' Which racists they have converted, and what data they showed them, are strangely not mentioned in the *Guardian*'s report. Malcolm says the same thing to a *Wall Street Journal* reporter when he is interviewed in September 2024, and is unchallenged.

The most controversial issue that the Collinses discuss in their media interviews is their use of a service to screen their embryos' genes to identify which ones will likely have the highest IQ. Their interviewers have asked them if this is not tantamount to eugenics, which Malcolm and Simone rigorously deny. 'We're absolutely, definitionally not eugenicists,' Simone tells NBC News.

They might not be happy being called eugenicists by the mainstream media, but it is less important behind closed doors. Malcolm and Simone introduce me to Lillian Tara, the CEO of their organisation, Pronatalist.org.† When I speak on an internet call to Lillian, a Harvard graduate

---

† She is now no longer involved in Pronatalist.org.

student, she uses the term 'eugenics' three times to describe her work. 'I don't care if you call me a eugenicist,' she says with a laugh.

Malcolm and Simone do not publicly use the term eugenics, but they do use a similar one: dysgenics. If eugenics is about improving humans by breeding desirable traits, dysgenics is the concern that humans are deteriorating because of undesirable traits. The term was proposed by William Shockley, the Pioneer-funded academic who, as mentioned in the last chapter, sought to sterilise low-IQ black people. Advocates of dysgenics, such as Richard Lynn, believe that because of advances in medicine and public health, it is no longer just the fittest in society who are surviving, but unintelligent genetic defectives. 'Dysgenics appears to be the primary cause that IQ was going down,' Malcolm says in a podcast on intelligence.

When we meet, he reiterates this belief. 'With IQ declining as much as it is,' he says, 'I'm never going to convince the general population to fix that problem, and I don't think that there's an ethical way that you can.' In his podcasts, he often talks about his fears that IQ is plummeting and will create a society of idiots. 'These people – the dumb ones – are going to be more and more of the general population as time goes on. And so they will be electing and building bureaucracies that make it harder and harder for the geniuses to do their jobs.'

The anxiety that society faces not only a population crisis but an intelligence crisis sounds frightening indeed. It reminds me of those catastrophising articles in *Spearhead* and *Action*.

But is IQ really falling? Is dysgenics real? Malcolm insists in one podcast that the data proving the fall in IQ 'has been well documented in many sources'. To make his case, he cites a study that claims the average IQ of US university students 'has been dropping by 0.2 points per year since the mid twentieth century'.

The actual study says something different. The paper, published in *Frontiers in Psychology*, does find that IQ scores of US university students were higher in 1939 than in 2022. However, the authors say this was a 'necessary consequence of college and university education becoming a new norm rather than the privilege of a few'. There were far fewer students in 1939. Approximately 10 per cent of young Americans went to university, compared to 60 per cent today. This does not prove IQ is falling, just that more Americans are going to university, lowering the average. Furthermore, the study's authors called for IQ 'not be used to make high-stakes decisions about individuals'. The Collinses' fear that IQ is falling, that dysgenics is occurring, has been rejected by mainstream scientists. One critical review of Richard Lynn's book on the topic is clear: 'The deterioration of average intelligence predicted by the eugenicists has not occurred.'

Malcolm and Simone's desire to protect themselves from dysgenic forces has taken them to strange places. They tell me on our first video call about a plan to build a new city and put their ideas into practice.

'We've already done a lot of outreach to UK policy-makers, but they are all acting like stone walls,' Malcolm says. 'Except for the Isle of Man.'

The Isle of Man?

'They're rapidly depopulating, they really need to keep tech talent in the region – as soon as someone gets college-educated they leave,' he says. What he and Simone have in mind is to build their own autonomous city on the Isle of Man where they can enjoy a low-tax, low-regulation lifestyle among their own.

This outlandish idea is the dream of some Silicon Valley inventors, who are experimenting with 'charter cities' – libertarian communities where they can do as they please. One is called Praxis, which hopes to find land in the Mediterranean. Its founder is reportedly inspired by the works of Julius Evola – the super-fascist philosopher popular among the Basketweavers – and has raised $19 million in funding. Another is called Próspera, which actually has its own land on the Honduran island of Roatán. Funded in part by the billionaires Peter Thiel, the Facebook investor, and Marc Andreessen, the venture capitalist who supports Ed Dutton, Próspera is at present a smattering of buildings in a semi-autonomous economic zone, hoping to attract start-ups and remote workers.

Malcolm sends me a fifteen-page PDF outlining his idea to build a city on the Isle of Man. It is called 'The Next Empire: Leveraging a Changing World to Save Civilization'. He suggests it as a possible project I might wish to invest in. The document is full of drawings of computer networks and robots. The community would be ruled by a dictator, known as an executor, 'who has full control of the government's laws and operational structure during their tenure'. The proposal adds:

> Existing governing systems assume that every citizen has equal value when they objectively do not. Our system assumes an individual's value is correlated with

their utility to the state and optimizes around those individuals with the most utility to the state – all to ensure the competent operation of a state that attracts productive immigrants.

The city would be funded, the document says, by becoming a hub for 'no-holds-barred' medical research. 'This attracts both extant and cutting-edge businesses to develop therapies and innovations (including artificial wombs and human genetic modification) that are in high demand but nearly impossible to develop in a heavily regulated environment.'

Artificial wombs? Human genetic modification? Malcolm is convinced that he will be able to circumvent international laws against gene editing on the Isle of Man. 'It's not under EU regulations so if they set aside a charter city for us it would be really safe,' he says on our call. 'It's really hard for them to dislodge us once we're there because they don't have their own military.'

Later, Malcolm says the Isle of Man was receptive to their idea. 'If you can get some billionaires signed on board with us, we can probably pass this,' a government representative allegedly told him.†

In October, I meet Malcolm and Simone face to face, in what will turn out to be a very strange encounter. They fly to the UK to attend a conference, and agree to meet me beforehand at a Hawksmoor restaurant in Canary Wharf. I wait for an hour before they finally show up, having got the time wrong.

---

† The Manx government did not respond to a request for comment.

Deciding what to eat is a struggle that lasts for ten long minutes. They bicker over what to have.

'Would you share with me if I got a steak frites?' asks Malcolm, enunciating each word, like he is explaining the options to a child.

'I wouldn't eat any of the French fries,' replies Simone.

'Would you share with me if I got a burger?'

'A burger patty, probably, is not as shareable.'

Waitresses keep coming to take our order, only to leave because Simone and Malcolm need more time analysing the menu. They debate the merits of chateaubriand (fancy) versus beef Wellington (local). That's before we get onto the sides. They finally decide on steak and bone-marrow pie, a dish of maple bacon and a pint of lager for Malcolm.

'This was a very thoughtful ordering session,' Simone declares when the menus are collected. Malcolm and Simone reassume their public characters, taking turns to speak while the other stays quiet.

Malcolm explains their pronatalism advocacy depends on finding 'one young non-white person to be the public face of everything'. He is insistent on this. 'We need one non-white young girl. That's the goal. You have to, right?'

'We're not allowed to say many things that they're allowed to say,' says Simone.

I spot an opening, and ask what those unsayable things might be. Malcolm compares his own output to the work of Aporia.

'I do think they go into one area which we will never, ever touch which is racial differences-slash-racialism,' Malcolm says. He pauses, moving closer to me. 'Like, obviously there are. But you've got to not say it. The world isn't ready for that. I understand interest in discussing differences between racial groups in the context of, like, "education should be different", because we know that people have different abilities . . . It's a hill that doesn't make sense to die on.'

I think of their video entitled 'Scientific Racism is for Midwits', which argued against ranking groups by IQ. 'All of these differences are gonna be irrelevant in three generations if they exist at all,' Malcolm says in that video, because soon gene editing technology will be able to drastically increase IQ scores. But it sounds like he privately thinks that racial differences in intelligence do exist, and that education policy should take this into account.

I feel unable to push him on this point, fearful of saying something suspicious.

Malcolm orders another pint, and asks Simone for a 'Pez'. She passes him a white pill. He says it is naltrexone, an anti-addiction drug, that he describes on his livestreams as 'a cure for alcoholism'. Malcolm takes the pill and can avoid drinking too much.

'You can tell by his genetic heritage that his family is good at inhaling beers,' says Simone.

How many did you drink a day?

'Forty-five beers a day,' replies Malcolm.

Forty-five beers a day?

'Yes,' he says. 'I had forty-five beers a day every day for over a decade. While I was graduating Stanford at the top of my class, while I started my first company.'

Cans? I ask.

'It's a lot of calories,' says Simone, ignoring my question. 'He was mostly not eating food.'

'Other people in my family drink a lot and are incredibly high-functioning,' Malcolm explains. 'This,' he says, meaning the pill, 'enables moderation. We discovered it right around the pandemic. Simone made a rule that I wasn't allowed to drink before 8 a.m., and I found that really difficult.'

'He does start working at 2 a.m.,' Simone clarifies.

Forty-five beers a day would mean Malcolm drank a beer every twenty minutes (factoring in eight hours for sleep). This is a preposterous amount of cans. Let's assume one beer was the average American can of 350ml. Forty-five of these amounts to fifteen litres of beer a day. Is such a thing possible? Malcolm was fond of Coors Light. At 4.2% ABV, this equates to a weekly intake of 420 alcohol units. The NHS recommends drinking fewer than 14 units.

Although my interest in Malcolm's beer consumption threatens to derail the meeting, it actually seems like a significant moment. Malcolm and Simone like to present themselves as superhuman figures predestined for greatness, capable of extraordinary feats. 'I consider myself an ultra high-value male,' Malcolm says in one podcast appearance. 'I'm attractive, quote-unquote successful, respected publicly, broadly speaking.' His bragging reminds me of Ryan Williams. How true is it?

Intriguing as it is to me, I can imagine that Patrik would not be pleased if Malcolm's per diem beer count is all I gleaned from our lunch. To get back on track, I ask them to describe their use of embryo screening.

When couples normally pursue IVF to have a baby, a doctor will look at their genetic data to identify any embryos that have serious genetic disorders like cystic fibrosis or sickle cell disease, and implant the one that looks healthiest. What the Collinses say they have done for their most recent two children is pick the embryos that have the highest IQ.

You can do that? I ask. I have no idea, although I'm about to find out.

Simone smiles, and pulls out her phone. She opens a website – I can't yet see the name of it – and shows me a bell curve of IQ. On it, little squares and circles are plotted on the graph, ranking the male and female embryos.

What company is this?

'We have signed an NDA.' She grins and points at one outlier, with a much higher predicted IQ than any of the others. 'That's going to be the next male,' she says proudly. 'We call him the Champion. On every statistic he's like this. He's going to come out super deformed.'

She sticks out her tongue, bugs her eyes, and goes 'blaaaaargh', imitating how deformed the Champion might be. I take this to mean his incredible brain will outweigh any disabilities he may have.

'We will never choose a child that is less privileged in IQ than either of us,' says Malcolm.

Simone shows me a list of other traits that she could select and reject using this secret company. In case my hidden camera can't capture her phone screen, I read the list out loud so that my microphone records it:

Stress, mood, brain fog, fatigue, anxiety, ADHD, infertility, thyroid, joint pain, MS, acne, H. pylori, PTSD, PCOS, inflammation, eczema, gut pain, migraines.

Simone says her eggs and Malcolm's sperm were combined by an IVF company to create these embryos. The embryos were then scanned for their genetic data by the secret company, who then ranked them for the possibility of having different traits.

At the end of lunch, Simone offers to introduce me to the secret company. I accept her offer, pay the bill, and am glad to leave. She promises to set me up shortly via email.

The Collinses' performances are so polished, so thought-through, that I think the only time I encounter an unscripted moment is when we order dinner. This makes them slippery. I don't think I can really pin them down, but I think that's the idea. More than anyone else I've met so far, Malcolm and Simone inhabit the mainstream world while dipping their toes into far-right waters, and it is important that they can deny holding extreme views while associating with racists and sharing some of their talking points. Can the strategy work forever?

8

One of the first things I learn about screening embryos for IQ is that, apparently, Elon Musk is a fan. I hear this from a man named Jonathan Anomaly (born Beres, he changed his name as a young man). Anomaly is an American philosophy professor turned entrepreneur, and he had lunch with Musk several weeks before we meet on a video call in late October 2023. 'I could not believe that we met for three hours one-on-one, which is, like, way more generous than I could have imagined with his time,' says Anomaly. He's still buzzing from talking to the world's richest man. Anomaly, like Musk, is involved in the tech scene of Austin, Texas. He was once in the same group chat as Musk and his former partner Claire Boucher, the singer known as Grimes.

For the first two and a half hours of their lunch, Anomaly and Musk spoke about artificial intelligence, game theory and whether the British Army's square formation was ever broken by enemy forces. (Anomaly asserted it had been impenetrable, Musk apparently replied: 'That's not true at all.')

Their conversation turned to embryo screening towards the end of their encounter. Anomaly showed him the same website that Simone Collins showed me: embryos plotted on a graph, displaying which ones would make the smartest people. Musk was enthusiastic about it, according to Anomaly. 'I know he supports us and is interested,' he says. 'He thinks it's cool, but he's not like, "Hey, here's a bunch of money."'

He beams into his laptop camera as he recounts this story. Meeting Elon Musk is probably at the top of the wish list for any entrepreneur and he has done it.

Jonathan Anomaly used to teach at the top-tier universities of Duke and Penn. He is a friend of Matt Frost and has hosted Aporia podcasts and live events with him. Anomaly tells me when we speak online that he is a 'race realist', which refers to the belief that races are distinct biological categories and can be meaningfully ranked by traits like intelligence. In December 2023, he appears on a panel at the Natalism conference in Austin, alongside Simone and Malcolm Collins.

His full-time job is now at a company called PolygenX, where he was an early employee. He claims to offer a service straight out of a science-fiction movie. Couples pursuing IVF can go to his company and have the genetic code of their embryos analysed. Anomaly says he can tell them which embryo will likely grow up to have the highest IQ. Parents can then choose to have that one implanted.

Whether this practice works is a matter of fierce debate, aside from the conversation about its ethical implications. In the UK, it is against the law to check for traits like intelligence. PolygenX purports to be one of the very few companies offering this service from its base in the US to clients around the world. It raises the question: at what point does giving your child the best start in life become a form of eugenics?

Like the issue of pronatalism, not everyone involved in making designer babies is necessarily an extremist. However, the more Patrik and I look into PolygenX, the more connections we find to the world of scientific racism and the wider far right, and the more shocked we become.

After lunch at Hawksmoor in late October, Simone Collins introduces me to Anomaly over email and we have the video call where I hear about Elon Musk. In turn, Anomaly arranges an online meeting with his two colleagues. In November, I speak to the CEO and founder of PolygenX, Michael Christensen, a former day trader from Denmark. Tobias Wolfram, a German academic with a PhD in sociogenomics, is introduced to me as the chief science officer. Anomaly cuts in and out, his Wi-Fi struggling to maintain a connection.

My preliminary chat with Anomaly was all smiles and friendly chit-chat. A week ago, he keenly described PolygenX as a screening service for 'IQ and the other naughty traits that everybody wants'.

Today the mood has curdled. Christensen looks at me with narrowed eyes. He says he has been looking me up online without success. Shouldn't there be a company page somewhere, listing my name? It's even odder, to them, that my wife is absent from this call. I'm meant to be posing as an aspiring father. Where's the mother?

Patrik and I had spoken about how to approach this, and we ultimately decided that it would be too risky to bring in my wife to the call. I didn't want to put her in the position of having to lie for me, nor did I want her to see me as Chris, who I have come to think of as a weaselly sycophant with terrible views. Instead, I make up an excuse that she has a family situation to deal with. They don't seem to buy it.

'Most people have some LinkedIn or whatever,' says Christensen. 'Like, do you have anything else? Or anyone who can vouch for you?'

I value my privacy a lot, I say. I mention mutual connections, like the Collinses and Matthew Frost, hoping they will act as my credentials.

Anomaly is more laid-back, the good cop to Christensen's bad cop. 'Hate to give you the third degree,' he says chummily. 'I had a journo on my case a few weeks ago. Not that you fit the file.'

I try to look calm. It feels like my heart is about to detonate.

Christensen has an idea. 'Do you have any close buddies who could just say, "Hey, I've known Chris for five years"?'

Sure, I say. In the awkward silence that follows, I assume Christensen is about to end the call while he checks my credentials. But then he carries on.

'I think we should just start our presentation,' he says. He tells me we can sort this out afterwards. To my enormous surprise, he begins to explain the inner workings of his company. I check once again that my audio and video recording devices are switched on.

Christensen and his colleagues talk me through the mechanics of PolygenX's service. First, I must pursue a standard course of IVF with my wife in which our embryos are made and frozen. Then we should request the genetic data of those embryos. This can't be done in the UK, where clinics do not provide this information to parents. I am instead recommended to go to the US, where there are no laws prohibiting embryo screening. Then I can hand over that data to PolygenX, who say they will be able to identify and rank which embryo will likely have the highest IQ. 'Once you've seen our report,' says Christensen, 'you can go back to the doctor – "I want number three to be implanted" – and he doesn't need to know the reasons.'

Only a certain type of embryonic screening is legal in the UK. Here, genetic counsellors will test for life-limiting diseases caused by a single gene, like muscular dystrophy or Tay Sachs. These are known as monogenic traits, because just one gene can cause them.

Height, sex and intelligence are polygenic traits. They are influenced, as the UCL geneticist Adam Rutherford writes, by 'dozens of genetic variants of very small effect, in aggregate and in concert with the environment'. It is not legal in this country to screen for polygenic traits.

The list of traits that PolygenX says it can identify, as Simone Collins showed me over lunch, is surprisingly long: it includes anxiety, brain fog, migraines. But the big one is IQ. Tobias Wolfram says IQ was 'basically the starting point of the company'. He says PolygenX has got hold of giant data sets from the UK Biobank, a repository of genetic information, and found a way to parse it to create a list of the many hundreds of genes that, he claims, influence IQ. With that list in mind, Wolfram and his colleagues say that they are able to check it against my future embryos and see which ones have the most genes that they say correspond to intelligence.

Wolfram explains that the effects of this are potentially enormous. 'The overall difference, for ten embryos, for a

British couple, is roughly 12 points,' he tells me. The average IQ is 100, and two-thirds of everyone who takes a test gets between 85 and 115 points. Twelve extra points could nudge someone up from the average range towards the level of gifted.

Christensen, near the end of the call, says PolygenX is working towards an analysis of traits like depression, creativity and beauty. He also says that he is interested in 'the dark triad', three traits – psychopathy, narcissism, Machiavellianism – that are united by hostility and a lack of empathy.

I am quoted a figure of $50,000 to use PolygenX's service. At the time I speak to them, thirteen couples have used it since PolygenX was founded in late 2022. The company, I learn, appeals to the tech elite. They have around $1.8 million in funding from venture capital sources, and, as Jonathan Anomaly says on a podcast: 'There's big demand for it among the wealthy already and among the well connected in Silicon Valley.'

The big question is: does it work? PolygenX's team assures me that it does. In their video presentation, they show me a slide that says 'by adulthood, general intelligence is 60–80% heritable'. However, this figure is in the upper range of what most geneticists claim. Different studies present different percentages, with some estimates of heritability as low as 5 per cent.

Their presentation slide lists four academic papers, but only two of them actually support the claim that intelligence is up to 80 per cent heritable. Another paper doesn't specify a percentage at all. A fourth paper is written by Emily Willoughby, a behavioural geneticist at the University of Minnesota. I recognise her name. She is a board member at the International Society for Intelligence Research, an annual conference that has hosted scientific racists like Emil Kirkegaard. She has also received funding from the Institute of Mental Chronometry, which was backed by the Pioneer Fund. Even her paper only estimated IQ to be 42 per cent heritable.

Perhaps some of these inflated claims could be explained by this being a sales call trying to convince me about the virtues of a product. But there are other moments that, after the conversation, make me wonder. Anomaly describes traits like height and IQ as 'continuous and additive'. 'The genes aren't just doing random things,' he says. 'Instead, they're adding fractional amounts of height or IQ or something like that. They're not also, I don't know, giving you breast cancer on the side. Evolution doesn't work like that, right? If you had mutations doing really egregious things like that, they'd be selected out pretty quickly.'

But this doesn't sound right to me. Some genetic components that are associated with desirable traits like intelligence are also correlated with negative traits, most famously the eating disorder anorexia.

After the call ends, I have to move quickly. I pick up my phone and dial Patrik's number. Despite the candour of the PolygenX team, they still want to be assured that I am a genuine person. As we are discovering, the world of scientific racism, eugenics, pronatalism and polygenic screening are all networked. If it gets out that there is something weird about Chris, then the rest of the project – and our attempts to extract Andrew Conru's name from HDF – will be put in jeopardy.

Michael Christensen had wanted to hear from a friend of mine as soon as possible, someone who has known me for five years. Patrik and I start frantically cooking up a backstory for him as my Scandinavian friend Nikko, sourcing a Facebook page that looks just about believable. On the phone together, pacing madly around my flat, we brainstorm all the questions that PolygenX is likely to ask. We conjure up an email account and WhatsApp number for Nikko. Jonathan Anomaly emails him. 'We always vet people before sending them to our partner clinic,' he writes. Around 10 p.m., Patrik calls him.

He talks to Anomaly using one phone on speaker mode. Using another device, he calls me so I can listen in. I hear Patrik's calculated vagueness in action. When Anomaly asks how long he has known me, Patrik purposely stalls – as you might, if someone asked how many years you had known your best friend. 'Since forever,' Patrik sighs, casting his mind back for the right date, talking about how our families went on summer holidays together, how our dads went to the same university.

Anomaly asks him where I work. 'He's, uh, a consultant,' Patrik replies uncertainly. 'Management? I don't know all the details. It's like a big management company. He gives, like, strategy advice to big companies.' A note of frustration comes into Patrik's voice – an excellent touch, given it's late at night and he's having to answer weird questions from an unknown source about his oddball friend Chris.

Anomaly wants to know the source of my fictitious wealth.

'It's family money,' Patrik replies. 'His dad was a big bank person. There's something with his grandfather as well. There's a lot of money there.'

'That pretty much answers my questions,' Anomaly says, satisfied. He is apologetic, telling Patrik that he vets all his clients, but as most of them 'have a big online presence', he has to take extra care with me. 'I was 99 per cent sure that everything he was saying checks out, but I have to be sure he's not some undercover journalist.'

Patrik asks why the need for all the questions. What is Chris up to? Anomaly replies that he probably shouldn't mention what it is. He tells Patrik not to worry – 'he's not going to transition his gender!' – but that when his company does launch, it will be international news. 'It's a really, really cool thing,' Anomaly says, unable to contain his excitement. 'Everyone we talk to thinks it's amazing. In the meantime, we have to be very, very careful.' Anomaly pauses. Unprompted, he goes on. 'Here's why. It's like a medical thing, it has to do with children.' Patrik doesn't push him, and says he'll find out the rest from me.

The call ends. Anomaly tells me that I passed the vetting stage. I slide to the floor, and feel the hidden wires that had been wrapped around my chest blissfully begin to loosen.

What PolygenX offers sounds a lot like eugenics. Jonathan Anomaly, in his published writings, calls for the term to be reinterpreted without its connotations of state-mandated sterilisations and euthanasia programmes. In his book *Creating Future People*, he cites the definition of Leonard Darwin, son of Charles, who chaired the British Eugenics Society in the early 1920s: 'Eugenics is the study of heredity as it may be applied to the betterment, mental and physical, of the human race.'

The impending arrival of polygenic screening has increasingly become a topic of conversation in the press. The *Spectator* magazine ran a feature in 2024 describing it as 'the opportunity to offer your children the best possible chance in life', further calling it 'a new kind of eugenics'. A decade ago, the political commentator Toby Young wondered if polygenic screening might be used for 'progressive eugenics'. He wrote: 'Why not offer it free of charge to parents on low incomes with below-average IQs?'

The possibility of 'improving' life at the embryonic stage has also been called private eugenics, positive eugenics and eugenics 2.0. Jonathan Anomaly calls it liberal eugenics, and in his book argues for the practice to be seen in a new light. 'Moral grandstanding has become so common in connection with the word that journalists often use "eugenics" to mean something like "unjust coercion of innocent parents",' he says. 'While people disagree about precisely which traits are worth promoting, what motivates eugenics is a concern that individual welfare depends in part on the average traits of a population, and that demographic trends matter to the extent that they influence the success or failure of entire populations.'

Positive, new or liberal, eugenics makes me feel queasy. Can it ever be divorced from its dark past? Anomaly also claims that Francis Galton, the Victorian inventor of the term eugenics, has been much misunderstood. 'A lot of the criticism of eugenics,' he writes, 'conflates what Galton and many modern academics in bioethics mean by "eugenics" with how the Nazis misused it.'

Historians of eugenics might disagree. Galton's views were indisputably malign. He said eugenics should 'give to the more suitable races or strains of blood a better chance of prevailing speedily over the less suitable'. Elsewhere, he wrote about the extinction of what he deemed to be inferior races: 'The gain would be immense to the whole civilized world if we were to out-breed and finally displace the negro.'

The same goes for Leonard Darwin. Although he defined eugenics merely as the study of heredity to improve the human race, he still advocated for brutal corrective measures: 'How can practical results be obtained? . . . By insisting that the palpably unfit and degenerate shall not reproduce and multiply their kind. This may be accomplished by segregation, and ultimately, perhaps, by sterilisation, voluntary or compulsory.'

To make its analytical models, PolygenX uses data from the UK Biobank. As mentioned in the chapter on HDF, this is a massive repository of genetic and cognitive data of 500,000 volunteers who also share their educational and medical records. The information is used to unlock the secrets of hereditary disease, and has been helpful in cancer research. It has also been very helpful to PolygenX. 'The UK Biobank is a godsend, that's basically the best thing that's ever happened for this field,' Anomaly tells me when we speak in October. Access to the UK Biobank is meant to be highly restricted. Although volunteers relinquish the rights to their information when they sign a consent form, I wonder how they would feel about the use of their data to screen embryos for intelligence in an overseas company developing a practice that is not legal in the UK.

The UK Biobank publishes a list of the projects they have approved and given genetic data. Patrik and I search through, but don't find any mention of PolygenX. We do, however, stumble on the name of Alexandros Giannelis, a professor of psychology at the University of Minnesota. In my final call with the PolygenX team in mid-November, Anomaly describes Giannelis as 'one of our colleagues'. On the UK Biobank's website, under the list of approved projects, Giannelis's name appears as the principal investigator for Heliospect Genomics. It's dated June 2023. 'We want to improve genetic risk predictions for these diseases and others by using advanced techniques on new genetic data,' he writes, hoping to 'answer broader questions about how genes and environments are connected'.

Heliospect Genomics' own website is fairly blank, and contains boilerplate descriptions about genetic research next to a doodle of a microscope and a double helix. No names of any staff members are listed on the website, except a business address in Sheridan, Wyoming. Although this address appears to be used by many companies – including the Human Diversity Foundation – it is intriguingly registered at the same location as PolygenX. Michael Christensen is furthermore listed on a research website as the point of contact for Heliospect. The division between the two companies appears to be somewhat porous. Later, we are able to confirm by contacting Heliospect that Christensen is actually also its CEO.

(The UK Biobank, in a statement in October 2024, says Heliospect's use of their data was 'entirely consistent with our access conditions', adding that it was acceptable for them to use their data in the US for polygenic screening, a practice that is forbidden in the UK. 'UK Biobank did not require companies to disclose the precise commercial applications of research,' adds a statement from Heliospect.)

The involvement of Alexandros Giannelis in Heliospect is additionally troubling. When Midgard, a neo-Nazi music website, was hacked in 2023, Giannelis's name appeared among the leaked customer data. According to the files, he had purchased four neo-Nazi propaganda posters and a book called *Invasion* by Ian Stuart Donaldson, the virulently racist founder of the Blood & Honour white nationalist network.

Later, when Patrik and I are compiling all this information for our reports at HOPE not hate, we contact Heliospect about Giannelis. His representative says he was removed from his role after the company 'became aware of some allegations about Mr Giannelis's political affiliations which, if true, were in conflict with the company's core values'. Giannelis, in his own letter, denies the allegations, writing: 'I do not sympathise in any way with far-right ideologies.'

He isn't the only person involved in this network of companies who troubles us. Online, I find the CV of a man named Curtis Dunkel, a former psychology professor at Western Illinois University. On it, he declares that he has been a research consultant for Heliospect Genomics since June 2023, around the time Giannelis's application for UK Biobank data was approved. Dunkel has written five articles for *Mankind Quarterly* and two for OpenPsych, both run by Emil Kirkegaard. He has published with Kirkegaard and Edward Dutton. Dunkel's paper on sex differences and brain size – which concludes that women are approximately 4 IQ points less intelligent than men – was presented at the 2016 London Conference on Intelligence, a gathering of scientific racists.

Dunkel later says he had been approached by Heliospect to work for them. 'I was offered a short-term consultancy with the task of developing a personality profile/ measure of a child with ADHD,' he replies. He justifies his work with scientific racists, adding: 'I have published in numerous outlets. I viewed it as my obligation to try and present my findings and was conscientious about trying to do my best. Some subjects are sensitive, but this sensitivity reflects their importance.'

Months later, we find records of Tobias Wolfram, the chief science officer at PolygenX, posting messages in the secret Telegram group of Martin Sellner, the Austrian far-right activist who leads the identitarian movement. In January 2024, Wolfram types an anti-immigrant slogan 'we were never asked' in the channel, which is closed to members of the public. He posts again in the same chat in April to criticise a leaflet organising a counter-protest against Martin Sellner in Steyregg, Austria. His representatives later tell us that Wolfram was unaware he had been posting in Martin Sellner's private chat group on Telegram. 'Immediately upon realising that the post was on Mr Sellner's channel, Mr Wolfram removed it,' they say. He added in a statement: 'I vehemently deny being associated with the "far-right". I am a scientist who founded the German Association of Humanist Students and am a member of the left-leaning Party of Humanists.'

Polygenic screening is controversial in the field of genetics. Adam Rutherford has written eloquently about the subject.

Patrik and I visit him at his campus office at UCL – where the eugenicist Francis Galton founded the labs in the early twentieth century – to ask him about the practice. Is it really possible to screen embryos to identify which will be the smartest?

Rutherford tells us he works in what used to be called the eugenics department, noting the irony that much of his current role involves countering the ideas that were once advanced in this very building.

'My starting point is that this is scientifically dubious as a practice. This technique has very limited power for individuals,' he says, explaining that PolygenX relies on genome-wide association studies, which make sense on the grand scale of a large population, but not necessarily on an individual level. Furthermore, the tiny genetic variations that PolygenX analyses are only *associated* with intelligence, they are not known to be causative in the same way that, say, mutations in the cystic fibrosis transmembrane conductance regulator gene will cause cystic fibrosis.

Rutherford says the impact of polygenic screening is unlikely to outcompete the error margin of IQ tests, which is around five points, plus or minus. 'In my view, it is just a waste of money. It may have a very marginal effect that we can't really account for, but you may be just nudging an embryo towards being a human who scores highly on those polygenic scores like educational attainment.' He tells us that there are better ways of improving your child's IQ. 'Read them books,' he says. 'Or, you know, be a better parent.'

Ultimately, Rutherford says this practice is unlikely to take off, mainly for the reason that IVF can be an 'unpleasant, gruelling' experience. Some find it painful, invasive, time-consuming, expensive, emotionally draining and, in the end, might only yield a handful of viable embryos. With fewer embryos, there are worse odds in screening them to find an outlier with especially high intelligence. Rutherford suspects most couples who can will choose to have children 'the old-fashioned way, rather than a very expensive roll of the dice'.

There is no amount of intellectual gymnastics or clever rebranding that can make eugenics anything other than frightening. Some of the main advocates of both eugenics and polygenic screening that I encountered have worrying links to far-right activism and race science. Their real power doesn't come from the product itself – which pretty obviously sounds like a waste of money – but in selling the idea that genetics is far more important than one's environment.

'Eugenics has never worked primarily by producing more intelligent babies,' writes Emily Klancher Merchant, a historian of science. 'Instead, it has worked by creating the illusion that intelligence is primarily genetic, absolving governments of responsibility for ameliorating social inequality. The illusion leads to policies that enhance the life chances of those who are already privileged while further diminishing the life chances of those who are not.'

In a statement sent in October 2024, Jonathan Anomaly said his work had been 'entirely misconceived'. Wolfram again denied belonging to Martin Sellner's Telegram channel, and said he was 'appalled' at attempts to 'mischaracterise' him as holding far-right views. Michael Christensen said: 'My work has been driven by my desire to reduce suffering, having seen close relatives suffer from hereditary conditions such as Alzheimer's and heart disease. As a small startup, we are dedicated to developing with rigorous ethical and scientific standards to meet the diverse health needs of a broad audience.'

9

In November, Malcolm and Simone Collins organise a dinner of British 'pronatalists and luminaries' at an Indian restaurant in central London. Twelve of us sit so close around the small table that our shoulders and knees almost touch. As I reach to pass around the dishes of Kashmiri lamb and tandoori grilled tiger prawns, I keep patting my pocket to make sure my camera wires haven't slipped out. Dinners are hard to film. Water jugs and wine bottles tend to obscure the camera lens, and the clatter of cutlery confuses the microphone. I switch on another audio recorder in my jacket as a backup.

Tonight, fortunately, my devices pick up just enough of the conversation to capture an astonishing moment. Apart from Malcolm and Simone, I'm not familiar with the other dinner guests, some of whom, I learn, are involved in the Conservative think-tank world. But I have heard about one person, on the other side of the table, wearing a crumpled white shirt over a creased black tee: Andrew Sabisky.

Andrew was hired to work for the government in January 2020 when Dominic Cummings, then the prime minister's chief adviser, requested that 'weirdos and misfits with odd skills' apply to join him. A self-described 'super-forecaster', Andrew was meant to bring his enthusiasm for data analysis to the Downing Street operation. Aged twenty-seven, he found himself in Boris Johnson's senior team, attending meetings with the prime minister.

He did not last long. Weeks into his employment, the press found Andrew's detailed writings on race differences and IQ. Among his comments was the claim that in America, there are 'a far greater percentage of blacks than whites in the range of IQs 75 or below, at which point we are close to the typical boundary for mild mental retardation'.

Andrew made his views on race and IQ perfectly clear. He wrote that 'anyone who has researched the issue for more than 5 minutes' could see that there are 'very real racial differences in intelligence'. These differences were, he claimed, 'significantly – even mostly – genetic in origin'. He concluded that IQ scores should inform how the UK controls immigration.

An active participant in the race-science movement, Andrew spoke at the 2015 London Conference on Intelligence, a secret gathering of race scientists. Some of his fellow speakers at the event, like Emil Kirkegaard and Edward Dutton, would go on to create the Human Diversity Foundation. 'The Efficacy of Early Childhood Interventions in Improving Cognitive Outcomes' was the title of Andrew's speech. He was followed by Noah Carl, a future editor of Aporia, and a British writer called Michael Woodley, whose paper on race was cited in the terrorist manifesto of the 2022 Buffalo gunman.

Like the race scientists he mingled with, Andrew had concerns that extended beyond the genetic. In one of his articles for a race-science website, he recommended a book sold by Richard Lynn's Pioneer-funded Ulster Institute, and in the same piece fretted about Britain becoming 'a majority Islamic nation by 2050'. He wrote that immigration was creating 'divergent genetic impulses', threatening the British constitution, further anticipating 'violent' resistance to this demographic trend.

Andrew also wrote about what he perceived to be the detrimental genetic impact of lower socio-economic classes. In the comments of Dominic Cummings's own blog, he wrote: 'One way to get around the problems of unplanned pregnancies creating a permanent underclass would be to legally enforce universal uptake of long-term contraception at the onset of puberty.'

He quit his job in February 2020, likely told to jump instead of waiting to be pushed. In his departing statement, Andrew complained that he had been selectively quoted, adding: 'The media hysteria about my old stuff online is mad.'

Andrew, who is now in his early thirties, was defended by his friends in the media on the grounds that he made these posts and spoke at these conferences as a much younger man. Perhaps, his friends said, his youthful views had changed. Have they?

Over dinner, Andrew bangs the table with his hand to punctuate his speech. I notice he shares the three interests of Ryan Williams: gambling, weightlifting and boasting. 'I put on muscle pretty easily,' he says, telling me about his high testosterone levels and lack of erectile problems. I'm glad that I've finished eating by this point in the conversation. When the subject of his departure from Number 10 arises, Andrew beams as the table turns to listen to him.

'I'm easily the most cancelled person,' he says. 'I don't think anyone's been cancelled harder than I have.'

Malcolm, who earlier had been struggling to navigate the restaurant menu with Simone, praises Andrew. 'I loved all your quotes,' he says. 'They seemed so rational. That was the thing, I looked up how you were cancelled. It was a bunch of really reasonable but offensive stuff . . . Getting cancelled for saying reasonable things is the best thing that could happen to you.'

I wonder what reasonable things Malcolm was referring to – the 'mild mental retardation' of black Americans? Or the impending civil war against British Muslims?

Andrew grins. When someone around the table says he's famous, he agrees. His friends call him 'Sabs' or 'Uncle Sabs', a nickname he uses to refer to himself in the third person.

The plates are cleared to reveal a white linen tablecloth spattered with sauce. Andrew stops his conversation when he hears in the cross-chatter that I am an investor.

'How much?' he asks quickly. His bluntness catches me off guard before I remember Patrik's advice to stay vague.

You're going to have to put a lot more glasses of wine into me before I tell you, I reply.

'Very roughly?'

No, I say.

'Sabs is one of the least socially concerned of any people I've ever met in my life,' says another diner around the table, tittering.

'I only ask because I have one super juicy thing I want funded right now,' Andrew says, realising he may have come on a little strong. 'I have a bountiful number of excellent, high-impact ideas and, as you can tell, I'm well-networked.'

Andrew had earlier said he was going to gamble in the Hippodrome casino after dinner, so I ask if he should instead make the money he needs by putting it all on red.

He clarifies that poker, not roulette, is his game, and can't resist a little brag. 'Out of 150 hours, I've won about ten grand this year,' he says proudly. He prefers to play in the casino, where the standard among inebriated tourists is lower than in more professional games online. Although he is improving, his skills at gambling are not yet so good that he can use his winnings to fund his projects, hence his interest in me.

Andrew tells me he now does geopolitical risk analysis for a small consultancy called Bismarck. When I look it up later, I notice his name does not appear on its main website, although I find him mentioned on a company blog. Samo Burja is the boss of Bismarck – he is a former writer in the neoreactionary subculture, an online, anti-democratic movement associated with Silicon Valley. Burja's Instagram page shows him travelling the world and hanging out at parties with the singer Grimes.

At dinner, Andrew demurs from telling me about the 'super juicy thing' he needs funding for. However, when the evening draws to a close, I spot a moment when he's alone, putting on his coat. I ask again. He can't resist from divulging, his eyes glowing. In a voice much quieter than the one he used to hold court at dinner, he says: 'I'm informally advising the government on a super urgent basis relating to energy.'

Surely not, I think. Andrew Sabisky, back working for the government?

'I'll fill you in privately,' he says, perhaps spotting my

surprise. 'I need someone to pay my company for, like, a month so I can do this full-time and help my buddy at Number 10. That's all we need. The work is being published in December. We're trying to get the government to commit to a few big things on nuclear power. Some regulatory and planning reform.'

We exchange phone numbers, and he says he will arrange a Zoom call in the coming days, preferring to avoid speaking among the group. 'It's just really sensitive,' he explains in a hushed tone. 'For instance, in my bag I've got a whole bunch of insider stuff right now.'†

I can hardly believe what he's saying. The other guests invite me to join them for a drink, but I bail. Once I've walked a safe distance in the opposite direction, I call Patrik.

Is Andrew lying? What on earth is he doing for the government? Who is his buddy at Number 10? Many of the diners tonight seemed to know him well – well enough to call him by his avuncular nickname. Why are they happy risking their careers associating with a man whose record of endorsing race science made him – by his own admission – famous?

Five days later, Andrew sets up a Zoom call, sending me a document beforehand. It is headlined 'Pitch'. Under a subhead marked 'What you are being asked to fund', he writes: 'Me to work unofficially and exclusively for No. 10 for a little over a month.' He doesn't say how much

---

† 'This was poetic licence,' Sabisky later said in a statement. 'I had my own notes and some other material but it wasn't "insider stuff". It was a harmless bit of showmanship.'

he needs, just that the money would be used to pay his employer while he takes a brief sabbatical from work.

Andrew's pitch asks 'Why isn't the government paying?' To which he responds:

> The government cannot hire me directly (obviously), and while they could in theory contract formally with Bismarck, getting Bismarck set up on the civil service framework would take too long and be a giant pain in the backside (especially because we don't have a UK corporation). Also it is semi-public knowledge that I work for Bismarck and the risks of leaks are way too high. In a sane world one of the big nuclear players would be paying for this kind of thing, but their PR people would never allow it or indeed understand the value.

He believes that his expertise on energy is integral to informing the government's forthcoming 'roadmap' for nuclear power, due to be published at the end of the year or start of the next one. It sounds like he has an indirect line to the current prime minister, Rishi Sunak.

'What the hell is going on?' Andrew asks in his pitch, then answers: 'A friend of mine is a spad [special adviser] in no. 10.' Andrew has already written a paper for the government on British energy. 'Rishi read it and liked it,' he adds, although he clarifies later the paper did not appear under his byline and Sunak does not know about Andrew's involvement. Other briefing papers have been slipped into the hands of the prime minister by Andrew's mysterious friend in Downing Street.

Intrigued, confused and more than a little alarmed, I dial into the Zoom call with Andrew. Like his friend Malcolm

Collins, he animatedly delivers minutes-long speeches about his grand plans. Unlike Malcolm, whose Isle of Man dream will never be realised, Andrew seems frighteningly close to the levers of power.

He wants £32,000 for a month's work – an extortionate sum – to pay his employer for a leave of absence, plus a 10 per cent commission for himself, to draft government policy.

At the beginning of our call, Andrew refers to his 'guy' in Number 10, keeping his name out of it. Twenty minutes in, he lets slip that his friend is called Will. While Andrew is speaking about South Korean nuclear power stations and his assessment of the Ministry of Defence ('lack of skills', apparently), I quietly google Number 10 advisers named Will. On a Tory blog, I find there are three of them. One has a distinctive name – Will Dry – and appears in a news story the previous year about lobbying for the Remain campaign in the Brexit years. I take a chance. During a gap in the conversation, I ask Andrew.

Is it Will Dry? The Remainer?

'Yeah yeah yeah,' he replies. 'He's one of the best people in government by miles.'

Once the thrill of confirming the name subsides, I marvel about how the prospect of a fat stack of money can prompt wild indiscretions, just as it did with the leaders of the Human Diversity Foundation. Andrew is meant to be a sophisticated political operator, and I'm amazed the ruse works on him.

Nobody else within Downing Street knows about Andrew's work. 'We're providing this secret service for Number 10, and trying to keep it as secret as possible.' He claims he has been sourcing internal documents 'through arm's length'. Surprisingly, he is happy to tell me about his hidden source, at great career risk to himself and his contact.

At the end of the call, I tell Andrew that I'm a bit unsure why he needs my money, and so much of it. Partly it's true, but also I want to signal my interest in hearing about other projects while turning down this one. We part amicably, him spotting, I hope, that this isn't for me.

An hour after the call, Andrew sends me a few WhatsApps:

- oh I forgot to mention btw
- we met Lord Adonis on Saturday morning
- for some quiet but extremely helpful advice on managing the Treasury and giving ourselves maximum flexibility to get stuff through this year
- he was great

Andrew has been hinting about his connections to the Conservative Party, but until this point he never suggested that he had contacts in the Labour Party. Lord Adonis, a Labour peer, is a former minister in both the Cabinets of Tony Blair and Gordon Brown. He even wrote an article in 2020 that questioned why the Conservative government would hire someone with 'ultra-right prejudices'. (Months later, when Patrik contacts Lord Adonis to ask why he took a meeting with Andrew, he says: 'I recollect a meeting with Will Dry and a few others to discuss infrastructure strategy. I wasn't aware Andrew Sabisky was going to be there. He seemed mainly concerned about nuclear power.')

The next day, maybe sensing my hesitation, Andrew

says he will seek another source of funding, someone who has paid for his work in the past.

- Why don't I ask [redacted] to do this round
- and then come back to you later, probably next year
- I imagine I may well need me to do work on this in 2024

As revelatory as my conversations with Andrew are, they come at a hectic time. He sends his texts about funding on 9 November, the day before I'm due to fly to Warsaw with Britain First. I spend the rest of the month focused on extracting the name of the Human Diversity Foundation's anonymous funder in London and Athens.

With all the hours I am spending preparing for, undertaking and debriefing meet-ups, there is little time to spare for Andrew. This work is also exacting a greater toll on me. The nightmares I have about exposure are increasingly vivid. It is getting difficult to perform the everyday tasks of being undercover – responding to messages, answering phone calls – without feeling panicked.

After Warsaw, Athens and two terrifying encounters at my last infiltration just before Christmas (see the Conclusion), Patrik and I agree to draw a line under the project as planned. There is luxurious relief, during the first few months of 2024, in watching my life as Chris become a memory. I shut off my undercover phone, stuff my shirt camera in a box at the back of a wardrobe, grateful to no longer dwell in that frantic space of my brain that houses Chris mode.

I start work at HOPE not hate, becoming a researcher,

enjoying the routine of an office job. And yet, as Patrik and I draft our reports on the last year, sifting through the hours of camera and audio footage, a question hangs over the story of Andrew Sabisky. In January 2024, a document appears on a government website, headlined 'Civil nuclear: roadmap to 2050'. Did he contribute to it?

When we start speaking to the *Guardian*, who agree to partner with us for a series of articles about our findings, the subject of Andrew's involvement becomes harder to ignore. Just how extensive are his connections to power? Does he advise policymakers on issues other than energy?

Although the thought of returning to life as Chris induces major dread, there are questions about Andrew's apparent role in the running of our country that demand answers. The curiosity becomes insatiable, and I decide to reactivate Chris in the spring of 2024 as an epilogue to the undercover project. I take the box back out of the wardrobe, and screw the camera into my shirt once again, and start muttering 'Chris Chris Chris' to myself. A handful of final meetings, I think, and then finished for good. In April, I text Andrew once again.

Apologies for radio silence, I say. I took the last few months off to travel . . . How have you been?

'OMG hello again!!' he replies. 'look who's back from the dead. let's meet up!!' We arrange to meet at a pub in Pimlico.

It's empty save for a handful of midweek afternoon boozers. We order non-alcoholic Heinekens and sit upstairs on a deserted mezzanine. I have a spiel prepared to explain my absence, but Andrew seems uninterested. Within minutes, he is telling me about his contribution to Rishi

Sunak's nuclear policy. 'I literally fed back on the roadmap while it was being written,' he says. 'It got better, which was good. And it got stronger.'

But this is yesterday's news and he is already looking ahead to his next scheme. Rishi Sunak's approval ratings are circling the drain, and it looks ever more likely that a Labour government led by Keir Starmer will win the next election. Andrew is hoping to build contacts within the Labour Party to continue influencing the next wave of policymakers. He says he has been having talks with Day One, a Labour-aligned organisation aiming to brief the Shadow Cabinet about their upcoming policies.† Tantalisingly, he says he 'made friends with a spad in Starmer's policy unit'. I ask as directly as I can who this might be, but he refuses to be drawn.

Andrew's claim, the night we met at dinner last year, that he was 'well-networked' was not bluster. Despite his defenestration from the government for supporting race science, he is back in politics, almost as powerful as before. It is baffling.

He is not just involved in energy policy. Andrew may not have changed since he first started talking about race and intelligence. He has, however, learned to alter his tactics. During our conversation, he reveals that he has been involved in pronatalist lobbying in the UK.

In the US, Malcolm and Simone Collins are publicly trying to divorce pronatalism from its far-right connotations, but on this side of the Atlantic, Andrew has subtler ideas. He says he has been lobbying to make childcare more affordable. Why? 'The vast majority of people do not use

† A representative of Day One did not answer a request for comment.

paid childcare,' he says, because they leave work or use grandparents. 'Paid childcare is unbelievably concentrated among a smallish group of professionals.' By lobbying for childcare to become cheaper, pronatalists are secretly targeting the group they most want to have children.

'Any time you're saying you want to make childcare cheaper you're already addressing a concern that only affects graduates, because they're the only people actually using paid childcare,' he says. 'The fact that your policies are going to be stuff like targeting tax and childcare costs, you are already targeting the fertility of the elite, you don't even need to fucking say it.' In January 2024, the Conservative MP Neil O'Brien, who Andrew claims to speak to, endorses a think tank report called the 'New Deal for Parents'. It is a title that Andrew claims to have thought up. Both the report, and O'Brien on his blog, mention reducing the cost of childcare.

(O'Brien later denies involvement with Andrew. A Conservative source says: 'These claims are a complete fabrication. Neil O'Brien has only spoken to Mr Sabisky once to discuss energy policy. Sabisky has never acted as an adviser nor provided advice to Neil on any subject.' The party source further says Andrew had nothing to do with the 'New Deal for Parents' title.)

I ask what other projects I might help with. I'm coming to this from a perspective that's pretty red-pilled, I say. I don't know where you stand.

'When you have immigration running at 700,000 a year, or whatever it is, you've made some problems for yourself,' Andrew begins, gearing up for a big speech. 'If you want to unpick all this, which you definitely should, right – this is not sustainable – the quality's not particularly good.

Frankly, we had way better immigration pre-Brexit. All this needs to be changed.'

He says there are a few small things that the government could change to 'increase the quality of the current flow and radically cut the number', principally by restricting access to benefits and housing for immigrants. 'Stop doing that, and even if you leave everything about the immigration system the same except access to public funds and access to housing, a lot of your problems start to go away.'

That sounds more realistic than repatriation, I say, using a word common among the far right.

'Yeah, you just get voluntary repatriation,' Andrew replies. 'People will want to go back if they don't have access to public funds. Even if they've got passports, they'll literally just go back because they can't afford it otherwise. If you don't have access to benefits, that's the deal. And you need a much longer pathway between being allowed to live here and the right to remain . . . The bar needs to be massively higher. All of this needs to be done, can only be done, through regular, democratic politics.'

What's the end goal? I ask.

'Obviously Britain should be only full of the smartest people. There's really no reason for us to be importing people unless they can probably earn forty, fifty K a year minimum. A really high salary goal will get around regression to the mean.'†

This sets off an alarm bell. 'Regression to the mean' is a

---

† In December 2023, Rishi Sunak's government announced a plan that immigrants to the UK would have to earn at least £38,700 in order to bring their families.

statistical term used by race scientists to express fears that IQ scores are falling because foreigners of low intelligence are coming into the UK.

I need to clarify whether this is what Andrew is talking about.

Regression to the mean of IQ? I ask.

'Yeah,' he replies. 'The whole system should probably, actually run on IQ. At the moment it runs on credentials, which is fucking insane, because so many Third World credentials are fake. We're importing people with fake credentials for nursing, medicine, social care, teaching. If they're not fake they're of massively lower quality. There's no quality adjustment being done by these departments. It is the biggest false economy imaginable.'

This is a repeat of what he wrote on a race-science blog back in 2014. It's what he still believes. As subtly as I can, I straighten my back and point my chest at Andrew to make sure this astounding conversation is captured by my shirt camera.

'I know,' he begins, lowering his voice, enunciating each word, '*I know* – most elites actually know the score. They won't talk about it, but they know. I know, because secretly, I'm still *persona grata*.' He grins. 'Obviously, not publicly, but unofficially, everyone comes to Uncle Sabs for wisdom.' He names a prominent political journalist he advises, plus Neil O'Brien MP. 'Same thing. Everyone knows. It's not some big fucking secret. People have got the message.'

I'm taking a risk by asking him directly, but I feel like it's vital to pin him down.

You're talking about race and IQ? I ask.

'Yeah, yeah. People know that.'

Just to be clear?

'Yeah. People know that. It's not some huge secret. The question is, what do you do about it?'

Our meeting barely lasts an hour, but by the time it's over, I stagger out of the pub, feeling a little nauseous. Back home, I replay my tapes to make sure I hadn't imagined what Andrew told me. His views on race and intelligence weren't 'old stuff'. He hasn't apologised for or recanted his views, and his political career, following his exit from Downing Street, has only advanced.

For someone who so openly supported eugenics – and much else besides – it is frightening that so many policy-makers and influential figures in the Westminster scene will meet him, not just among the Conservatives but also the Labour Party. Does he really have private conversations with them about race and IQ? Is he genuinely *persona grata*, feeding Britain's most powerful people ideas on how to achieve racist ends with legitimate means?

Andrew invites me into a private chatroom on Slack, a social media messaging app. The group is called Sabs Central, and it contains almost sixty of his political contacts. Inside, there are journalists working for main-stream, respectable publications, political advisers, think-tank workers and parliamentary researchers. Will Dry is a member. So is the GB News presenter Charlie Peters. For legal reasons, it is not possible to name everyone else.

'This is actually a pretty right-centrist gang, insofar as my pals go,' Andrew texts me, adding: 'All the Angels are in there.' Sabs's Angels is a term that he uses to describe his protégés. When I ask about how spicy – how extreme – the conversations are, Andrew replies: 'Mild spice only.'

The chatroom is divided up by topic, one of them being 'demographics'. I see messages bemoaning the ethnic makeup of different parts of the UK, and complaints about a 'migration blackpill', an online term for a despairing fact, this time applied to the '10-year route' to British citizenship being deemed excessively lenient. Another post hints at the prescience of Enoch Powell, the Conservative MP who gave the infamous 'Rivers of Blood' speech against immigration in 1968.

The membership tends to be young – there are men and women here in their twenties and thirties. 'I expect many of you here to become eminent figures in public life,' Andrew says. He frequently invites them for drinks in the Hippodrome casino, where he hones his poker skills late into the night. When they publish articles or reports online, they share a link and ask fellow members of Sabs Central to promote it on social media. In September 2024, Andrew posts a link to an essay on the state of the British economy. 'Can we please aggressively promote this on twitter,' he writes, 'especially b/c I had a big influence on and wrote some of the energy section (keep that secret tho).' The Angels duly share it on their social media profiles, where the article racks up millions of views.

Andrew and I make another date to speak in June, after the election has been called. We meet at the same Pimlico pub. This time, Andrew invites his friend Will Dry, the former Downing Street special adviser. Will's name was plastered over the newspapers in January. He was identified as a turncoat formerly at the top of Rishi Sunak's team, now involved in a plot to oust him. 'Sadly, it became clear to me we weren't providing the bold, decisive action to overcome those challenges,' Will said in a statement at the time. Only twenty-six, he was named as a plotter belonging to a group of Conservative MPs, advisers and donors who had commissioned polling that predicted their party would be wiped out at the next election.

'He's going to be a real mover and shaker over the next decade or more,' Andrew tells me. Will arrives in a creased white T-shirt and talks with Andrew about their work together on nuclear policy.

'We made a bit of progress,' says Will.

'We made a little bit,' agrees Andrew.

'We could have done more, the scale of the disaster,' says Will.†

He curses his former colleagues in Downing Street. They are 'completely unserious', their manifesto made 'fuck all difference', their views are 'crap and wrong' and 'a thousand times more socially liberal than most people in this country', especially their policies on tackling illegal migration.

I ask Will for his views on fixing the problem. His answer, given his proximity to power, is scarcely believable.

'The quality of the population matters a lot,' he says. 'We've neglected that fact massively, to our detriment, over the last two decades. Particularly in the last four years, the amount of dross that's come in is, like, horrific. And we're

† In a statement, Dry later said of Sabisky's involvement in the nuclear roadmap: 'I asked him various questions. He did not contribute to the roadmap and none of his writing appears in it.' However, in his own statement, Sabisky says something a bit different: 'I believe that I influenced Will's thinking and I hope that he influenced others.'

going to be living with the consequences of that for quite a long time. I agree with Sabs that the most politically feasible way to address this is essentially a hostile environment for unproductive people you don't want in the country. I would then be very supportive of a state that's got the capacity to deport people who are illegally here.'

It is harder, he says, to get 'rid of people who are legally here'. He pauses, turning to Andrew. 'Has anything been done on taxing remittances?' A remittance is money sent by someone in a diaspora community to their family abroad.

'Interesting question,' Andrew replies. 'I don't know a lot about this.'

'I think that would be very politically feasible,' Will says.

'And it would probably be another quite good way to cut the incentives,' Andrew responds.

Will says he hopes the Conservatives fare badly at the election – he laughs at the prospect – and wants a new leader on the right of the party to replace Rishi Sunak. 'I know a fair amount of the different players,' he says. 'I just want to try and make sure that something good emerges from the wreckage.'

I watch, stunned, as he leaves the pub for another meeting.

'Having good demographics is very important,' Andrew tells me. 'Quality matters as well as quantity. You want to have good quantity – that's pronatalism. You want to have good quality – that's migration control.'

Will has a place at Civic Future, which, like the Sabs Central chatroom, is a talent incubator for rising stars in Westminster. Andrew tells me about his own involvement in it. Civic Future is run by Munira Mirza, a former director of the Number 10 policy unit under Boris Johnson. A communist in her youth, she joined a Conservative think tank in the mid-noughties. She has called British Muslim communities 'a nation within a nation'.

Civic Future, according to its website, seeks to put 'our most capable citizens' into public life. Over the course of a year, Civic Future interns are given part-time lessons on the mechanics of government and policymaking, listening to lectures and attending workshops designed to accelerate their political careers. At a meeting in the Corinthia Hotel bar in central London, Andrew introduces me to Jack Hutchison, programme director at Civic Future.

'Andrew's been influential,' says Jack. 'We run this fellowship programme and Andrew put a lot of the new fellows in touch with us originally.' Andrew says he put forward eight candidates, friends of his, for a Civic Future fellowship. Three were ultimately accepted out of a total cohort of fourteen.†

Over the course of our meetings together in the spring and summer of 2024, Andrew mentions a dizzying number of his political contacts. In addition to Lord Adonis, there is Peter Thiel, Dominic Cummings, Sam Gyimah (a former Conservative MP now working for Goldman Sachs) and

---

† Much later, when Patrik contacts Civic Future for comment, Jack replies: 'No candidates were interviewed nor selected for the Civic Future Fellowship based on the recommendation of Mr Sabisky. To be clear, dozens of people make informal recommendations to us, some as a result of being asked to do so, others on an unsolicited basis. Mr Sabisky was in the latter category. We know each other because we attend the same church and have had occasional contact elsewhere. He wrote to me personally with his ideas. I thanked him politely but gave no indication as to the status of his names.'

a load of other up-and-coming political figures not yet in the public eye. What is most surprising and dispiriting are the number of journalists he claims to be friends with who have not reported his influence on public life.

Back at our meeting in April, Andrew says something that continues to haunt me. His 'cancellation', as he puts it, has taught him a lesson. 'In the UK you either lose or you do democratic politics and you win,' he says emphatically. 'Personally, I like to win. I don't want to be a heroic loser, I just want to win. Glory to my name? I don't care, I just want to win.' Each time he says the word 'win', he pounds the table with his fist. 'You win in Britain through the long march through the institutions. Everyone puts on the mask and they get into the machine and that's how it works. It's how everything has ever worked, pretty much.'

Ten years ago, Andrew used to openly post his views on the internet. Since he was first exposed for endorsing race science, he has learned, poker player that he is, to conceal his hand and put on a mask.

At one of our last meetings in July – green tea and orange juice in a Westminster hotel – he describes the repercussions of losing his Downing Street job. 'Effectively zero,' he says. 'The people I meet – journalists or business people or politicians, often people with impeccable centrist-level bona fides – we get on surprisingly well.' He smiles. 'It increasingly makes me think that everyone knows I'm right.'

Conclusion

The Traditional Britain Group is a far-right organisation based in London, and tonight it's their Christmas party. A few of their associates meet in a pub near Paddington Station for a drink beforehand. When I get there, four men are sitting round the table with a space at the head. I recognise Nathan, who I met in Tallinn and hung out with in St James's Park. He introduces me to a conspiracy theory YouTuber named Thomas.

Thomas shakes my hand as I take a seat. Then he hits me with a sentence I will never forget.

'These guys have been telling me you're a fed.'

The vacuum of the ensuing silence yanks the air out of my chest. Four pairs of eyes are on me.

I think about how to respond, and repeat the joke I made when I joined Identity England. Pulling down my sleeve, I pretend to talk into a cuff mic to say I've been compromised, I need to escape.

There's a lame chuckle around the table.

Although Thomas has a smile on his face, he's watching me intently. 'How did you get into all this stuff?' he asks.

I want to grab my coat and sprint out the door. Instead I force myself to act naturally, taking a sip of my pint. If I appear flustered, that will be odd. And if my answer is word-perfect, that will sound rehearsed. The table is silent as they await my answer.

Christ, I huff, there wasn't a single red-pill moment. Moving to London after growing up in the countryside was really different to what I expected. I didn't have anyone to talk to about it.

Thomas nods at me to go on.

I describe searching online for YouTubers who could explain my feelings of loneliness and alienation, naming two: Carl Benjamin (aka Sargon of Akkad) and Colin Robertson (aka Millennial Woes).

'Millennial Woes had a huge influence on me from 2015 onwards,' he says. Something in his voice has softened.

I praise Tom's own videos, including a recent one that made fun of Neema Parvini for being out of touch with his followers. Together, we mock Parvini and his courses on economics and entrepreneurship. Each time I make Tom laugh, I imagine an eraser rubbing out his suspicions of me.

We get another round in, and Nathan tells us how police stopped him at the airport and demanded he hand over his phone under counter-terrorism laws. I take this opportunity to teasingly question whether he is now working with the feds. The others join in, and before long we are all tipsily accusing each other of being rats.

I feel like I'm back on firmer ground. We down our drinks and walk to another, much bigger pub in Mayfair, where the Traditional Britain Group event is being held. Its founder, Gregory Lauder-Frost, is an advocate of remigration, and was fined by a court in 2019 for racially abusing a British citizen of Hong Kong origin. On Facebook, he wrote that she had 'no right to be in our country or arguing with a superior race'.

TBG hosts an annual conference with speakers like Ed Dutton plus a Christmas pub meet-up and a spring dinner – which the Conservative MP Jacob Rees-Mogg attended in 2013 and later apologised for.

When we reach the pub, we greet the other guests having a smoke on the pavement. It's the last Saturday before Christmas, and the street is packed. I look around the crowd and freeze. It's my brother-in-law. He's barely two metres away, half turned towards me, chatting to a friend. What the hell is he doing here?

My biggest fear while undercover has been bumping into someone I know and being stuck in the group while they approach, shouting my real name. Fizzing with alarm, I push my way out of the crush and pull out my phone, muttering that I need to take a work call. I jog down the street and call my brother-in-law. The phone rings and rings and finally he picks up. He says he's at a wedding reception at a pub in Mayfair. I stammer at him that we're at the same venue by coincidence – our event must be on a different floor. I'm working undercover, I say. Please, please do not acknowledge me. Just ignore me. He sounds confused, but says if he sees me, he'll leave me alone.

Adrenaline surging, I head back to my group. This is a mistake. I should have waited a minute to regain my breath. When I rejoin the other TBG guests, a woman I've not met before looks at me askance. I must still be a little agitated. 'There are always infiltrators at these events,' she says, glaring. 'I can always tell who they are. Who do you know here?' I point out half a dozen people, including Nathan who luckily forgets how long we've known each other and accidentally exaggerates to say we met several years ago. She is not impressed, and as we head indoors I see her whisper to a friend, covering her mouth with her hand, scowling at me.

We go upstairs to our hired room, which is mercifully on the top floor so there is no chance of running into my brother-in-law again. I spot Rhodri Phillips, whose aristocratic title is Viscount St Davids. In 2017, he was jailed for offering his friends £5,000 to run over an anti-Brexit activist. There's also Robin Tilbrook, the head of a far-right party called the English Democrats. I've written articles about him before and try to avoid catching his eye. Members of Patriotic Alternative and the Homeland Party, a new white nationalist organisation, have shown up. Nick from Britain First and Charlie from Identity England are here and they tell me about their very expensive visit to a Warsaw strip club. They talk about going to Germany in the new year to rekindle their relationship with the European identitarians – but they're worried about getting stopped at the border.

Gunnar Beck, a former law lecturer at the School of Oriental and African Studies in London, is invited to address the hundred or so present. He steps onto the banquette and introduces himself as an ex-MEP with Alternative für Deutschland. 'The plight has reached a very critical point,' he says, telling us he wants to talk about 'climate insanity' and immigration. 'We are all used to hearing "Ah well, they'll integrate, it'll be fine, they'll be just like natives". No, they aren't. Their education level will remain much lower. They will not work with the same regularity and, of course, the kinds of jobs they are getting won't mirror those held by the indigenous population.'

In Germany, he says, the percentage of people of foreign descent is around 30 per cent.

'Ugh!' shouts a voice from the crowd.

'Yeah,' agrees Gunnar.

He is asked what the AfD will do about immigration. Gunnar predicts that 'a complete economic collapse' brought about by the implementation of climate change policies might sweep the party to power. He gets the biggest cheer when talking about the AfD's support in the polls, which is surging. As the crowd applauds him at the end of his speech, I become worried that tomorrow belongs to him.

This is my final undercover assignment. Or it is meant to be, until I have those few extra meet-ups with Andrew Sabisky the following spring. Still, I think of the December event as the climax of my life as Chris. I am so relieved to stop. When Gunnar Beck finishes his talk, I say happy Christmas to Nick, Charlie and my other associates. I walk away, leaving Chris on the mucky floor in the back room of a pub where he belongs. For so long I have thought that Chris mode would end with an incorrigible mistake and a fist in the face. Some have had their doubts about me, but they don't know for sure that I am a rat. What a relief it feels to slip out unnoticed.

When I began this project, the pace of undercover meetings was slow. I met the Basketweavers once a fortnight. Now I am pretending to be Chris almost every day with the Human Diversity Foundation team. The strain has become intolerable, the escapes too narrow. I can no longer distinguish between a genuine crisis and a small challenge: an unexpected phone call gives me the same feeling of panicky despair as an accusation of being a fed.

Hanging around far-right activists has also become deeply depressing. A year ago, infiltrating these groups was a thrill; I was sneaking past a closed door and peering inside. But it is unbearably bleak to listen to extreme racism and either say nothing or, worse, have to nod my head and agree.

In the last few weeks of being undercover I meet:

- A young man who complained that his fellow university students were mean to him online. What did you do? I ask. 'I insulted a negress on Instagram,' was his reply. He called her 'a big fat brown hippo'. It didn't damage his job prospects. He moved to Brussels to become the assistant of an MEP in Alternative für Deutschland.
- An activist who rants about women. 'As long as you go through life knowing that women are completely pathetic, you'll be really successful,' he tells me.
- A mixed-race man who had been posting in a chat group about the evils of race-mixing. I later learn he has been kicked out of his family home after spending his allowance on sex workers.
- A conference guest who says a white woman in her early twenties got onto his train carriage holding hands with a South Asian man. 'I just thought, *eurgh*. I didn't know it was that bad, and I live here. Disgusting.'

- An influencer who complains about 'negrophilia' in the US.
- A writer who says: 'My religion is antisemitism.'

I've had enough of this poison. Nearly all of those people described above were young men, who, in addition to being frighteningly extreme, expressed a deep loneliness. The romantic and platonic relationships they yearn for have not yet materialised, and many of the men I met as Chris sought community. Rank-and-file members of extremist groups like the Basketweavers openly expressed the need for warmth and welcome that they otherwise felt had been denied to them in their families or among their friends at school or university or work. While their political beliefs are without doubt objectionable, their life circumstances deserve empathy.

The same cannot be said of the leaders of far-right groups who prey on the isolation and purposelessness of their members.

It can be difficult to pinpoint the exact reasons why someone ends up joining an extremist group. Arie Kruglanski, a psychologist at the University of Maryland, makes a compelling argument that radicalisation is driven in part by the need to feel significant, the need to matter. If it is shaken by difficult life events – loneliness comes to mind – then someone might seek to reclaim their lost significance by doing something drastic, like believing in far-right talking points and making extremist connections. One in ten young people between fifteen and twenty-four say they feel lonely most or all of the time. Not all are going to join Neo Byzantium tomorrow, but as long as people lack social connections there is a risk that a malicious organisation like it might seek to take advantage of them.

When the story broke in October 2024 about this undercover project, first with a series of articles in the *Guardian* about HDF, then the announcement that Channel 4 would broadcast a documentary about HOPE not hate, I wanted the followers of extremist groups to see their leaders for who they really were. The far-right leaders I spent time with were certainly concerned about their bottom lines. Matthew Frost and Erik Ahrens thought a lot about how to squeeze every penny from their followers.

Just as important to the leaders of HDF and the other groups I infiltrated was the prospect of power. It meant different things in each organisation. To the senior Basketweavers, it is being in charge of a heretical, dissident underground group. To Ryan Williams, power brings a group of adoring fans to enjoy his boasting and bolster his ego. Charlie Fox has a gang of drinking buddies who can indulge his beery nostalgia for Generation Identity. In Paul Golding's case, his quest for power has a more nakedly financial element: the near-daily emails begging for donations speak to obsession with parting his members from their money. (He exploded at a drunken member who complained about donations at the summer camp, calling his dissenters 'fucking wankers'.)

What about the others? Alison Chabloz has a small team of friends who can feed her fantasy as a hero of the far right. The HDF network seeks power by persuading policymakers that race science is real. Simone and Malcolm Collins, according to their Isle of Man pitch, are seemingly after a very real form of power – it ends with them as dictators of a city state in the Irish Sea, conducting medical experiments on artificial wombs and constructing their isolated and differential breeding network. Jonathan Anomaly, one of the brains behind PolygenX, wants a world that accepts eugenics. Andrew Sabisky takes a long-term view: in the decades to come, he wants to have installed a like-minded ally behind every lever of power.

Whether or not these groups succeed depends on their maintenance of an illusion, that they are less extreme than they appear to be. Even though many of them believe a silent majority supports them, they know that their views are unpalatable to many. That is why they obfuscate their true intentions: Britain First with their leaflets claiming to be anti-racist, while refusing to knock on the doors of non-white households; HDF with their claims of scientific impartiality yet ignoring evidence that contradicts their conspiratorial fantasies; Andrew Sabisky, with his extreme views about race and IQ, going into the Westminster machine with a mask on his face.

The far right have rarely been more visible in this country. There are five Reform UK MPs sitting in Parliament, led by Nigel Farage, an admirer of Enoch Powell. More than a hundred Reform candidates were barred from standing at the last election for belonging to the BNP, or supporting Hitler's views, or even saying Africans have 'diluted' national IQ scores. Reform's manifesto calls for the deportation of British citizens of foreign descent if they commit crimes. This would create a two-tier justice system by making British citizenship conditional on good behaviour. It sends a message that no matter how many years and generations after the granting of citizenship, there are some people who can never be considered fully British.

Reform also scapegoats immigrants as the reason why wages are stagnating. 'The unprecedented population explosion has pushed Britain to breaking point,' Nigel Farage has written. It is not enough to make the case against voting for a party because it is far right. Four million people voted for Reform at the last election in part because it offered easy, if misguided, solutions to the cost-of-living crisis. The best way to undercut support for the far right is by addressing high energy bills and broken public services and offering a more hopeful alternative.

The danger of Reform's breakthrough (plus the re-election of Donald Trump) is that it legitimises far-right views and pushes the Conservative Party to adopt a more hard-line position on immigration. Kemi Badenoch, leader of the Tories, has already signalled her position, writing in a newspaper article: 'We cannot be naïve and assume immigrants will automatically abandon ancestral ethnic hostilities at the border, or that all cultures are equally valid. They are not.' A more concerning prospect, however, is that the Labour Party, now in power, might decide to address the Conservatives and Reform by borrowing their ideas. This would be a victory for the far right, widening the Overton Window, the scope of acceptable ideas, which I heard so much about while undercover.

While I was writing this book, the largest wave of far-right violence in the post-war period swept through the UK. In twenty-seven towns and cities, mobs set fire to asylum-seeker accommodation, beat up Muslims – or people they believed to be Muslims – and trashed shops. They targeted mosques, immigration solicitors, police officers, a Citizens Advice Bureau, and, in one particularly sad incident, a Merseyside library, which was burned down.

The nightmare began when a teenager entered a children's Taylor Swift-themed dance class in Southport on 29 July and stabbed three girls to death. Axel Rudakubana was not named by the police because he was under eighteen at the time. Far-right activists, influencers and politicians took this to mean he was actually a Muslim immigrant and that the establishment was trying to whitewash the crime of yet another violent foreigner.

Further unevidenced claims circulated online: that Rudakubana had an Arab name, that he was an anti-white racist, that he had recently crossed the English Channel in a small boat. 'The evidence is stacking up that the Southport attack was carried out by a migrant,' wrote Paul Golding on X/Twitter.

Nigel Farage, head of the Reform Party, posted his own conspiratorial video. 'I just wonder whether the truth is being withheld from us,' he said. 'I don't know the answer, but I think it is a fair and legitimate question.'

Rudakubana's attack was met with calls for extreme action from the far right. 'We need to permanently remove Islam from Great Britain,' said Laurence Fox, the former TV actor turned agitator. 'Completely and entirely.'

Six days of vicious rioting thus began. 'Pakis get out', 'we want our country back' and 'stop the boats' were common phrases shouted by the rioters.

When a hotel temporarily housing asylum seekers was attacked in Rotherham, the crowd cheered as the building's glass doors were smashed open. 'Get 'em out! Get 'em out!' a man shouted. A masked thug, filmed by a refugee upstairs, ran his finger across his neck in the universal gesture of violent intent.

In Middlesbrough, a crowd set up roadblocks that stopped cars, checking that drivers were white before allowing them to pass. In the same city, mobs tore through Muslim neighbourhoods to break the windows of houses and cars.

In Hull, rioters stopped a car because they thought the driver was 'foreign'. They dragged him and his companions out of the vehicle and beat them, shouting: 'Yeah! Fucking kill them!'

And in Cyprus, the far-right activist known as Tommy Robinson lay on a sunlounger at a five-star hotel as he sent his followers a list of meeting points for anti-immigrant events, including at asylum-seeker accommodation. 'Get there and show your support,' he said. 'People need to rise up.'

Rioters in Southport coordinated their activities in a group on Telegram. One of the members complained about their enemies being 'spiteful mutants', a term popularised by Ed Dutton in his race-science articles to refer to people who have, in his view, inferior genetics and left-wing beliefs.

For the asylum seekers within these hotels, the riots probably did not come as a surprise. Their temporary accommodation sites have been targeted for years by far-right activists who show up to hassle refugees. Activists follow a model made by Nigel Farage, who in July 2020 went to a hotel in Worcestershire to film African and Asian men on the premises. 'We've no idea who some of these people are,' Farage said in a video he posted on his YouTube channel. 'We've no idea whether some of these might be ISIS. It's possible, I don't know.'

In making this video, Farage launched a new form of far-right activism. Some are full-time 'migrant hunters' who go to hotels housing asylum seekers and shout at residents and staff. Others, like Paul Golding, incorporate the tactic into their activism, as I found out when I went with him to the refugee accommodation sites in Wethersfield in Essex and Napier in Kent.

Paul Golding and other so-called 'migrant hunters' make these videos too. They are useful for feeding a narrative that the government is both ignoring its own and being hoodwinked by manipulative foreigners. 'They come here to abuse our hospitality,' he said on a repeat visit to the Napier barracks in November 2023 (that I didn't join). 'If we didn't roll out the red carpet for them, they wouldn't come.' The reality is that the conditions at Napier are so inhospitable, the buildings so decrepit and the facilities so dirty that a third of the residents there have reported feeling suicidal. But Paul seems to genuinely believe that the refugees within the walls are not only exploitative con artists but part of a grand conspiracy to replace white Britons.

When I went leafletting with Britain First in their Tamworth by-election campaign of October 2023, we handed out dozens of flyers that read 'KEEP TAMWORTH BRITISH' and 'CLOSE DOWN THE TAMWORTH MIGRANT HOTEL'. In the centre of the town, a Holiday Inn Express was being used to house refugees and immigrants. During the riots that following summer, a mob smashed the hotel's windows, hurling petrol bombs at it, incinerating a hallway. 'Fuck Pakis' and 'Get out' were graffitied on the outer walls. Around 180 refugees were in the building when the attack took place – they thought they were about to die. For ninety minutes, rioters did everything they could to break into the hotel, clashing with police who ultimately took control of the situation. 'I will bite your fucking face,' one rioter snarled at an officer.

After the riots ended, in part due to the speedy convictions of participants, right-wing commentators moved to justify the violence. Some sought to excuse the violence as an outburst of legitimate anger against a multicultural society. There was a particular emphasis on not identifying the rioters as far right. 'Anybody who breaks the law should be arrested,' wrote Matthew Goodwin, an author and former professor of politics at the University of Kent. 'But what you are also witnessing in the UK right now is a concerted & most likely coordinated effort by the elite class to inflate "far right" to stigmatise & silence millions of ordinary people who object to mass immigration and its effects.'†

After initially condemning the first riot, a further way of minimising the violence came from Reform's MP Lee Anderson, a former deputy chairman of the Conservative Party. 'These are not far-right thugs, they're just young

† The strange trajectory of Matthew Goodwin is a story for another day. He once investigated far-right groups from a critical perspective. I quote and draw on some of his analysis of the BNP in Chapter 4. 'There were countless examples,' he wrote of Nigel Farage's previous party a decade ago, 'that UKIP was a racist or extreme party that was filled with amateurs.' Goodwin has since become a vocal opponent of multiculturalism and begun working with Farage and his Reform Party.

idiots who got carried away,' he said, adding that they 'probably had one too many'.

This is a very generous interpretation of what happened. Far-right activists were among the rioters. A number of Britain First members, in addition to associates of Patriotic Alternative and National Action, a proscribed terrorist group, were keen participants. Warren Gilchrest, a Britain First activist before my time, was jailed for three years after shouting 'kill him' and 'stamp on his fucking face' as a crowd attacked a lone black man in central Manchester.

I used to listen to the rantings of Britain First members discussing ethnic civil war or the Basketweavers chat about remigration and think they were fantasists. Aggressive and conspiratorial, yes. But violent? I wasn't always sure. The riots clarified things for me. Suddenly there were gangs of racists rampaging through English towns looking to hurt anyone without a white skin tone. At the time of writing, around 1,280 individuals have been arrested, and at least eight hundred charged. Their actions did not take place in a vacuum, they were motivated to hurt Muslims and people of colour deemed too alien to belong in this country.

There is a targeted, well-funded effort to influence society into believing that races cannot live together because of irreconcilable genetic factors. And there are a number of people across the country who have taken this message to heart and are willing to hurt anyone who they think doesn't fit into their vision for Britain. Luckily the majority do not agree. There were massive counter-protests that mobilised against the far right, and even at the first riot in Southport the day after the stabbings, a woman who bravely held up a sign that read: 'ONE RACE – HUMAN. HOPE NOT HATE. RACISM NOT WELCOME HERE.'

Cas Mudde, the political scientist whose definition of the far right is quoted in the introduction, writes that he is often asked what can be done to stop the far right. There is no silver bullet, he says. 'Even after more than two decades, I still do not have the answer.'

Neither do I. But I do think about an old TV programme featuring Oswald Mosley. On the rare occasions that he would get invited on TV, Mosley would deny having ever said or done anything antisemitic. So it was a powerful moment when, on an ITV chat show in 1967, a member of the audience stood up and recited to Mosley the telegram he sent Julius Streicher, the Nazi politician, about the need to defeat 'the forces of Jewish corruption'. Shifting uncomfortably in his chair, hunching over the desk, Mosley looked like the liar he was. If we are to counteract the growing influence of the far right, we cannot take at face value their claims of moderation. 'Everyone puts on the mask and they get into the machine and that's how it works,' said Andrew Sabisky. It's up to us to make sure the mask comes off.

Select Bibliography

I hesitate to point readers towards extremist material such as terrorist manifestos, and have omitted these sources from the bibliography. Some of the secondary material that informed or is quoted in this book is listed below.

Evans, Gavin, *Skin Deep: Dispelling the Science of Race*, Oneworld Publications, 2019.

Goodwin, Matthew, *New British Fascism: Rise of the British National Party*, Routledge, 2011.

Kruglanski, Arie W., Daniel Koehler and David Webber, *The Radical's Journey: How German Neo-Nazis Voyaged to the Edge and Back*, Oxford University Press, 2022.

Merchant, Emily R. Klancher, 'Breeding for IQ', *Los Angeles Review of Books*, 22 August 2024.

Mudde, Cas, *The Far Right Today*, Polity Press, 2019.

Purdue, Simon A., 'A Battle of the Groin': The Reproductive Politics of the Global Extreme-Right, 1969–2009*, Palgrave Macmillan, 2022.

Rutherford, Adam, *How to Argue With a Racist: History, Science, Race and Reality*, Weidenfeld & Nicolson, 2020.

Rutherford, Adam, *Control: The Dark History and Troubling Present of Eugenics*, Weidenfeld & Nicolson, 2022.

Saini, Angela, *Superior: The Return of Race Science*, Fourth Estate, 2019.

Tucker, William H., *The Science and Politics of Racial Research*, University of Illinois Press, 1996.

Tucker, William H., *The Funding of Scientific Racism: Wickliffe Draper and the Pioneer Fund*, University of Illinois Press, 2007.

Walmsley, Jan, 'Women and the Mental Deficiency Act of 1913: citizenship, sexuality and regulation', *British Journal of Learning Disabilities*, Volume 28, Issue 2, June 2000.

Wilmoth, John, 'Review of *Dysgenics: Genetic Deterioration in Modern Populations* by Richard Lynn', in *Population and Development Review*, Volume 23, Number 3, September 1997.

Wise, Sarah, *The Undesirables: The Law that Locked Away a Generation*, Oneworld Publications, 2024.

Acknowledgements

I would like to thank all the staff at HOPE not hate, especially David Lawrence, Gregory Davis, Joe Mulhall, Marcus North and Nick Lowles. A special thanks to Patrik Hermansson, who kept me safe and sane while undercover. Thanks to my family and friends and those who read early drafts. Thanks to Adam Rutherford for lending his expertise on race science (any mistakes are my own). Enormous credit to Havana Marking, Natasha Dack, Tom Turner and the rest of the documentary crew for making *Undercover: Exposing the Far Right*, plus Channel 4 for broadcasting it. Thank you, Doug Young at PEW Literary and the team at Chatto & Windus, for working with me. Thanks to my copy-editor. By far the biggest thank-you goes to my partner Hattie, whose patience, enthusiasm and love made this project possible.

About the Author

Harry Shukman is a researcher at HOPE not hate, an anti-fascist organisation. Formerly a journalist, he worked as a news reporter for *The Times* and then a writer and editor for the *Manchester Mill* – an investigative online newspaper – and its sister sites in Liverpool and Sheffield.